but when he pulled up on it, it came out like the sliding lid of a box so — & the very strength & firmness of his grip would just add to the violence of the fall – He was never careless; & I have never seen him climb more carefully than that day. He apologised for slowness — saying he had … climbed for a fortnight & dared not hurr… like you, that he would be so annoyed … suspicion of fault — Well, there is …

Mabel Barker in 1938. Drawn by G E Gascoigne

And Nobody Woke up Dead

The Life and Times of Mabel Barker – Climber and Educational Pioneer

by

Jan Levi

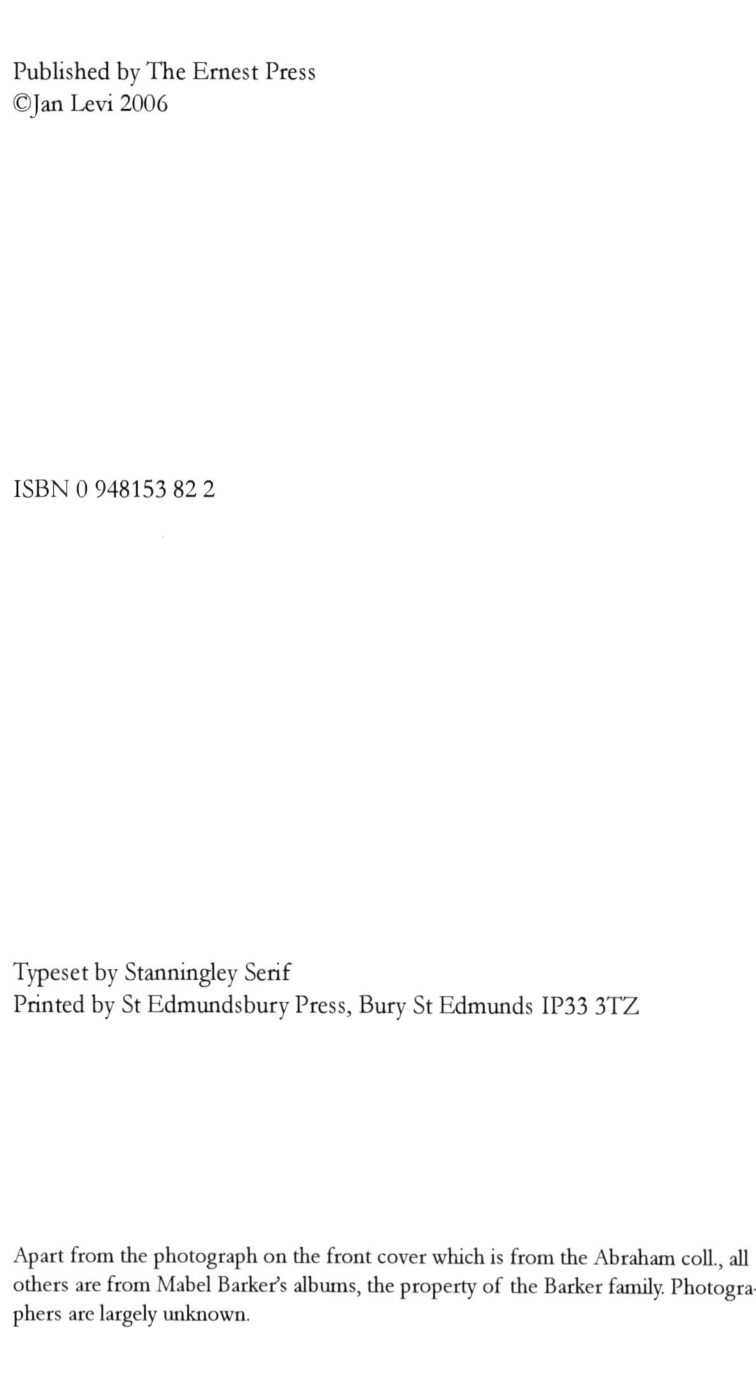

Published by The Ernest Press

ISBN 0 948153 82 2

Typeset by Stanningley Serif
Printed by St Edmundsbury Press, Bury St Edmunds IP33 3TZ

Apart from the photograph on the front cover which is from the Abraham coll., all others are from Mabel Barker's albums, the property of the Barker family. Photographers are largely unknown.

CONTENTS

Acknowledgements

This book would not have been possible without the help, advice and encouragement of so many people. I have been heartened by the interest and enthusiasm of the mountaineering literature and outdoor education communities of Great Britain and further afield, which are going strong.

I owe a special debt to: Lindsay and Mina Barker, who have so often welcomed me into their home, made photographs and documents available, and trusted me to write this book; John Frankland, who started the ball rolling when he lent me his grandfather's journals; Jonathan Reid, who played an important part in the origin of the book; Tim Barker, for providing valuable help and information; Graham Wilde, for his prior research, informative letters and discussions; Marianne Nevel, for her fascinating letters, and for trusting me with documents and photographs relating to her late husband; Jack Carswell, for sharing with me so many of his memories.

I owe thanks to many other people for pointing me in the right direction, providing information, help and encouragement, for lending me books, sending articles and answering my queries. They include: the late Julian Atterton, Shirley Angell (of the Pinnacle Club), Ian Angell, Kathleen Ashbridge, Margaret Ashbridge, Chris Barker, Andrew Bennet, Ray Bromley, Maureen Camrass, Lord Roger Chorley, Margaret Clennett (of the Pinnacle Club), Geoff Cram, Kirsteen Croll and Angela Seenan (of the Sir Patrick Geddes Collection, University of Strathclyde), the late Jammy Cross, Trevor Elliott and Judith Bunten (of the King's School, Peterborough), the late Harvey Frieze, Terry Gifford, Verena Johnston, Janet King (of the Scottish Ladies' Climbing Club), Dave Musgrove, Gwen Moffat, Jim Perrin, Colin Reid, Stephen Reid (of Needle Sports, Keswick), Dorothy Russell, Gordon Baddely, Audrey Salkeld, Dr Helgard Schröder, Ian Thomson, William Todd (of the Yorkshire Ramblers' Club), Colin Wells, Iain Whitmey (of the FRCC), Ken Wilson, Cathy Woodhead, Brian Zimmerman, and members of 'Women, Mountains, Words'. Thanks, too, to Helen, for help on the very last lap.

Finally, I should like to thank Peter Hodgkiss of The Ernest Press for his help and advice throughout the project.

To Barbara, Wolfe, Sam and Jake
for many gifts of support
and especially the gift of time

'Of those that hearken to the mystic quest
A score return unscathed, one pays the price -'

The Last Hold

Sunday, 31st July 1927: Great Gable in The Lake District

Mabel and Claude sit at the foot of Napes Needle, eating lunch and talking of their longing to return to Scavaig on Skye; they have just climbed Eagle's Corner in boots, made even more delightful by finding an egg in the Eagle's Nest. Now they stop to savour the rhythm of the climbing day, with its time for action, interspersed with rest and reflection. The sky is clear, the sun warm, and they can see for miles. Wasdale lies before them. Far below, Lingmell Beck surges past, then turns southwards and laces its way through a patchwork of fields and stone walls, a few buildings quilted into the picture – Burnthwaite Farm, Wasdale Inn, and the tiny church, which is more a place of pilgrimage than worship. Then it runs onwards to the lake, which lies shimmering and silent below the waiting screes. Strands of whiteness stand out against the emerald green of the fields, the inscrutable blue of the lake, and the austere grey of the screes.

Mabel is forty-one years old, slim and sunburned, her long dark hair coiled in catherine wheels, worn pinned over her ears. Her clothing is old and well worn; she looks more like a gypsy than a schoolmistress, at home in this steep landscape of rock and sky. Claude is forty-nine, fit and vigorous as ever, eyes twinkling behind his round spectacles. He too is a teacher, a headmaster, but now school is over for the year; at last both can forget the commitments and demands of everyday life. Sometimes Claude wonders why he is here, when he should be with Kitty and the children back in Leeds: but the urge is too strong, and he cannot fight it, nor give up friendships that have grown through sharing these wild places with others.

'Shall we join the Wood-Johnsons on the Ennerdale Face after lunch?' Mabel asks.

'No, let's stay in the sun,' says Claude. 'Let's go and find Miss Curtis.'

Mabel is pleased at his kindness; for 'Harry' Curtis is lame, and while Claude admires her spirit and pluck, and loves her beautiful voice, yet her determination to go wherever the rest go, and the consequent delay, often worries him. Perhaps they could all do an easy scramble together in the sunshine.

So both set off from the Needle, but at once see a party on Chantry Buttress.

'What's it like?' Claude shouts up.

'Oh, all right,' says Arthur Wood-Johnson.

'Let's do it quickly, and then find Miss C.'

Claude ties up with Arthur, and Mabel with Billy Cain, who wants to join them. Then Lawson Cook arrives and ties onto Mabel's rope. Claude stands at the bottom of the first pitch.

'Chorley did well with your article on Skye,' he says to Mabel over his shoulder, preparing to make the first move. 'The latest Fell and Rock journal is the best yet.'

'Then my piece is in good company,' says Mabel. 'And we are both wearing the same stockings as we did in Skye. Had you noticed?'

'Don't you think Mason's picture of Pillar wonderful?'

Claude sets off upwards. Their conversations are often so. Held in the ebb and flow of their progress up the climb, taken up again on a stance, often fleeting, leaving questions to be answered, threads to be taken up later.

Claude arrives at the top of the first pitch, and brings up Arthur. Mabel starts her ascent, now launched into a different conversation with her two companions. High above, Claude negotiates the slab and moves up the steep crack. Suddenly there is an explosion of sound. Mabel freezes. Claude plunges, his body turning a half somersault. On the stance, Arthur jerks in the slack rope but it is too late. Claude hits a rib of rock forty feet below, then hits the ground. Lawson Cook rushes forwards to try and prevent further injury, but it is no use. Blood pools on the ground. Mabel hurriedly reverses the moves she has made and kneels at his side. She cradles his broken head and talks to him softly, while sending a party to Wasdale for help to carry him down. A doctor who is climbing nearby is summoned. All to no avail. Claude does not reply to their questions.

Twenty minutes later, he is dead, the broken handhold still tightly clutched in his hand.

On Great Gable – 1927

I can be glad that my friend is dead –
    My friend is dead, being yet my friend.
In the hands he trusted I hold his head –
    (But the things we trusted can break and rend)

'Shall wc go climb on the other side?'
    'No, let's stay in the sun,' he said.
(For the mists had lifted that eventide)
    So shines the sun on the grass grown red.

Never a cloud of the many that are
    That form and threaten and roll and dip
Never a cloud had risen to mar
    The lovely radiance of comradeship.

Never a word of the words we spoke
    On the hills we trod, O my mountain brother,
Never a thought of the mind that broke
    From either's dreaming has hurt the other.

Comrade, the end of the pitch is here –
    The life blood streaming that bathes my breast
Is thy last great gift: there is nought to fear,
    And the mighty mountains shall keep the rest.

MMB.

To Mary from Mabel

FRIAR ROW,
CALDBECK,
CUMBERLAND.
23/8/27

Dear Mary,

Thank you very much indeed for your letter. It was a great solace to me somehow, to know that you cared to be certain that nobody was careless – your father least of all. The Wood-Johnson boys and Mr Basterfield went over the rock very carefully later. The loose piece had been in a kind of slot – one couldn't see it, it could never fall out; it was probably pretty firm to the test (they fitted the bits in), and would feel like the back of the block – but when he pulled up on it, it came out like the sliding lid of a box so: -

& the very strength and firmness of his grip would just add to the violence of the fall. He was never careless, & I have never seen him climb more carefully than that day. He apologised for slowness – saying he had not climbed for a fortnight and dared not hurry! I feel, like you, that he would be so annoyed at any suspicion of fault – Well, there is none.

And I wish I could tell you how deeply he had won the hearts of all my rather mixed little camping crowd – men & women & lads & lasses. They have written of him and spoken to me in a way that is a touching proof of his greatness, as a man, not only as a climber. One boy (with us in Skye in 1925) writes 'Cumberland is dearer to me than ever – & Great Gable will always be a monument to one of the finest men I have ever known' – Another said 'He was the kind of man you meet once & never meet again' & a boy with me this year & 2 years ago, exploded over some stupid tourist criticism of climbing with 'How dare they! They are not fit to mention his name'! Mary Steele sums it up with, 'What a very gallant gentleman he was'!

If there is anything else that I can do, or any details that I can tell you I will do so gladly. Gertrude Walmsley & I are coming to Leeds for the meeting of the British Assn. & will be staying at 39 Mt Preston. I tell you so that you may meet us or not, as you like.

And I wonder if you would care to have prints of any snap shots that we have? Probably you have lots of them already – but if there are –

Please remember me with enduring sympathy, to your mother & Basil. And again, thanks for writing –

Yours sincerely

Mabel M. Barker

Twenty Questions

May 1996, Leeds, England

Another busy school day, no chance to think. Hardly time to glance at the staffroom noticeboard in passing. Damn! Last lesson, cover for an absent colleague. Just when I'd hoped to catch up on marking and a million other tasks. Nothing to be done. At 2.20 p.m., I dismiss the scallywags in Year 7 bottom set English, and head out for one of the huts that passes for a temporary classroom, to teach Year 10 GCSE P.E. theory.

There's a pile of textbooks and a scrap of paper with a few page numbers on it, and a group of students who think that they might just get away without doing any work. But we all know that we have a game to play, so we share out the textbooks and give out the paper. Exercise physiology. Aerobic and anaerobic exercise.

'Why can't we just play football?' says Duane, looking out onto the playing fields. There's a chorus of agreement.

I am about to launch into reasons why not when John Frankland, senior master and geography teacher, arrives.

'Hello,' he says, looking surprised to see me, and it transpires that he usually supports the group.

John has taught at the school for many years, but still has a glint in his eye, and a hearty laugh to go with it. He has a strong voice, one that I can always recognise even when I can't see its owner. John is known for his love of the hills, and likes to share anecdotes on the ironies and anomalies of life in a large comprehensive school, especially the foibles of some of its clientele.

'We can do a double act. Soon get this lot sorted out,' he says, nodding to a few of the renegades. 'Won't we, Duane?'

Then we work out that the page numbers and questions set don't tally, and that we've got the wrong set of textbooks, and that Miss has got the key to the cupboard with the right ones in.

'Okay, Plan B, then,' we agree, and find a page on the general topic being studied, and read through some theory together, and answer a few questions; but there's still at least twenty minutes left. We look from the windows of our 'temporary' hut, which has been there for at least ten years, out onto the fields, where the sky looks blue and the grass looks green, and there's no point in starting anything new. I think wistfully of the days when I used to teach outdoor education in the Lake District, days spent out on the fells.

'Okay,' I say to the class. 'Twenty questions. Guess my sport.'

The fact that I'm seven months pregnant may put them off the scent and prolong matters, I think. Mind you, there are not many sports that it's easy to imagine your pregnant teacher doing, other than prenatal synchronised swimming.

'I'll keep score,' says John. 'Let's go.'

The boredom lifts and the class springs into action. Do you need any specialist equipment? Yes. Do you play it on a pitch? Well, yes, there are pitches. Do you need a lot of stamina? Usually. Do you need a lot of strength? Ye-es. Is it hockey? No. Do you play it with a ball? No. Is it a water sport? No, although sometimes you do get very wet. Do you need good balance? Yep. Is it competitive? No, although you can enter competitions these days. Is it a martial art? No.

'That's ten questions,' says John. 'Be careful. Don't waste them.'

On we go. Is it an indoor or outdoor sport? Mainly outdoors, although sometimes you can do it inside. Do you use rackets? No. Do you need flexibility? Very much so. Gymnastics? No. Is it a team sport? In a way, because you usually do have to work as a team. '

'Miss, can we have a clue?'

'That's another question. How many's that, Mr Frankland?'

'Sixteen.'

'Miss, is it airborne?'

'One hopes not.'

'Do we play it at this school?'

'Some students do, but not in the school grounds.'

'Miss, Miss, I've got it! Archery.'

'No, you're off the target.'

'Is it an Olympic sport?'

'No.'

'That's it,' says John. 'You've used up all your questions. Now I'm going to ask some.' He looks at me thoughtfully. 'Would you say that in this sport, some of the difficulties are mental?'

'I think you would.'

'And does it take place in a countryside environment?'

'Yes.'

'Then I know what it is,' says John Frankland. 'Any more guesses?'

The P.E. students scratch their heads.

'Rock climbing!'

'You've got it, Mr Frankland.'

'Aw, Sir! It's not fair!'

The buzzer goes, and the students scramble out, looking mystified.

'I didn't know you were a climber,' says John.

'I used to be,' I say, looking down at the bump, and thinking of the previous one. 'But it's been somewhat curtailed.'

'Funny thing – my grandfather was a climber. Put up a few routes in his day. He used to climb a lot at Almscliff. He was quite well known.'

Suddenly, it dawns on me. Frankland's 'Green Crack'.

1996-2002, Leeds, England

We occasionally manage rushed conversations over the following years, about climbing and the Lake District – usually in between half drunk cups of coffee and teaching groups of children with more than a passing similarity to the Bash Street Kids. John is a keen walker, and knows the Lake District well. He tells me that his grandfather died while climbing on Great Gable, and is now buried in the tiny churchyard in Wasdale facing the mountain. What a furore it caused in the family! He was only forty-nine when he died and left a wife and a son and daughter; John's father, Basil (also known as Paul), had just turned twenty when the accident happened. John wished he had found out more about Claude during his father's lifetime. But he still had some of his grandfather's climbing books; an old copy of O.G. Jones' book, *Climbing in the English Lake District*, full of notes in the margins and diagrams and sketches of climbs he'd done. It was so different in those days, he tells me; they had old hemp ropes and nailed boots, and none of the protection we use today. The only way to climb then was not to fall, because if you did, you were likely to be dead.

I tell John of my own interest in mountaineering literature; and one November day in 2002, he brings some articles and journals of his grandfather's to school to show me. I browse through them at lunchtime. There is Mabel's letter of 1927. For some reason, it speaks to me directly from all those years ago. And I wonder, who was this climber of the 1920s, Mabel Barker? What else did she have to say? What was the nature of her relationship with Claude Frankland? Now I have twenty questions of my own to ask, or more.

The rest, as they say, is biography.

Early Days

Mabel Mary Barker was born at Sunnyside, Silloth, Cumbria, on 14th December 1885, not long before Haskett Smith made his first historic ascent of Napes Needle and so began the modern sport of rock climbing. Silloth is tucked into the northwest corner of Cumbria, wide open to the elements with views across the Solway to Scotland. Mabel grew up in a large, old house there, the entrance of which was marked by the jawbones of a whale.

The Barker family originated in Tadcaster, Yorkshire, where traces of Mabel's ancestors can still be found in St. Mary's Church. The earliest positively identified ancestor is John Barker, a farmer, who died there in 1672 and from whom a further ten generations of the Barker family descended. The last generation to live in Tadcaster was that of Emmanuel Barker who was born in 1713. Descendants then moved to York and Sheffield. On 9th December 1822, Mabel's grandfather, Thomas Barker, was born in Sheffield, where he worked for the Hallamshire Bank of Sheffield from 1838 to 1852. At the age of 23, after admiring a painting of his sister, Anne Barker, done by one Catherine Anne Morison, Thomas wrote a letter to Catherine asking for a copy. Soon afterwards he met her in Perth and they were married about six months later, in 1845.

Their first daughter, Grace, was born in 1847. They had a further five children, three sons and two more daughters. None of the three girls, Grace, Margaret or Katherine, ever married. In 1854, Thomas co-founded the Queen Steel Works in Sheffield, but quite soon the company failed and he was obliged to move to a smaller house where his wife started a school for girls. A few years later, Thomas got the business going again, but he and his wife separated in 1862, and she took the children to live in Perth. From 1872 to 1887, Mrs Catherine Anne Barker operated a boarding school at 17 Athol Street in Perth. Very little is known of the last 25 years of Thomas' life, except that he died at Algiers on January 9th 1887, probably on winter vacation; mystery surrounds the family split, although it is thought that another woman was involved.

Henry Lindsay Barker was the second son of Thomas and Catherine, born in Sheffield in 1854, but he spent most of his formative years in Perth. At this time he met a certain Patrick Geddes, who was also born in 1854, at Ballater on the Dee. He walked to school in Perth every day, equipped with a penny and a 'piece' for his midday meal. It is possible that the two attended Perth Academy together; they remained in contact throughout their lives, and Geddes was to have a profound impact on Mabel's life, becoming an eminent biologist, sociologist and town planner, one of the most influential thinkers of his day. Henry appears to have been a very likeable man who had a healthy disrespect for authority. He became a chemical engineer and manager of the Maxwell Brothers Plant at Silloth, where he was well liked by the workers, and looked after their welfare. He married Mary Smith, and the couple had four children together; Grace Lindsay died at 18 months and Rose Catherine at 9 months old. A family story has it that one of these little girls died of poisoning from eating matches. Mabel Mary was born in 1885, and was the first child to survive infancy. Her little brother, Arnold, was born in Silloth in 1891, and Mabel clearly adored him.

Mabel had a happy early childhood in the midst of a stable, loving, middle-class family, and believed strongly all her life that a very important form of education begins in the early years at home. Silloth was then a busy, bustling town, well known for golf, and had become prosperous as a result of the railway, which regularly brought trainloads of tourists. It had a port and a fishing industry, Carr's Biscuit Factory, and an active community life, including a troupe of Pierrots who delighted the small Mabel. One of Mabel's early memories was walking with her beloved godfather, Patrick Geddes, as a seven-year-old at the seaside. He had shown her some curious and beautiful things, and returning home through the garden, they passed an old upturned boat, half-rotten. She would often give it a kick in passing, and say, with the carefree attitude of the child, 'Look at that old boat!'

'Yes,' said Geddes. 'Look how pretty it is: look how the fallen leaves have made a crimson pattern on the side.'

'Yes, it's really pretty,' said Mabel. And she remembered adding to herself: 'And if that is pretty, then there is beauty everywhere.' It was her first memory of having understood an abstract idea.

At an early age she became an enthusiastic botanist, with the help and encouragement of two friends of her mother's, Miss Lizzie and Martha Glaister. She said that they were both 'true naturalists and local historians of a type very rare today. They were really the equals of naturalists like Gilbert White and James Macpherson.' Mabel always felt a deep sense of gratitude towards them. With them, she developed the foundations of a love for observing nature and a quest for knowledge that stayed with her always.

Mabel looked back at her earliest introduction to the fells in her article for the Pinnacle Club Journal, *The Way of a Neophyte,* published in 1934:

> The Solway shore does not seem a very hopeful milieu for the making of a mountaineer, but I suppose the will to climb was there from the time when, a delicate and undersized infant, I walked and ran at nine months old. ('The very smallest thing I ever saw walking.') All children climb, more or less, and by the fortune of circumstance, I never stopped. There are a few trees, even in Silloth, and our house had a very useful roof on it. The understructure of the pier offered a good field for adventure to a young brother and me, as, I am glad to see, it does still to my young nephews. There was also a fine 'sailor's ladder', now, to my regret, filled up with concrete – down the side of the old dock gates. Derelict chemical works also provided us with a varied, and as I should now suppose, a highly dangerous climbing ground, but there was nobody much concerned to call us to heel in the holidays, and neither of us ever had an accident. People are, as a rule, too much afraid for their children, and should have the courage to let them take their risks. Do the clumsy or the agile children come to grief more often? I wonder.
>
> But the fells were another matter, and very far away. Daily I looked at the hills: English and Scottish hills, as my nurse told me; and though Criffel, just across the Solway, was the nearer and looked the more imposing, my heart yearned to Skiddaw.
>
> When seven years old I was taken for a long drive in a dog-cart. Seated back to the horse, I have no memories of the journey, till suddenly my mother said, 'Look where you are going.' I turned, and Skiddaw was there, close, close above me. It was one of those poignantly vivid moments which can never be forgotten, becoming part of us for the rest of life; but I don't suppose the

child said anything – she probably disappointed the rest of the party by a lack of enthusiasm. It is hard to know what children are thinking, and impossible to tell what they will remember.

After that, said Mabel, it was years until she went in the fells again, not until she became the owner of a bicycle in her teens.

Schooldays

In Mabel's PhD. thesis, first published in 1926, Mabel talked of her early schooling:

> When I was a child, school interested me enormously. I loved the camaraderie, the friendly competition and the lessons, which I never found very difficult (except for arithmetic and grammar, which have always eluded me). I had a reputation for being particularly able in geography. I went to a little school near my home (at Silloth) for the first three years of my school life, from seven to ten years (I was never the youngest in my class). I learnt the definitions of headlands and bays and estuaries with great speed and ease, and I found the examples in the atlas very easily. But at two kilometres from our house was the sandy point of Skinburness, protecting a bay from which two small rivers flow. No one ever explained to me that we had a headland so close by; that we were living in the bay of Silloth; that the Solway was itself a splendid example of an estuary! I ran about all over the sands and the dunes and the marshes, and I learnt for myself all these aspects of the Solway. The 'Golf Course' was a wonderful place to play and explore, and it exercised an extreme fascination for me (and its interest was all the greater because I was not the least bit interested in playing golf!) but the geography that I learnt at school in the Gill text book never seemed to have any connection with all this!
>
> In the same way, we heard about the Norman Conquests (from a brown book) yet Carlisle Castle itself was built by Guillame Rufus during a northern excursion, in an attempt to complete the conquest that his father never achieved over my ancestors in those distant lands (and which, it is true to say, has never been fully achieved in our mountain valleys), but nobody explained that there was a connection between these things and my brown book. For me, this is almost unbelievable now, but it is only too true.
>
> We learnt something that we called 'Latin declensions'. I was in the habit, together with my friends, of remembering only the English words, or of working out, from my place, which word would be asked of me; and if it happened by chance that we changed places, or that the teacher started by asking someone other than the first in the class, that was too bad! But we were close to the

eastern end of the great Roman wall, between two Roman settlements, and in one of the richest parts of England for Latin monuments and inscriptions, yet no one noticed this at school! I strongly doubt that these facts were even known to our teacher!

Something of the richness of traditions, of the beauty of history, of the legends and songs of this area known as 'The Border', the whole variety and charm of my county (many times acknowledged as being one of the most beautiful regions in the world), I understood to some extent while still a child; later this grew, and continued to do so throughout my life. To write the story of my childhood explorations, experiences that remain in my memory as some of the most important events of my true development, would be to repeat what I have already said about the development of a child who is a naturalist. But school! That was a totally different matter; for me, as it happened, it was fairly interesting, at least while I attended my little school in Cumberland.'

A subject that Mabel disliked was Mathematics: 'We used to spend many monotonous hours doing arithmetical exercises known as "practice". But practice for what? It has certainly never helped me solve any problems in mathematics, or anything else for that matter, and in fact, referring to it here is the only time it has ever been of any use to me!'

It is clear from Mabel's thesis that she had strong ideas about the education of young children:

Here is another idea: the education of a child is always for the future. Why is this? One must not forget that children are already vibrant beings with a life of their own which is complete in the moment. How many times does one hear: 'Yes, this subject is very difficult, but that will certainly change', or 'The work gives little satisfaction, but perhaps it will pay off later on.'

It seems to me that it is a mistake that we do nothing for children now, but only for what they will later become. It is a shame to spoil such a period of life. These unhappy children are kept going in the hope that an approaching change which will ease their misery, but is it not sad that it should be like this? And that during this part of their life when they want to be so active, and are so full of beauty and joy, that they should be shut away for so many hours each day, sitting still on a bench, having nothing but books and paper to deal with.

'Luckily,' stated Mabel, 'the success of this method is never complete. The human body has infinite and unexpected capabilities.'

However, when Mabel was ten years old, tragedy struck; her beloved mother died of pneumonia, at the age of thirty-three. This must have been a traumatic time for the little girl, but she never referred to it in any of her later writings, and one can assume that she had developed such a strong and secure foundation in life that she was able to cope with the emotional aftermath. Soon after this, she was sent to Perth to live with her father's three sisters, all maiden ladies, where she attended Miss Burton's School. These must have been austere times for the young Mabel, whose life had always been so full of outdoor freedom and adventure. Religion played a big part in her life in Perth; on the Sabbath there were lengthy sessions of worship and bible reading and the active little girl must have struggled terribly to sit still. Religion was never again to play a role in her personal life, save as a topic of cultural and historical interest.

There survives from this time a sampler, dated April 27th 1894; Mabel clearly resented every stitch! Instead, she must have gazed longingly out of the windows at the hills, wondering why she could not be outside among them. At school in Perth, Mabel found 'not the slightest connection between what I learnt, and the world I knew as a child'. From her earliest days, she was a bookworm, but at this time she became an even more avid reader – she was well known for walking around reading, with a book in her hand. Perhaps one of her solaces was being able to spend time with the Geddes family, then based in Edinburgh: Patrick Geddes' daughter, Norah, was of a similar age, and the younger boys, Alasdair and Arthur, were probably good company too. Mabel corresponded with her father regularly during this time and communicated how she felt; it was the holidays, back home in Silloth, which kept her going. At these times she was free to roam, even though nobody talked of the fells or suggested going there.

Henry Barker eventually acted upon Mabel's unhappiness. At the age of nearly fifteen years she was sent to a school in Cornwall where Alice M. Morison, one of her relatives, was headmistress. Here she thrived, benefiting from the many opportunities for experiential learning. She wrote of this time in her life:

At the high school in Truro, I had the joy of doing my first real scientific experiments! How fascinating that was! We actually studied botany, we had proper gardens, and we had a laboratory. My teachers were intelligent and devoted; I loved that school, and I am still full of gratitude and acknowledgement when I think about it. Everyone, at that time, was helpful and encouraging towards me. Nonetheless, as a boarder, I see now that I must have made many sole excursions on Saturdays – to the river, in woodland, to the coast or to the wild expanses of the area. During the holidays I often stayed in Cornwall, too far from home to make the journey three times a year, and completely alone, I explored the coasts for whole days, covering many kilometres over the rocks or on the cliffs that I climbed, exploring the many beautiful caves. I searched for flowers, shellfish and other small animals in the rock pools; I returned drunk with the beauty of the sea, the sky, all the wild places I had experienced, turned golden by the gorse and the broom.

(This was clearly a very formative time in her life. Later, she said:)

Education in school can be real and effective, according to whether it encourages and increases, rather than hinders, those experiences and personal connections, as well as the dreams and ideals that result from them.

It goes without saying that we have never been short of schools and educationists who act in this way, by making use of all that they find around them, to widen and bring to life all the abstract things learnt about in books. But, despite this, it is outside the school system that we have found, in the last fifty years, the most lively educational methods; and the formation of the greatest and most interesting personalities, has for the most part, taken place outside it. We have cases of those who give up school, who make a stand against the school system, and who create for themselves alternative, vital experiences in the fresh air. A typical example is that of Charles Darwin! He never wanted to go to school. He preferred to explore on his own. Who could say that he could not justify the method?

A Secret Passion

Mabel's passion for wilderness could not be kept in check.

In my early teens, I became the owner of a bicycle, and in the holidays, took to cycling from Silloth to the fells round Bassenthwaite, and exploring them alone. There was a day when I left the cycle at a farm near Bassenthwaite village, thought out and took a route up the long ridge by Ullock Pike and Carl Side, and stood at last on Skiddaw. In an ecstasy of joyful emotion I tidied up the signs of human heedlessness which even in those days desecrated the summit cairn of my beloved mountain; and then sat on it and read Swinburne's 'Hertha'.

On another occasion, somewhere on the west side of the lake, I deliberately went up into the mist to see what it felt like (surely I had achieved a map and compass by then?) and wandered for a long time in a grey and mysterious fairyland. I question if anyone ever enjoyed mist more than I did on that first experience of it; I felt it as a thin veil hiding unimaginable things: enclosing me in a secret intimacy with something intangible, far from the world of men. In a small green hollow I found three witches' brooms. But I came down out of fairyland safely, and alone as I had entered it.

Indeed, I seem in retrospect to have been alone with the fells for a long time; but I have no records of those early wanderings and cannot date them, nor does that matter. The only point of these very personal confessions is that I was doing something that it does not seem possible for any young thing to do now. For I not only went there alone – I met nobody. The fells were empty, and they were mine, mine with a great emotion of possession, like a secret love, a passion which could not even be shared with the beloved. It seemed impossible that anyone should find their way into my kingdom; should love the hills as I did; and the discovery, years later, that others loved and knew them intimately came as a strange discovery, rather slowly grasped.

Nobody bothered much about my doings, till my father perplexed and astonished me by spasmodic efforts to do so when I was well on in my twenties! (Too late by far!) But my brother began to join me sometimes, and once we induced Mary Crosby to come with us, our one-time nurse, and since our mother's death, our very dear housekeeper. That excursion is chiefly memorable because on the return journey, we nearly ran into a large grey horse, loose on the road somewhere near Bothel.

Mabel told of the cycle tours they went on, when they stayed out overnight in order to cover more ground, and how friends who came to stay found themselves press-ganged into taking part in their expeditions. Their father knew the Lake District well and sometimes accompanied them. He had been an enthusiastic cyclist from the days of the penny farthing solid tyre, and later took up motorcycling, an interest he kept until he was eighty.

One of her first serious fell walks was with a friend called Mary Briggs of Aspatria, in around 1906.

We cycled to Seathwaite, took a room for the night, and went up Scawfell Pike. It was April, and a dense mist came on when we were part way up. She had been to the top before, so I offered to turn back, but to my great satisfaction she wanted to go on. We had started far too late, and when, after a brief stay on the summit, we turned to go down, it was already growing dark, and very soon it was completely so. For the upper part of the way there was a covering of snow in which we could follow our own tracks, and it was not till we left it that we found ourselves in the most perfect darkness I have ever experienced in the open; for there was no moon, and the mist hid the stars. Literally one could not see one's own hands, and the track was not cairned then as it is now.

Mary was a fine companion, equally devoid of funk or a sense of direction. On Esk Hause she wanted to turn to the right and make for Langdale. I said, shortly, 'Very well, *I* am going home,' and she came. I had some matches (no flash lights then) and struck one occasionally to see if we were on any sort of a track. I had not been there before, but remembered the map, and knew our route was left at Esk Hause, and right on the Sty Head, and that if we overshot the track there, as we very well might, we should begin to go up Great Gable. My one real anxiety was to avoid bogs near the tarn – that, and a fear lest Mary should twist an ankle or damage herself in any way, for she was built on a generous scale. Slowly and very carefully we worked our way down, and four hours after leaving the summit reached the farm, where the anxious

Richardsons had hung out a lantern for our guidance, and were meditating a search party. The effect of this adventure was exhilarating and encouraging: it was a kind of deeper initiation. If I could do that safely, and enjoy doing it, then the fells were mine by night as well as by day; there was nothing to fear on them ever, save results of my own carelessness.

(I can well imagine a few caustic comments here from some into whose hands these confessions may fall. 'Rotten habit of hers getting benighted' – 'Yes, we've had some!')

Sometimes, about this time, I wrote stories and verses. They were influenced by William Morris and other romantics, yet were also, as I read them now, an attempt to find expression for the moods resulting from such contacts with the beloved earth. None of them ever saw the light, and have seldom been owned to before now. And the habit faded as solitary wandering gave way to guiding others.

Unhappy Evidence ...

Mabel left Truro High School with strongly developed ideas about what learning should be: a living, dynamic process, closely related to nature and the earth, not something that came out of books. She was lucky. Her father recognised her lively intelligence and her potential; he saw that she was not the sort of young lady who would be satisfied with marriage and motherhood, but needed to pursue her own path. He was willing to continue financing her education in 1904 by sending her to Cheltenham Ladies College, where she trained to be a teacher. In 1907, she obtained her BSc from London University, where she studied geology. At this point, she fervently wanted to assist Patrick Geddes, who not only held a Chair in Botany at Dundee, but was also busy pioneering new ways of thinking about society and its development, using the natural sciences as a basis. He initiated a host of experimental practical projects to support his ideas, and Mabel wrote to him asking if she could take part in this work. He thought about the proposal very carefully, writing back with a number of possibilities, but saying that she must be aware of the risks, and that he was fighting an 'ever losing battle' – not everyone viewed his attempts with approval. Mabel took his advice on board: she managed to assist him in many ways over the following years and throughout his life, as well as develop her teaching career, eventually finding a way of integrating his work into her own. She was adaptable and resourceful, and wanted to gain a variety of experiences: from February to April 1908, she taught Botany at the Convent of our Lady of Mercy in Limerick. In June 1908, she then went to Dundee to assist Patrick Geddes at University College, and in September that year, she took up her first full teaching post at Gowerton County School in Glamorgan.

Very few records remain from this time in her life, but it was around this point that her father, Henry Lindsay Barker, remarried. His new bride was Sarah Wilson, and in 1908, a half-brother was born, named Patrick Geddes Barker. Mabel's relationship with her new stepmother appears to have been a warm and harmonious one. Mabel adored the new baby in the family; she was 22 at the time of his birth, and perhaps he was a substitute for the child she never had. He was certainly to prove most useful as a subject for conducting educational experiments in later years! In 1909, she was offered and accepted a post at Saffron Walden Teacher Training College, where she spent several happy years, making many long-term friendships.

Mabel's first real 'walking tour' was in the Scottish Highlands in 1910. The same year, she volunteered to take two Welsh girls walking in the Lake District.

> We met at Ambleside, most unsuitably clad, and in pouring rain set off up Langdale, our destination Wasdale Head. Knowing of no track there, I led them up the bed of Rossett Ghyll. By the time we were on Esk Hause in gathering dusk we would have passed for the three witches in Macbeth. All had very long hair, now down and dripping. There wasn't a dry rag among us, either on our persons or in our home-made kit bags. With no desire to make a fuss, but merely anxious to be getting on with it if necessary, one of my companions asked quietly, 'Isn't it about time to lie down and die now?' 'Die? No! We're going to Wasdale,' said I cheerfully, and eventually we got there, my wretched victims half-dead with fatigue, but uncomplaining. That was my first visit to Mrs. Whiting, and three more bedraggled objects never entered that hall. Soon we were all warm and dry, dressed in her clothes!'

(Mabel remarked that she met with no rock climbers in those days.)

> I knew that they existed, but they were as the gods, and far beyond my ken. I wanted to get onto Scawfell though, and hunting about on Mickledore one day was delighted to find a narrow cleft with evident signs of use in it. This must be the path, so I took it unhesitatingly, more than once. On one such occasion, I came down what we now call Mickledore Chimney. I did lots of scrambling up and down gullies, with no fear of accident, and never seeing a climber on a rope. Sometimes I have thought it a pity that I was not caught really young, but in fact I was more inclined to hide from stray pedestrians than to seek them, being still, when alone, rather like a shy wild animal.
>
> But once, in an inn, I don't know when or where, I met a Mr. Raeburn, and he, finding that I knew the fells, told me a thrilling yarn about a rock climb. Now I know that this was an incident on the first ascent of the Central Buttress. Which of us would have been the more surprised, I wonder, to know that I myself should feel those rocks one day, make, in fact, in two hours, with C.D. Frankland, its fourth ascent?

How much Henry Barker knew about Mabel's secret passion is uncertain. However, he was clearly concerned about his 26-year-old daughter's future, and so was Anna Geddes, Patrick's wife, who took a motherly interest in her. It appears that Anna had suggested the possibility of Mabel going to America to work with the psychologist, G. Stanley Hall, who had put forward the theory of recapitulation. Patrick Geddes was interested in his work, and the two had visited each other. On 7th November 1911, Henry replied to a letter from Anna in which they discussed Mabel's future prospects. Some months earlier, he had met Mabel's old headmistress, Miss Morison, from the school at Truro. She had said to Henry, 'You'll have to look after Mabel, she is too attractive to go on walking tours with gentlemen.' Henry continued: 'I said to Miss Morison (and to Mabel later) that I had no anxiety about Mabel with four boys – but I did not like her running from Mrs Taylor to Mr. Taylor and meeting the latter and going about town with him. Mabel said – 'Father – I know things – it is all right – Mr. Taylor is most desperately in love with his wife – Mrs Taylor knows that I very occasionally meet him – Aunt Anna knows.'

Henry's letter continued. 'I could not say much to Mabel, fearing to lose even the little confidence she still reposes in me now – it was about the above that I meant to write to you – but you open a much wider field.

'I have unhappy evidence that Mabel is not cut out for domestic cares and anxieties – she is very untidy, careless and extravagant – seems to have little notion of the value of money – and I despair of her ever saving any even if she earned some. Were she to marry, it would have to be, if she is to be happy, a man of comparatively abundant means, who would let her intellect follow its natural inclination – I am sure that worries about ways and means and a nagging husband and the grinding cares of a household would kill Mabel's spirit – I have dreaded that she might marry a poor curate or mediocre schoolmaster – and think I may thank you and Pat for saving her from that possible danger.

'She appreciates her advantage in having so much leisure to devote to pursuits apart from professional duties – she has not since going to S. Walden spoken as though she was anything but satisfied with her present life – in fact she said to me only recently that she had lost the distinction between work and play.'

It is clear from Henry's letter that Mabel had been through a time of some uncertainty as regards what to do next, and Geddes had wanted her to go to Montpellier to see more of the world and perfect her French. Henry continued: 'She spoke of Canada also some years ago as a place of high involvement for such as she – Recently she has only said vaguely that she had no definite plans, but did not contemplate settling down to a life of teaching – America is a new idea altogether.

'Now as to my feeling and my power in the matter – if it can be assured that to go to America is the best thing for Mabel – well – I would not seek to hinder or embarrass her in going, much as I would grieve at the separation to such a distance. I agree with you that it is more important to consider her welfare. I have my selfish desire to keep her near to me – and if she goes there she should have at least a three-month term under Stanley Hall as you say – but and what follows it is very humiliating for me to have to say – but I think you must here be told – that I have no money to play with, having in the past 25 years or so had no better success in my other investment directions than the Town and Gown! (*a company formed by Geddes to make university accommodation available in Edinburgh*) Of the few hundreds I have in various ventures I had to find a proportion last year to save my brother from arranging with his creditors (and I fear that it only postponed). I have done a good deal for Mabel but she has so splendidly proved it the right thing to have done for her that I feel that I must somehow try to help her further if necessary. I have long felt that the best I can hope for now is to see Mabel and Arnold 'on their legs' and self-supporting at more or less congenial work.

'I am going to keep your letter a profound secret between ourselves, more particularly that Mabel might find a husband as the outcome of this idea – Because I don't like that part of it – and I am not at all sure that I can see it as you do – a good many years ago when Mabel was at school in Perth my sister Grace wrote to me too candidly that I need never expect Mabel to come home and settle down 'to be a comfort to Papa' – and I have since reluctantly had to agree with this and feel rather sorry for the man who marries Mabel ... I will suggest to Mabel at once that she avoids 'signing on' at S. Walden beyond the summer term which ends 30th July (perhaps dear old worked to death Pat would be able to write a few lines about agreement with Stanley Hall etc) ...

'I wonder if you will agree with me that it can only be wholesome for her to 'economise' as you put it – she may be stimulated to do so to some extent if she believed that she cannot make such a great change without doing it herself – it is true that she does not ask me for money and has not cost me anything worth mentioning for some years – but I feel that beyond her insurance she has saved nothing out of her fairly liberal earnings. But I have no right to find fault with her on that score.

You and Pat will read a lot between the lines in all this – I write as my pen runs and it is a pleasure to do so to you two ... '

This letter, although very telling of the attitudes of the time, raises more questions than it answers. First of all, why were Anna and Pat Geddes to be thanked for saving her from what Henry thought was an inappropriate marriage? Could the schoolmaster in question possibly have been George Morris, her colleague at Saffron Walden, whom Mabel was reported to have spoken of with a certain degree of enthusiasm? And if so, what became of any romantic intentions? Had Patrick Geddes, who was highly influential to them, tried to put one or both of them off? Secondly, who exactly were the Taylors, and what was the nature of Mabel's relationship with the Mr. Taylor mentioned in the letter? Thirdly, why did Henry think that Mabel had lost confidence in him? Lastly, for what reason did the proposed posting in the United States never materialise? Could this be due to Mabel's growing interest in the 'sport of the gods', rock climbing, and the growth of opportunities to participate on her home ground? There are no direct answers to these questions. However, it would seem that in 1912, she attended St. Hilda's College, Oxford, to complete a Diploma in Geography.

No further records remain of courtships with eligible young men, yet Mabel must have known many. Vera Brittain, in her chronicle of these times, *Testament of Youth*, wrote how schools in those days were regarded by middle-class parents 'as a means of equipping girls to be men's decorative and contented inferiors'. She described how this form of schooling was, not surprisingly, quite a stultifying experience. If a girl was clever, it could serve as a handicap; if she showed signs of original thought, this was an even greater deterrent to eligible men. As Mabel's father was clearly aware, she would have none of this! Perhaps she was simply too clever, too different or too assertive to attract the usual suitors. Henry Barker was only too perceptive when he observed that her leisure pursuits and working life, which she had successfully blended together, were more important than romantic entanglement or the trappings of marriage. But soon, the onset of the Great War was to disrupt all the usual pathways through life; the old social order would change, and new priorities come to the fore.

Patrick Geddes and the Regional Survey

At Saffron Walden Teacher Training College, Mabel played a central role in the life of the establishment. She loved drama and country dancing, literature and mythology, history and prehistory, and everything to do with outdoor activities and nature. This enthusiasm she communicated to her female students in every way. Her philosophy of education was strongly based around the theories and example of Patrick Geddes, and his simple motto 'Vivendo Discimus' – by living we learn. Discussing her ideas and theories was not enough; she lost no opportunity to put them into practice.

Mabel had naturally imbibed the ideas of Patrick Geddes throughout her youth. Through him, she was exposed to the ideology of many of the influential thinkers of the day, and he had a profound influence on her development and world view. As well as being part-time Professor of Botany at Dundee for many years, Geddes was also an eminent sociologist and town planner, who directed his fierce intelligence to a wide range of disciplines. He was a prepossessing figure, with fiery eyes, thick eyebrows and a bushy beard, who worked with feverish, almost evangelical intensity at a variety of projects, all aimed at social betterment and improvement of the environment through better understanding and closer connection. 'Our greatest need today,' he said, 'is to grasp life as a whole, to see its many sides in their proper relations, but we must have a practical as well as a philosophic interest in such an integrated view of life.' He was constantly moving on to the next grand scheme, whether renovating Edinburgh's slums, resettling Armenian refugees in Cyprus, rushing about the world lecturing and setting up international exhibitions, doing Regional Surveys in India or town planning in Jerusalem. He was also a prolific writer, his books including *The Evolution of Sex* (with J. Arthur Thomson, 1890), *Cities in Evolution* (1915) and *The Coming Polity* (with Victor Branford, 1917). His strong personality and energetic demeanour attracted many followers and assistants, all running in his wake in order to keep up with a plethora of new ideas, and waiting to see what he would turn to next. However, the academic world looked on with some discomfort, unable to pin him down to a specific discipline; at times, his trailblazing fervour caused resentment, and some felt that his ideas were over-simplistic and idealised. His attempts to synthesise facts and values, science and arts, the practical and the poetic, did not always lend themselves to being taken seriously.

Nonetheless, Mabel was his natural disciple; he provided a vital framework for the ideas that she was to apply to education for the rest of her life. His ideas on the subject were strong, as can be seen from a letter to an Indian friend, when he described western education as a 'sub-Napoleonic cram-shop and castration-shed which are the vicious antitheses of any real education – however well camouflaged by all the methods of that art'. Geddes advocated a regional method of teaching, of leading students step by step from the most familiar facts of daily experience to the wider relations of life and the remoter phenomena of nature. He, in turn, was heavily influenced by the social philosopher, Frédéric Le Play, whose work had a socio-biological viewpoint, advocating three determinants to society – Place, Work and Family – and who looked at the interaction between humans and nature. He was also influenced by the geographer Elisée Reclus, and his brother Elie, a sociologist. Important in Geddes' scheme was 'The Section of the Valley', which he used to explain the origins of different occupations and social structures.

Geddes was a humanist, with a distinctively unmaterialistic approach to life; 'This is a green world,' he said, 'with animals comparatively few and small, and all dependent on the leaves. Some people have strange ideas that they live by money. They think that energy is generated by the coins. Whereas the world is a vast leaf colony, growing on and forming a leafy soil, not a mere mineral mass: and we should live not by the jingling of our coins, but by the fullness of our harvests.' This attitude clearly rubbed off on Mabel, who never had the least interest in amassing material wealth. She agreed with Geddes that 'Our cosmopolitan and mechanical contrivances tend to blind us to the profounder and more human intelligence of the rural and regional cultures that they corrupt and exploit.'

Geddes lectured to groups of teachers about his ideas, and soon after the Paris Exhibition of 1900, an International Association for the Advancement of Science, Arts and Education was formed. He organised a series of Summer Schools in Edinburgh, which ranged widely over the arts and sciences, and formed the Sociological Society with his colleague, Victor Branford. At an early stage he had premonitions about the probable outbreak of war, and at his travelling Cities Exhibition of 1911, one of his main themes was the idea of social and civic renewal as a 'moral substitute for war'. Later, in 1915, Mabel, as secretary of the Sociological Society, helped to organise a conference of relief organisations where Geddes gave his interpretation of the war and views on reconstruction. He coined the term 'Peacedom' and discussed how societies could prepare for such a state – the forerunner for the modern idea of 'Peace Studies'. He foresaw that if the world really wanted peace, it would not be achieved by crushing Germany, disarming her, and making new treaties and boundaries.

Mabel discussed the contribution of Geddes at length in her PhD. thesis. His use of the Regional Survey was the cornerstone of her work in education.

> Professor Geddes, knowing well the fundamental character of Le Play's three factors: *Place-Work-Folk*, showed that these were the social equivalents of *Environment-Function-Being,* that he knew so well from his biological studies as the triple harmony of life. He then understood that social reform must have as its foundation a complete and in-depth study of these factors, that is to say, a Regional Survey. He had also been the student of the grand master of geography, Elisée Reclus, and he brought his geographical ideas into the synthesis.
>
> In summary, he saw that 'a village, a town, a city, are not just a Location in Space, but a Drama in Time' and he sought to persuade and teach that a plan for social reform, no matter what kind, should be preceded by the study and understanding of the environment and its inhabitants, and that one must know the reciprocal influence of one on the other – that is to say, their work and their history. For him and his colleagues, the Regional Survey is truly 'the diagnosis before the treatment'.
>
> It is clear that testing out such a theory needs to be done in the surroundings in which one finds oneself. As a result, they started off in Edinburgh. Professor Geddes and his wife took the experiment to the degree of living for seven years in a slum area (James Court). A study of the city in relation to its environment had begun: it is still taking place.
>
> It goes without saying that it is the true nature of a Regional Survey never to be finished. Nonetheless, results and analyses of this Survey were published

in 1911, in a brochure entitled *The Civic Survey of Edinburgh*. This Regional Survey has influenced all the literature on the subject and the survey of Edinburgh has been very much a model for all others, being the most advanced, as one can see in the Edinburgh Room of the Outlook Tower.

It was in the Outlook Tower that the Survey and the summer schools found their home in 1892. This building, located at nearly the highest point in Edinburgh, at the entrance to the castle, has been the origin of many ideas and experiments since that time, a true 'Sociological Laboratory'. Due to the influence of the survey, and its recommendations, an effort has been made to improve the city; and objects of great value and historical interest, which were in danger of disappearing, have been saved. As a practical example of this work, the use of free space in parts of the old, densely populated city, to make gardens, can be cited ...

In 1910, the Survey was shown at the Town Planning Exhibition held in London, and the idea that a Survey should precede the drawing up of urbanisation plans, has since that time made continuing progress. From this modest start at a stand at the 1910 Exhibition, Geddes then assembled a major travelling exhibition, which has been shown in Edinburgh, Belfast, Dublin, Paris, Ghent (1913) and Dublin again (1914).

At this point in time, with a sociology summer school (of which I am secretary), the exhibition with its many plans and models of cities, ancient and modern, has been occupying the walls of an old barracks, and is accompanied by plans for the improvement of Dublin and for the building of a large cathedral. We also show examples of other Surveys, like those of Lambeth, Saffron Walden, Salisbury, Croydon, etc. done in connection with the educational ideas that were mentioned earlier. This display was used for demonstration and instruction with students, and we were in the midst of this activity when war broke out. Nevertheless, we continued for five weeks, and in autumn of that year the exhibition went to India. All the material, which was aboard the *Clan Grant*, was lost when the ship was sunk by the *Emdem*. Professor Geddes and his son, who were already in Bombay, and their British friends, started to rebuild the Exhibition immediately. This was held in Madras, Calcutta and Bombay, even more impressive than before, and also in many other cities.

Mabel had clearly been closely involved with the organisation of these exhibitions, and had undertaken the Saffron Walden Survey with the students she worked with as part of their teacher training.

> I found myself, in 1910, at the teacher training school in the little town of Saffron Walden. Professor Geddes had asked me to prepare a Regional Survey to form part of the Town Planning Exhibition in London. I replied that I did not know much about doing Surveys, but that I would try. I asked for advice from Miss Hardy in London, and returned to Saffron Walden with the information she gave me.
>
> ... I have already explained that we began the study of Saffron Walden at the teacher training school. We had 60 students, and it would be true to say that in the beginning we were as ignorant as them! Miss Fraser (later Mrs. Fraser-Davies) and myself assembled the students. We explained to them what we were attempting to do; a kind of exploration of our environment, and that we hoped they would help us with it. They accepted, a little intrigued, finding the idea quite amusing. So we told them some of our goals, such as the exploration of old pathways, Roman remains, the church and its history, geology, preparation of maps, the river and its sources, vegetation etc. These young girls started to work immediately in little groups of three or four. Activities were done, for the most part, during their recreation, but we also organised some general outings. In the school there was already a small museum, that was quite neglected. Being a teacher of sciences, it was up to me to make use of it. Helped by my pupils, we organised this with the idea of showing the results of our research in a clear and organised manner, starting with the physical, geological and botanical data, and continuing the historical findings right up to contemporary events in the city itself. In working this way, our ideas became clearer, as often happens.
>
> We soon needed a larger number of maps. This was when I went to ask G. Morris, at the nearby school, to join with us in the enterprise; and I found in him a very well disposed colleague. We needed some information on the Roman era; I went to the city museum, and I found another valuable advisor in G. Maynard. With the help of this 'triple entente', the survey progressed a little faster after this. But we were very much beginners, and I remember one day

when my students and I were researching a Roman camp and its surroundings. We followed a land shape that we believed was the edge of the camp, only to find out that it was the embankment of an old railway!

Clearly, Mabel made many enduring friendships during this period and enjoyed the collaboration with colleagues. George Morris, of the Friends School, was someone whom she spoke of often; whether or not there was a romantic interest, they both enjoyed a warm and friendly relationship for many years. Mabel continued:

> Even in this initial period, we were all aware that we were doing something positive, which could be developed in the future into something of practical use. We established some parallels between this small town and the large town of Edinburgh. Mr. Frank Mears came to help us for several days and we prepared some picturesque reconstructions of Saffron Walden in the Middle Ages ... With the help of our pupils (which I will tell you more about soon) we made a little leaflet of this borough, and the documents and tables we made formed part of the Town Planning Exhibition, and followed it on its various routes until it was shipwrecked in the Indian Ocean. ... We gave the results of our work to Professor Geddes but we also kept some copies. Then we asked Dr. Atkinson, the Mayor of the Town, to use the Town Hall for an exhibition. Professor Geddes came to give an address, and we displayed the results of our work to make it accessible to the residents of Saffron Walden. Later, improvements were made to the Public Museum, a museum already remarkable for a small provincial town, a tribute to the devoted work of Guy Maynard and his father. A series of rooms were put at the disposal of the Survey, which has been on public display since that day and is no longer a private affair of the two schools. In this way, the findings of the studies by G. Morris, G. Maynard, Miss Fraser, Miss Gibson (my successor at the school in Saffron Walden) and of the many other people involved in the local community, have been of service to all the other educators in the area.
>
> There were also practical results in the town. For instance, many old buildings were saved and restored with care and with good taste; trees have been planted in the streets; the history of the town has been re-enacted in a dramatic pageant; a unique maze from the time of Elizabeth I has been

restored and maintained. There has been a realisation that the beauty of the town is something very precious that our ancestors have entrusted us with, and that we can then hand on to our descendants, improved, where possible, and certainly not diminished.

Millican Dalton

The idea of 'School Journeys' played an important part in Mabel's ideology. Her friend, George Morris, organised excursions on foot during the holidays, when about 30 children took part. These were conducted in different parts of England – this was long before the establishment of the Youth Hostels Association in 1930. Rooms had to be booked in advance and each child carried a haversack with the things they would need during the week. The stages for each day were short and they explored interesting places en route. Mabel most probably accompanied such excursions, and perhaps also did reconnaissance tours with the 'four boys' her father had talked about in his letter to Anna Geddes. It was the planning of her own college camping expedition that first brought Mabel into contact with Millican Dalton.

Millican Dalton was an unusual character. Nobody knew exactly why he had given up conventional life as an insurance clerk to live wild in caves and home-made shelters. For the summer months each year he based himself in the Borrowdale Valley, and retreated to Epping Forest in winter for the warmer climate of the south. Millican became known as the 'Professor of Adventure', a title he liked very much. He made his living by hiring out lightweight camping equipment (he was adept with a sewing machine), and organising 'Camping Holidays, Mountain Rapid Shooting, Rafting, Hairbreadth Escapes'. He loved ghyll-scrambling, and for water transport, made rafts from materials he found. A later model was named 'Rogue Herries' (after Hugh Walpole's novel, published in 1930).

Born in 1867, Millican came from a Quaker background, and was one of the early members of the Fell and Rock Climbing Club of the English Lake District (FRCC), whose aims were to promote and encourage fell walking and rock climbing there. Unlike most clubs at the time, the FRCC permitted membership by women. The first list of members, issued in March 1907, numbered 104, and four of them were women, mostly wives, daughters or sisters of members. Women, however, were charged a lower subscription than men – 3s 6d instead of 7s 6d – possibly because they were not expected to attend the annual dinners. However, very soon the committee minutes included the statement: 'The question of ladies being invited to the Annual Dinner was then discussed and it was decided that *They must be asked.*' The next year, at the fourth annual dinner at Coniston, there were fourteen women in the company.

Millican was lean, tall and bearded, and always wore shorts; he strongly refuted the story that Baden-Powell had invented them, and claimed that he himself was responsible. Apparently, his legs were almost indistinguishable from the shorts, so tanned were they by Lakeland weather. At the entrance to his cave on the flanks of Castle Crag in Borrowdale (which he called 'The Cave Hotel') was the cryptic inscription: 'Don't!! Waste words. Jump to conclusions.' He was an ardent pacifist and socialist, reading the left-wing *Daily Herald* every day; the cornerstone of his philosophy was the right to personal freedom. He preferred to avoid money if he could. As he said: 'I am free as the buzzard mewing by day or the owl hooting by night.' He idolised George Bernard Shaw, and considered him to be one of the few sensible people in the world, apart from himself. On the occasion of his fiftieth ascent of Napes Needle, he even built a fire on top, brewed a billycan of coffee and smoked his Woodbines, at peace with the world. Although sometimes labelled 'The Lakeland Hermit', he enjoyed companionship and conversation, and liked friends to visit. He was happy to share his lifestyle, but was not concerned with spreading a message of any kind; he simply wanted to be his own man, steadfast in his views, and unconcerned with the approval or disapproval of others.

It is easy to see why he and Mabel got on so well. They both shared a deep philosophy of living close to nature. Millican wrote in the FRCC Journal of 1913 a piece entitled *A Camping Holiday,* in which he said: 'Camping provides the completest possible change from ordinary civilised town existence; and being the healthiest kind of life, as well as the jolliest and the most unconventional, is the best antidote to the rush and stress of city work ... Among the many advantages that camping has over house or hotel, the chief is that one is in the open air in view of the ever-varying aspects of mountain, lake and river, from getting up to bedtime. Camping also combines perfectly with other open-air sports and pursuits – such as rowing, mountaineering, fishing, swimming, painting, botanising, and the study of wildlife.'

In *Memories of My First Leader*, a tribute written by Mabel in the FRCC

Journal of 1947, the year of his death, she described how she first heard of Millican Dalton long before she had met him, through their mutual friend, George Morris.

> I gathered that he had tried without success to lure George on to the rocks. The first mention of him rose through a discussion on literature: 'I know the original of the chief character in *Rest Harrow*,' said George. 'At least, he is like enough to have suggested him.' And he described the friend who had left an office job to live on a tiny income on a piece of land in Billericay. Later, he had deserted even that for a tent among the Cumbrian mountains, and augmented the little income by making tents and rucksacks, and by initiation of budding mountaineers. I suppose he was, in a way, our first Lakeland Guide. But in long association, I never knew him to charge anything for his services beyond a trifle for camping expenses; and I wonder how many owed to him their first thrills on rock and rope; in camp and in caves in all weathers; in forest and in water, and in the cunning management of wood fires. Personally, I owe him much.
>
> When in 1913, I first took a party of students from Saffron Walden to camp at Seathwaite, I got his address, and wrote to ask if we could hire tents from him. The tents materialised, and one evening he walked into camp to see how they and their occupants were faring.

Mabel brought a party of about 25 of her students from Saffron Walden to camp at Seathwaite. This may have been one of the first camps for girls, and they were an unusual sight. She called her charges the 'Walden Gypsies' and they could be seen in their student uniform, the habitual gymslip, some also wearing ties (though God knows why) posing for group photographs with the tents and the fells behind them. Mabel was clearly game for anything, and it sounds like so were many of the students she led. However, even they must have looked on in some trepidation, as they saw their schoolmistress vanish into the vertical distance!

> Then and thereafter, he reminded me of pictures of Robinson Crusoe. He made his own clothes, very strong and efficient, and entirely to his own design, and of a dull green, toning with the fells. But whether from choice or a streak of laziness (I do not think I ever saw him in a hurry) they were never

quite finished, the edges remaining unhemmed. A red plaid added colour and was put to innumerable uses. A slouch hat always bore a pheasant's feather. Bright blue eyes sparkled in a permanently tanned face, and a little pointed beard was slightly grey even then. He used a bicycle, not for personal transport, but as a wheelbarrow, in which capacity it carried incredible burdens and got into extraordinary places. At that time, and for many years, his summer camping ground was a small flat space above High Lodore Farm, and his winter quarters a hut in Epping Forest.

That evening he sat by our campfire, and probably erected a really efficient bar to support kettle or billy cans. His own preference in this line was a varied assortment of tins, pierced for a wire, and his choicest brew was excellent coffee. ('The only recipe for making good coffee is to use plenty of it.')

He was at home throughout his life by any campfire, certainly so at mine. But when, years later, he visited me at Friar Row, it was a problem whether it would do him the greater honour and pleasure to put him in the best bedroom or the garage – I forget which it was; probably a tent in the garden!

One of our rather large company, that first year, had boots to be mended. He took them away with him, and we heard later that, Plaskett's shop being shut, he just left them on the doorstep. They returned safely in due time. Would we do that today – even in Borrowdale?

Skirt Detachable?

It was probably Mabel who brought up the subject of rock climbing as they all sat round the campfire, talking and singing. Quite casually Millican offered to take anyone who wanted for a climb. Mabel could hardly believe her ears. Was such a wild and impossible dream about to be realised, at the age of twenty seven? She and her students turned up in some force in the Needle Gully the next day. As she later wrote: ' – and so climbing for me began – officially, so to speak.'

Mabel continued the story:

On July 31st, 1913, we stood at the foot of the Needle.

"Skirt detachable?" said he.

"Yes."

"Take it off." I obeyed and knew the feel of the rope for the first time.

Several more of the party, including a young Japanese student, who took excellent photographs, were taken up in turn. But while he was on the rope I wanted to get a photograph of the top, and have still a faded old print of a startled Dalton turning towards my camera, level with the top block from somewhere on the Needle Ridge. Later in the day he took eleven of us up the Ridge on one rope – rather an achievement, and a test even for his immense patience.

A week later, some of us were with him again, and were taken on Kern Knotts. He was very careful never to take a novice on anything beyond their power, and his patience with them was wonderful. He really *taught* his initiates, explaining and showing the use of belays, knots (I was never really happy in the use of any knots but his), the safe length of a pitch, care for the leader, and the general safety of the whole party. Probably, by modern methods, he was overcautious, but it's a good fault. He climbed until he was in his 80th year, and I never heard of an accident to anyone under his guidance.

War broke out and interrupted the glorious adventures of the fells. But in September 1914, on a walking tour with Norah Geddes, we met him somehow, and were both led by glimmering and guttering candles through Dove's Nest Caves. On that ascent, and so lit, I was greatly impressed to note the seat of his breeches – one huge patch of Willesden canvas, so ensuring that his waterproof ground-seat went with him!

On another day that same summer we did *Eagle's Nest* and *Arrowhead.*

Then a blank – years in which there were other things to do and think about – the terrible war years of 1914-1918.

Mabel went on to have many more adventures with Millican Dalton; she climbed with him and his party 'for a few precious days each summer, hesitating to intrude among the gods lest my slower pace should keep the party back and I be a hindrance to them'. His way of life fascinated her, and one wonders whether the educational theories she later expounded were influenced by him, or were already formed by the time she met him. In her PhD thesis, one of her principal topics was the primitive occupations of humanity in prehistoric times. She talked of the miner, woodsman and hunter, the fisherman, the herdsman and the farmer. Mabel had a deep interest in prehistory and the evolution of humanity. 'It is the experience of the earth that gives us the comprehension of life,' she stated, as the opening line to the second part of her thesis:

> It is a truism to say that we are children of the earth. We all say it; we know it; but it is still necessary to fully understand that this is so; it is necessary to believe it literally. This is a fundamental idea, included and developed by Elisée Reclus, in his monumental works, his *Nouvelle Géographie Universelle* and *L'Homme et la Terre.*

In Millican, Mabel found a contemporary who acted as a prototype of the kind of primitive human being she promoted in her work. His lifestyle was as near self-sufficient as he could make it. He was teetotal and vegetarian, his staple diet consisting mainly of nuts, wild and dried fruits, porridge, potatoes, which he grew, and 'bread', which he baked himself. This was an unleavened wholemeal concoction, with plenty of currants and sultanas. Millican claimed that man could live by bread alone. His worst vices were Woodbine cigarettes and coffee.

Wrote Mabel:

> These days we are totally taken up with the complicated systems of industrialism and financial interests; the most honest of our economists frankly confess that they do not understand the financial systems of the world. We return, for the moment, to the one real and simple fact, that there exists *nothing*

but 'The Earth'; that we have no other means of production, and that all aspects of existence are the results of actions and reciprocal actions between man and earth.'

Mabel believed that the earth determines the occupation of human beings, and that these occupations, in their turn, determine the social organisation and the characteristics of those that practise them; and that they always lead us back to simple and fundamental connections between ourselves and the earth. One of her main points was the idea that different occupations engendered traits to evolve in different characters. She believed that if humans have made progress since prehistoric times, it was because of their work, which impelled them to use their hands and their brains. Without these occupations, they would not have evolved. Mabel felt passionately that children must be taught to understand this connection with the earth; she was to feel so even more urgently after the tragic years of the Great War. Many conversations on these topics must have been held with Millican over his campfires; for although known to be a man of the wild, he had many deeply held beliefs. Of one primitive occupation, the hunter, Mabel wrote:

> Should there always be hunters and 'squaws'? The hunter certainly has superb qualities, courage and hardiness; the ideal athletic quality and good health; knowledge of the forests; superior wisdom to that of the beasts they pursue; stoicism and self-sacrifice; all this is glorified in innumerable stories and legends.
>
> It is possible, nonetheless, to find other occupations and other qualities to add to those of the hunters. For hunters do not create very stable civilisations. We admire the qualities of the American Indians, but it is impossible for them to remain as hunters in this modern world. Weapons must be replaced by ploughs; for it is foolish to let them destroy the land we value by this terrible hunt, modern warfare. It is necessary to research ways to stop it, using methods that are more serious and effective than games, sports, the accumulation of arms and of scraps of paper.

Mabel hated the school regime of 'immobility and learning from books'. What children need, she said, is the recapitulation of the experience of the occupations of primitive man; they need to follow the activities of their ancestors, not just read about them in books. She believed strongly in the importance of practical work for children, stressing that this should come about by force of circumstance. In her view, this was the only way to truly reach an education for life, by experience of the earth itself, and by practising the essential occupations needed to live.

What truer embodiment of this ideology could be found than in Millican Dalton? Millican lived close to the earth all his days. He was the perfect role model for her students, and when he walked into Mabel's life, the effects were profound. In her tribute to him, Mabel wrote that not long before he died, she received a letter written from his cave in Borrowdale, posted without an envelope, concerning a difference of opinion with the Astronomer Royal ('He said I was wrong, but I have reason to believe he was'). She finished by saying:

> He was not ever, I think, among the great climbers. He had no ambition to be so. In a way, he had no ambition at all. It is difficult to strike a fair balance between his firm belief in his own opinions and his innate modesty; to assess his curious self-assertiveness, and the absence of any self-seeking. In his latter years it was quite impossible to argue with him, though he delighted in trying to make one do so ... He had, I think, early worked out a theory of life for himself, and if ever anyone did so, he lived up to it consistently and completely. He had found something and was well content with it.
>
> Into this theory and practice of life, climbing fitted as a natural part. He did things on the rocks, as everywhere else, to please himself, but not for self-seeking; to fit in with his theory of life, and of earth and his relation to it. He believed that people (astronomers included) were 'shutting their eyes to the foundations of the universe'. Perhaps he was wiser than most of us, and his long and happy life indeed trod a pathway to the stars.

New Century – New Ideas

What was the climate a hundred years ago in relation to education and outdoor recreation? Other than Patrick Geddes, what were the main influences that led Mabel along the path she took?

By the turn of the century, Mabel had just turned fifteen. She already held strong opinions about many aspects of the world and had a well-developed sense of social justice. She was old enough to know that she wanted to take an active part in the change going on around her, whether it involved social conditions or the struggle for individual freedom. She was also lucky in that she had a degree of freedom, not experienced by all young ladies at the time, and social and gender expectations were not placed too rigidly. She was in a position to benefit from the growing interest in the use of the outdoors for recreation, giving rise to the formation of many new hiking and cycling clubs. She was also strongly drawn to the Arts and Crafts Movement, led by William Morris. In 1891, his book, *News from Nowhere*, had set down ideas on art, politics, human nature, work, sex, love and economics – in the context of what today would be called an ecological society, but one in which the liberation of humans and nature were both important. Mabel wholeheartedly agreed with Morris's ideas of ending the separation between work and leisure. It was an ideal that Mabel strove for in her own life, successfully managing to achieve integration between her work in education and her outdoor life.

In the first decade of the Twentieth Century, Baden-Powell's Scouting Movement had a strong impact on young people. *Scouting for Boys* was published in 1908, quickly becoming a best seller. Girls also clamoured for inclusion, and a separate organisation was set up for them, aiming to make girls 'better mothers and guides to the next generation'. However, the Girl Guide Movement had a similar structure to the Scouting Movement, with girls to be treated as 'partners and comrades rather than dolls'.

Like Mabel, Baden-Powell had a strong antipathy to rote learning and the attempt to cram children with information and abstract ideas that were not related to practical expression. He wanted to find ways of allowing young people to enlarge their experience, and placed a special value on adventure, and 'learning through doing'. 'Boys are full of romance, and they love "make believe" to a greater extent than they like to show,' Baden-Powell said. 'All you have to do is play up to this and give rein to your imagination to meet their requirements.' His view of character formation was wrapped up with notions of training for active citizenship. 'Keep before your mind in all your teaching that the whole ulterior motive of this scheme is to form character in the boys – to make them manly, good citizens ... Aim for making each individual into a useful member of society, and the whole will automatically come to a high standard.' Clearly, the Scouting Movement served the national interest well, with its strong imperial ethos and its key words of honour, loyalty and duty.

Baden-Powell himself was influenced by the work of Ernest Thompson Seton in the United States, who sent him a book in 1906, entitled *The Birch Bark Roll of the Woodcraft Indians.* This described a scheme of activities based around camp life. In Seton's plan, groups of boys and young men were organised into a band supervised by a 'medicine man'. Seton also used a scheme of non-competitive badges linked to various activities in the programme, together with the use of a totem in the form of a bird or an animal to identify each group. Baden-Powell incorporated this new area of 'woodcraft', assisted by a young man called John Hargrave, who was later to break away from Scouting to form Kibbo Kift, and become a collaborator and friend of Mabel.

Mabel's most passionate interest was in new educational thought. John Dewey, Montessori, Froebel, Charlotte Mason and Margaret Macmillan all conducted innovative experiments and published theories about giving children greater freedom and chance for individual expression, aiming to develop more balanced human beings. Some of these ideas also appealed strongly to progressive headmasters, such as Cecil Reddie at Abbotsholme School. Geoffrey Winthrop Young, a School Inspector and leading light in the climbing world, increasingly felt that British schools were narrow and blinkered and failed to train young people for a full, rounded adulthood. He often discussed the topic with his young friend, George Mallory. At the time, Mallory was a teacher at Charterhouse School, taking parties of boys on mountain holidays in North Wales, but finding it hard to accept the educational methods of the public school.

After the war, Winthrop Young and Mallory discussed an antidote to the flaws of the public school system. 'We outlined together the scheme for a new type of school,' Winthrop Young wrote years later, 'to be half the year classwork, probably in towns; and all the summer months in permanent camp, engaged on practical open-air activities and crafts. David Pye, afterwards Provost of University College, London, joined in our plan-making; which we completed in considerable detail.' In their ideal school of the future, there would be more liaison between teachers and parents; the boys would be taught about the lives of ordinary working people around them – the school would include a working farm, experience of useful employment and instruction in crafts; and there would be less emphasis on team games. There would be an atmosphere friendly to intellectual effort, cutting down barriers between free time and class time – the school would be able to reduce the formal curriculum, while still preparing boys for exams. In his obituary in the FRCC Journal, fellow Everest climber, Howard Somervell, recounted how Mallory 'had wonderful schemes for doing something to draw classes together and thwart the appalling scourge of class consciousness that is being thrust upon the present generation; and I believe that, had he lived, he would have spent some years of his life to that end.' Here, there is a striking agreement with many of Mabel's ideas; it is not known whether she ever discussed them with Geoffrey Winthrop Young, but she certainly met and talked at length with George Mallory, the subject of their shared interest being an Austrian boy called Franz Nevel who lived with the Mallory family for a year after the war.

Winthrop Young was commissioned by Baden-Powell to write about 'climbing as an educative activity for Boy Scouts'. In her thesis, Mabel quoted Baden-Powell's 1922 article entitled *The Art of Climbing in Education*, in which children's need to climb was described as a hereditary one. 'It is certainly possible to allow all children to practise this sport on trees and on rocks, and this can provide excellent exercise. But the best of all is to climb in the mountains. (As General Bruce said: It is not the height; it is the difficulties that one must surmount.)' Mabel thoroughly supported these attempts to introduce young people to outdoor activities in their natural environment. 'In the mountains,' she wrote, 'one can find a joy that approaches bliss. What Baden-Powell is saying is that the religion of the mountains is really the religion of joy, of liberation of spirit from all its worries and sadness.'

Meanwhile, in Europe, a number of movements were advocating oneness with nature, some of which rejected conventional, urban, consumer society. At the turn of the century, hiking societies proliferated in Germany, and the success of one Berlin group led to the formation of the *Wandervogel* in 1901. Out of it, a huge youth movement grew, composed mainly of German children between the ages of 14 and 18. *Wandervogel,* roughly translated as 'Birds of Passage' was in some ways a movement against the values of the time, and an attempt to re-evaluate the social situation with the idea of creating better human conditions. Many of its members were ideologically charged, wanting to gain a new sense of values through experiences of hardship and raw nature. It adopted a specific style of dress (woollen capes, Tyrolean hats and shorts), had a ranking system and a way of addressing fellow members, which involved raising the right arm, accompanied by a 'Heil!' There was a focus on traditional German folk stories, folk songs and folk heroes. Members pooled their money and took long hikes in the country, where they camped wild. They established 'nests' in towns, or sometimes in ruined castles, where they met to plan trips, recite poetry and play folk music, away from the authority of adults. Short weekend trips led to much longer journeys, and as a result, permanent campsites and cheap hostels were set up. This formed a precedent for the youth hostel movement, which began in 1907, when Richard Schirmann opened the first hostel in Altena, Germany. The *Wandervogel* had some similarities to the Scouts, but were highly nationalistic in outlook, never attempting to be international. Mostly, they sought communion with nature and one another, exalting an idealised Nordic past and traditional peasant culture.

Mabel had many international friends and was aware of new trends in Europe as well as at home. She felt excited by ideologies that led people of all ages into the open air, to work with the earth and natural materials, and to gain a fuller appreciation of nature. She felt uncomfortable with notions of nationalism and boundaries. Hers was a vigorous, fresh air, folk singing-and-dancing approach, putting people in touch with their roots, with humanist values at its core. Unlike her friend, Millican Dalton, Mabel would never be a 'dropout'; her beliefs always led her to work from within society, rather than its margins.

The Outlook Tower

In the summer of 1913, Mabel travelled to Ghent for the International Exhibition, helping Alasdair Geddes arrange the exhibits for the Civic Section. Alasdair was one of Patrick Geddes' three children. At that time he was 22 years old and was studying botany in Montpellier under his father's old friend, Professor Flahault. It was from Montpellier that he went to Ghent and took over the arrangement of the Edinburgh collection, which won the grand prix there. Later, Mabel wrote about this time:

> 'In 1913, when we were in Ghent at the time of the Exhibition, George Morris suggested that it was perhaps now time to interest other teachers in this method. In 1914, I therefore went to Edinburgh, to work in the Outlook Tower, and there I organised that Easter the first 'Congress' of the Regional Surveys, from the point of view of education. About thirty teachers arrived from all corners of the British Isles. My colleagues from Saffron Walden and myself were all very enthusiastic but also somewhat afraid! C.C. Fagg, V.A. Bell and Miss Mary Champneys came; and we spent fifteen very happy days, full of interest and excitement. During the first week, we studied the general principles of the Regional Survey and we discussed with great interest the possibility of using each of the points of view that we have already discussed here, and how we would apply them to children attending very different kinds of schools. We found that there were many subjects to discuss! During the second week, we explored the town and its surroundings, with the helpful assistance of the most distinguished experts of the region; in the evenings, we would have discussions and conferences on the subjects dealt with during the day, alternating with social evenings, where we had songs, dances and plays, always in connection with the locality.
>
> At the end of the fifteen days, the whole congress formed itself into a 'Committee for the Development of the Regional Survey'. Under this title, we have worked together for many years. The first honorary secretary was George Morris. He worked to further these ideas with the greatest of patience, understanding and devotion, and the advancement of these methods in education owe a great deal to him. This little group grew bigger and has now

become the Regional Association. When Morris was mobilised, the secretariat passed to Mrs Fraser Davies, and then to myself. Now, for the last year, this association has joined with Le Play House of London. At this point in time, we have two or three hundred members, but we have never had the intention of becoming a particularly large organisation. On the contrary, we have always had the idea of introducing these methods to other societies, pedagogical and scientific, and to schools – primary, secondary and private. Our plan was for the advancement of the Regional Survey in education by the organisation, from time to time, of conferences and holiday courses to study and practise the Regional Survey, and also by publishing literature connected with the subject.

In 1911, the Exhibition had been displayed in Dublin, and Patrick Geddes' daughter, Norah, spent much of the next three years there, building gardens for its children in corners of the old town. Norah was a close friend of Mabel; in July, 1915 she married Frank Mears, an Edinburgh architect who also worked closely with her father. Mabel, who had a great love of Ireland, certainly went to visit her there. This was one of the critical moments in the political history of Ireland; while Europe was on the brink of catastrophe, the bill for Irish Home Rule was being debated in Parliament. In the early days of the war, Mabel was in Dublin as the organising secretary for a School of Civics run by Patrick Geddes. One anecdote comes from a letter she wrote to a newspaper. She related how one day, she was in the office of George Russell, the editor of the *Irish Economist.* A group of young Irish enthusiasts were also there, and their conversation soon got onto the subject of the wrongdoings of England. Mabel had much sympathy with the cause of Irish Home Rule, but after a while could remain silent no longer and remarked, 'Alas! My poor country!'

Russell rounded on her immediately. '*You're* not English.' 'I *am* English,' replied Mabel, stung by violent patriotism. She had to repeat it more than once. 'It doesn't matter if you sat there all day and said you were English; you're *not,*' declared Russell emphatically. 'I *am* English. I'm *Cumbrian,*' said Mabel finally. 'Ah,' said Russell, in quite a changed tone, 'that's different. They are real people up there.'

Mabel continued to work in the Outlook Tower between 1914 and 1915, staying with the Geddes family at Ramsay Garden in Edinburgh. She regularly conducted tours from the Outlook Tower and a little card was printed in 1914 to advertise these. It read:

> Local Geography and Nature Study
>
> Excursions for the study of local Geography are being arranged on Saturday mornings, May 9th to July 11th inclusive, and will start from the Outlook Tower at 10.30 a.m. unless other arrangements are decided upon.
>
> The excursions are intended primarily for teachers and those desirous of bringing children with them are welcome to do so at a charge of 1d for each child.
>
> Leader – Miss Mabel Barker, B.Sc. Fee – 3s 6d for the Course Half-fee to members and season ticket Holders of the Outlook Tower. Single excursion 6d.

She wrote in her thesis:

> In the month of May 1915, I had the opportunity to try out some experiments with a small class at the Outlook Tower in Edinburgh. I was not solely in charge of the education of these children, but they spent two hours with me every afternoon. They were mostly aged between six and ten years. On Friday afternoon, more older children joined us, some of them as old as sixteen.
>
> We made a plan of the esplanade in front of the castle. The children counted steps in order to establish a method of working, and then made a plan to scale, so that they were using an arithmetical constant. They then wanted to know the height of the rock on which the castle is built. We tried to calculate it, by counting the rungs of the long ladder from the esplanade to Grassmarket below, and by measuring the height between each rung.
>
> We then visited the castle itself. It was obviously too big and complicated to allow us to continue our original method, of making a plan by counting steps. But the children tried to draw up the plan from memory; they drew St. Margaret's Chapel, and made a plasticine model. Each of the children also made a small model of the rock, which they carried all the way round the rock

to help them complete it. But these models were very small, and the fingers of the children also, and they did not please everyone! So we resolved to all work together on a big model of the castle rock, and to achieve this the small plans done from memory were not good enough. I therefore looked for the largest scale map that I could find (1:1056). They understood it without the least difficulty. They then traced it and used it as a base for the model that we worked on, from time to time, over several months. For this, it was necessary to visit the castle often.

We also made many other visits into the neighbourhood, to the 'Historic Mile' which I have already mentioned, and they started to take note of the legends and stories of the area. We spoke often of St. Margaret, of King James, of Queen Mary, of the Dukes of Montrose and Argyll, of the history of a lake once found in the northern part of the city, the 'Nor Loch'; and many other things which were starting points to better study the history of Scotland.

Each Friday we would go a little further, and we began to study the town in a more precise and systematic way. The older children, after returning to the tower or their homes, then looked for supplementary materials relating to what we had just seen.

On Saturdays I organised excursions for adults, over a more extensive area; but the children nearly always came as well. We would go to neighbouring villages, to Gorebridge, to Roslin (of the famous chapel), Cramond and Musselburgh (with the remains of the Roman occupation) and the Pentland Hills. Our primary aim was to get to know more about our environment; but it turned out that we also studied the botany and the geology (at the seaside, for example). We had already started the study of geology on the great rock of the castle.

In one of the rooms in the tower, there is a great map of Scotland, laid out on the ground. After our visits to Musselburgh and Cramond, the children built in plasticine on this map the two great Roman walls, that of Antoninus, from the Forth to the Clyde, and that of Hadrian, from the Tyne to the Solway; and we then started the study of the Roman Conquest. At this point, I felt it necessary to give some concrete ideas of time, so we made a synoptic chart to make the ideas more concrete. We worked on this from time to time during the class.

From the top of the tower, we had a magnificent view of the city, located between the mountains and the sea. We visited it frequently, and we also used a telescope. We studied biology, for there were some doves to look after, an aquarium (where we followed attentively the metamorphosis of tadpoles) and some plants. It was hardly worth the trouble of returning to the classroom, being next door to a large garden of plants, or the Zoological Gardens, the City Observatory, and the magnificent museums of Edinburgh and Scotland to further our studies. We certainly had an ideal environment for education.

Literature was studied early on. An afternoon on Arthur's Seat, the big hill in the park at Edinburgh, was followed by reading the stories of King Arthur, but that was an enormous subject, much too big for us to make a great deal of progress with. We read ballads, and the stories of Kipling on the Great Roman Wall, and also the stories of St. Colomba and the Island of Iona. The older children read much more on their own. As the ages were so varied, the smallest child did not know how to read, but he listened attentively.

The following term, we continued to work in this fashion, but we added the ambitious project of making performances of our stories and legends, and presented them to parents and friends in the month of December. We performed some of the scenes from the stories of the Great Wall, and made living tableaux of King Arthur and the Round Table (Excalibur; his marriage; Sir Gawain and the Green Knight); and also of St. Colomba (who has a church named after him opposite the Tower). This was done as simply as possible, with few theatrical artifices, but the children took great interest in it.

I noticed, during these sessions, if one could follow the individual child well enough, that what interested one did not necessarily interest his neighbour, and that there were very large variations on this point. I did not make too much effort to try to fix their attention on one thing, but for the most part let them follow their interests, and their enthusiasm never waned.

The difficulties of the war meant the dispersion of this little class; I went to work for a year in the concentration camps for Belgian refugees in Holland, but already the results were so encouraging that I was enthusiastic about starting again as soon as possible.

Clearly, throughout this time, Mabel had merged work and leisure, and this took up the major part of her life.

I have already mentioned the sociology school that was held in Dublin during the summer of 1914, and at which we assisted. In January of 1915, we assisted at the general Conference of Pedagogy, and five individual works were published in the *Geographical Teacher,* and were reprinted in a brochure *A Conference on Regional Surveys,* which was for many years the only publication on this subject.

During the following years, and despite the difficulties of this troubled time, we organised meetings at Ludlow, Newbury, Malvern, Glastonbury, Edinburgh (many times, notably in 1920), at Durham and Carlisle.

The manner of working, though different in every location, was similar to the way we worked at the first congress at Edinburgh. It was a mixture of practical survey, quite quick and general, done with the help of local experts; a way of teaching our methods to the students who assisted at such conferences for the first time; and also discussions between the most experienced members on the most effective ways of making progress and perfecting Regional Surveys. Perhaps something was lost in the fact that we were never able to concentrate our efforts on any one of these aspects, to the exclusion of others. Sometimes, without doubt, our local friends have done too much for us, and we will always run the risk of being very well guided tourists! But always, these meetings had excellent results, not only for the visitors, but for the localities where we have always, I hope, left our mark. These results were reinforced by the exhibitions of Surveys organised during the meetings. We would take to them the work of our students, and borrow the work of others. On many occasions we presented work from the same school. But that did not matter; it served to make the progress of our experiments more visible; and if we old initiates recognised some map or photograph that was already an old friend of ours, there was always a novice or some curious person for whom this was a new acquaintance to make!

Arnold's War

When the war started in August 1914, everyone expected a short campaign. Instead, it dragged on for four years, and millions of people were killed. Mabel looked on in horror: to help the war effort, she did voluntary work in the Garlands Hospital in Carlisle, while Arnold, her younger brother signed up and went off to the front. Arnold had been educated at St. Bede's School, but was taken away in his last year because he did not work hard enough, and sent to work in a bank at Liverpool instead. He was doing well there when war broke out, but signed up together with the four other young men.

These must have been worrying times for Mabel, knowing that her brother, and many close friends, such as Alasdair Geddes, were at the front, or in danger. Arnold wrote a letter home on 25th January 1916, which was passed on to relatives in Perth and was then published in *The Perthshire Constitutional and Journal* on February 14th of that year. It read as follows:

> Yours of the 21st meets me as I come 'out' for a spell. You seem to be keen on personal experiences, and I will always try to let you know as much as possible. Previously it was hard to tell you much as it would have been all about the different places we stopped on our travels, and descriptions of places without any names would be silly. Moreover, the places have all been dull and uninteresting, but now we have settled down for a bit, at any rate, and I shall try to tell you a little about our life. We do four day spells in the trenches as a rule, and four days out. Of the spells out, every alternate one is spent in garrison or fatigue duty, almost immediately behind our front line in the remains of a village, which has been knocked absolutely to pieces, and the other is passed in 'rest' in another village some three or four miles back. Both of these villages are subjected to intermittent shell fire, and at the 'rest' one gets it worst, but there are plenty of civilians, cafes, and little shops. So it is quite a treat to go there, as happens one in, say, every sixteen days.
>
> Going into the trenches – sounds easy, doesn't it! Imagine some half-mile of narrow, muddy communication trench, down which one can just manage to squeeze oneself, loaded up with gear i.e. rifle and bayonet,

mess tin and cup, entrenching tool, ammunition, haversack, water bottle, great-coat, leather lined jerkin, muffler, gloves, electric flask, lamp, oil sheet, a pair of gum boots which reach to your thighs, your walking boots hanging round your neck and as many rations as ever you can carry in an old sack (the Army rations are not to be relied on, unless you are willing to risk a period of semi-starvation. They may be alright, and more probably won't be), in my case, a pair of field glasses, perhaps a periscope, and, oh, lots of other odds and ends, besides such as an extra bottle of water and a cooking stove. These things vary according to the fancy of the individual. But you can now perhaps understand our craze for having things small and light as possible. The process of getting in and out of the trenches takes anything from 1/2 to 2 hours, according to the particular difficulties which there are to be overcome in the communication trench which leads to the piece of line you've been allotted. This place is usually different each time (although this is not always the case) and I think that's a pity, as one would take more trouble to improve a place if certain of coming back to it again.

To get a wounded man up from the front line is absolute plain **** for him, if he's conscious, and always for his bearers. I know, 'cause I've been one of the latter. The night before last I was in another advance post, 35 yards from the German front line, and 90 yards in front of ours. This place was connected with our front line by a very **** of a communication trench, knee deep in mud and shallow so that one couldn't stand upright, unless you wished your head to show over the top. The sides are slime, and there are holes in the floor, when one goes down to the thigh unexpectedly as you squelch along in your slippery rubber boots. There was one of my pals shot through the head while standing alongside me on guard, and as it was impossible to get a stretcher along the trench. — — and I and two others as relief carried him back to our front line. The poor chap died in my arms on the way. It was heart-breaking to lose him after the way we worked to get him out without dropping him in the mud. We had hoped to save him. I could write sheets about that particular spot but I haven't time. Still, I'll have good stories for you later on. Can you picture that little hole in the ground right under the enemy's nose, far from your own chaps, and just a few (no, not picked men, that's unnecessary) of your pals in a little shelter behind you with the Corporal where you can kick him with your heel in case of trouble, and the whole blamed lot sleeping quite as peacefully as they would at home, except you and your mate all eyes and ears. The Gerries keep on snipe, snipe, sniping at you all the time, but they can't see you, and it will be bad luck if they hit you, provided you don't put too much of your head up. Still, you can't see with your head as low as that, and up it goes a bit further. It comes down again as one of the snipers' bullets hits the sandbag just alongside it though; those explosive bullets which they almost always use make such a bang when they come close. Your ears sing for a bit, and you can't hear, so you look a little harder if possible, and you think what a glorious game it was, and what a mixture of excitement and monotony, when suddenly your pal (——— in this case) grips your arm and says, ' ***** **** look at that'. You look and for a moment you get excitement in the superlative. There, creeping up, nearer and nearer, is a line of shadowy figures.

There's comfort in the nice little egg-shaped thing you hold in your hand though and now they're in range, just a nice 20 yards away, and they are trying to see your exact position now, before they can bomb you. Now, let 'em have it, and away goes your first bomb, and the earth round you even reels as it explodes. On the particular occasion I have been describing (it's only one of hundreds similar which take place all along the line) I heaved three bombs in as many seconds and you should have heard the row. Old ——, who had spotted the blighters first, is a careless bounder, and couldn't find his bombs until it was all over. But he threw one after, 'just to cheer up any of them who might be staying behind,' as he said. They are brave men, those Germans!

It was rather a curious experience to look through a periscope into 'no man's land' for the first time, and see the bodies of dead Germans lying about, the result of an attack upon a cheeky English outpost such as I have described. Our men would not lie there. What does the word 'dug-out' convey to you? An underground room with men squatting about in it. Have you thought of the floor, in most cases a foot deep in mud? That is what one can't get away from, mud! You get it on your person, in your food, in your bed, in your rifle, and in your dreams! A dug-out is necessarily small, and the beds (wire netting stretched over horizontal poles) are limited, so that often men have to stand up for two of their four hours 'off', while another man gets a little sleep, and when he goes on duty, they get their much coveted hour or two on the bed. It follows that when one is absolutely fagged out and has to stand for a couple of hours in mud and cold, waiting a turn to snatch some sleep, that tempers are a bit tried, and sometimes there's trouble about how long so and so's been sleeping, but it's wonderful how seldom this trouble occurs, and generally it's a case of 'get down here, old chap, you're on a rottener track than me tonight,' etc., etc.

It is splendid to see how fellows help each other. If a chap is ill, the others will carry his gear somehow to help him along, and he will take his turn at helping someone else, later on, when the occasion arises. The principle of each for himself is a proven failure in this life, and if you're not up to the mark, you will find some pal whom you have helped in the past has got you spotted, and will come and take your rifle and pack away by force. It is the finest thing the war has shown me.

To return to the dug-out. One can seldom stand upright in it, and the room is so limited everyone is in the way, and gear gets wonderfully mixed up. The smoke is so thick that one's eyes run when coming in from the fresh air, and you cough and can't see at first. But you get used to it after a bit. Some chaps would light a fire in — well, a place I won't mention. Corporal ——, a friend who was wounded yesterday, was a terror to light a fire. He has smoked us out of the dug-out any amount of times. Now he's gone to 'blighty' (home and hospital) with 12 bits of shrapnel in him. So we'll get a bit more peace. The door is a small hole, and its position is actually chosen so as to make it as hard as possible to get in and out. I suppose to guard against wearing it out too soon. And the roof has a mania for falling and trying to bury one alive. It is particularly good at this if a shell lands on it.

I don't think I acknowledged your letters of the 10th and the 13th with enclosures.

'Daddy ——' used to split the Boardman tobacco with me, and just because he's been wounded, he's sent that 1½ lbs. of baccy to-day. He is a nuisance, that chap.

I must stop now. Love to all at home. Just a 14th page to break the unlucky number. We get awfully superstitious, you know. – A.

P.S. Please send 'Spiritine' refills. I understand it can be got in ½ lb. and 1 lb. tins.

Not surprisingly, Arnold shouted in his sleep for years afterwards, often waking up his three sons. 'Did you hear father last night?' they would say. 'He was at it again.'

Mabel's War

In April 1916, Mabel went to Holland to work for the War Victim's Relief Committee of the Society of Friends, which had first been active during the Franco-Prussian War of 1870-1. When the German lines retreated from the battlefield of the Marne, the Society of Friends, part financed by the French Government, began to work among the ruined villages. They erected solid wooden huts, strong enough to house the population for the next five years if necessary. They distributed food, clothes, seeds and agricultural implements, to help the local peasants get back to work again.

When Holland was inundated with thousands of destitute refugees from Belgium, the Dutch Government erected large camps of wooden barracks, generally placed in heather moorland, far away from the towns. The largest of the camps was at Uden in South Brabant, which housed about 6000 inhabitants. This was where Mabel arrived in 1916. She described her first day there in a letter to her father: 'Today is Sunday and the whole unit has turned out for a picnic! ... 'We have come out on the moor by the lake, brought food, lit a fire & camped here for the day. It is a lovely day of sun & light wind & one revels in it: but far away & faint, but almost continuous as I write I can hear the boom of guns -' Mabel soon made friends with the inhabitants of the camps, teaching them a whole range of skills and trading their folk songs and dances for her own. She wrote long letters to her father, which had to go through the censor and sometimes arrived with bits torn off. She took everything in excitedly, describing her various journeys and giving details of the terrain, the villages and towns she passed. She wrote of her interactions with the people, often showing the amusing side of events. She took the opportunity to see as much of Holland as she could.

Mabel described the camp as 'a community collected together and organised at sudden need from the broken sweepings of a nation', yet with the organisation of a town, too – with a central government under Dutch soldiers, including government offices, post office, shops, school, hospital, church, theatre, even a financial system. Families often had only a part of a hut to live in, and there was very little privacy. To begin with, Mabel worked in a 'Zaal' or workroom. Here she had to use her initiative in developing productive craftwork for the camp inhabitants. She showed the workers how to do stencilling on lampshades and book covers, and tried out basket making, using rushes found nearby. She also began to experiment with paper pulp in an attempt to model dolls' heads – in the workshops they made dolls and dressed them in local costumes, but Mabel thought the heads were terrible. The men made brushes and mats, shoes and slippers, and had a woodworking shop. The workers were paid in 'points', cards, which they could exchange for goods at the shop.

As well as the big refugee camps, there were also internment camps, and small villages of wooden huts put up for the wives and families of the interned. It was at one of these, Elisabethdorp, at Amersfoort, that Mabel spent the greatest part of her time in Holland. She was sent there after only a few weeks at Uden. Amersfoort was for the wives and families of Belgian soldiers interned at Zeist, nearby. The refugees were housed, fed and cared for as much as possible, but Mabel observed that they suffered greatly from the lack of employment. Her role was to help to organise this. Conditions were very crowded and Mabel described how, on her first Sunday there, as an interlude at tea-time, she helped the priest make a confessional in their living room out of a piano, a curtain, string and drawing pins – the church was not built yet. How convenient it was, she commented, to be able to hear the sermon in her bed without actually having to go to it! Workrooms were run for both men and women. The men mainly took part in brushmaking, until the markets dried up, and then started a chair-making industry. Raffia shoes were also made and worn by the refugees. Other work included toy making, carpentry and mats. In the women's rooms, they made woollen rugs, linen bags and cushion covers.

Life was often harsh in the wooden huts, especially when the temperature fell as low as 18 degrees in winter. Mabel and her co-workers tried to make life as tolerable as they could for the refugees. In the evenings they ran classes, including sewing, country dancing, English lessons, raffia work, gardening, and socials. She also helped organise concerts where ballads and dancing were performed. Mabel kept her usual humorous commentary on events:

> On Friday 26th (May 1916) there was a romantic little incident. A <u>huge</u>

bunch of lovely flowers arrived from our good friends the Rants, labelled 'Heartiest felicitations with the birthday of your lovely queen' – ! We were all of us rather breathless over it for we had forgotten the auspicious occasion! Of course we put them in the workroom and told the women why they were there, and really felt as though we were representatives of the English nation and had to behave (and feel) accordingly!

Later, when Monsieur Rant was touring the camp with a number of Countesses, Mabel pointed out the flowers to him.

He said, 'The next thing is the King's birthday' and I am ashamed to say that I asked 'when is that?' He gravely said, '3rd June' and I tried to stammer some excuse about our having kept Queen Victoria's birthday for so long and its being Empire Day, that these others, so near to it, got rather forgotten. And on June 3rd came a huge cake for 'our Ladies in Elisabethdorp' and inside the envelope – 'Ladies! God Save the King' – Family Rant 3rd June 1916.' And another Dutch friend gave us a lovely red ensign specially bought for us in Amsterdam – which we pinned up in the workroom in the morning, and rigged up on the roof in the afternoon, and we ate the King's birthday cake, and felt desperately British and loyal.'

It was not long after this that Mabel received the shocking news that Arnold was reported killed in action on 28th June 1916. In a strange turn of events, Mabel's father received a letter from Arnold, dated 3rd July, sent from Aberdeen, where his condition was reported as 'not very serious'. Henry Barker reputedly ran around the streets of Silloth, shouting 'He's alive! He's alive!' Arnold lost one of his lungs; the family story goes that he was knocked out in the Somme, and came to in Aberdeen. Of the five colleagues who joined up from his Liverpool bank, he was the only one to survive.

Soon after her arrival at Amersfoort, Mabel played a part in establishing a Boy Scout troop. At first, she went round the huts to find the older boys, and attempted to make gardens with them. She said;

'The boys are awfully funny. They steal each other's seeds, encroach on the common paths, squabble over the tools, and altogether are a lively lot!'

In July 1916, she wrote;

We put up a notice in the village some days before, and had a miscellaneous rabble of about 30 boys waiting for us. Many of them are unfortunately much too little – but we took down the names of about twenty and then went off to the wood with 14 of the biggest. There was a sprinkling of tears among the small fry left behind, but later they will be formed into little patrols of their own, of 'Wolf Cubs' – We made three patrols (not with full numbers) – with temporary leaders. The men taught them a 'tracking' game and gave them some drill and some coaching of the working of the patrols and obedience to the leader – patrol calls and colours and so on. We gave them shoulder ribbons and are making 3 little flags.

You can imagine how the lads enjoyed it; and it is extraordinary how quickly one sees which ones are likely good lads and which the lazy wastrels! Of course a lot of them have been working at gardens with me for some time, and I already know them pretty well. We are going to do this every Saturday afternoon and I'll probably take them in the evenings some times. In about two months probably they will be ready to pass tests, and be enrolled as scouts proper, and then we shall see about uniforms. We are fortunate in finding a Dutchman and a Belgian who are friends and <u>want</u> to work together! and who are both quite strongly anti-militarist, and so will run the scouts on lines in accordance with S.O.F. ideas – We are therefore a little puzzled by the dictum of the S.O.F. Committee here who want us to include a Belgian <u>officer</u> trained in the management of scouts! I hope they will find it impossible to discover one suitable! ...

The scouts (to be) here are really very funny. They are the quaintest mixture of slippery naughtiness and aggressive virtue at present. One never knows what they will be up to next, and my life is a succession of interviews with boys who have been doing something they shouldn't. They are perfectly <u>horrid</u> the way they tell tales of each other. The great matter at present is poles, really broomsticks left over from making our fence ... I am always finding (or being told of) someone who has one. The order of events is generally:- catch the culprit, interview him, perhaps solitary confinement for a while, tears, 'attention!' 'Parole d'un scout est toujours vrai'; promises of amendment, salute! Dismiss!! One scamp who we came down on severely a few weeks ago for stealing toys (Josef Peeters) has been a model of virtue so far. He salutes me every time I see him – (most of them do) – and if you meet him one side of a hut and then go round it and see him the other he does it twice! & as I have to politely return it every time I really begin to sympathise with the officer evading privates in the street - ! ...

Last week we played at rescuing a prisoner. One patrol guarded beautifully, but the rescue came not. When tracked, they were all found to be bathing in a pool – Such is life! Last Thursday, a boy doing a garden clawed a girl with a rake. I arrived on the scene shortly after, talked to the villain for the good of his soul, interviewed a very irate papa, and went off with papa and culprit to the former's home. There, before the door, wide open, an excited crowd of infants were enjoying the spectacle of a weeping mother and daughter, the latter streaming with blood! We shut the door (the villain inside), saw there was really no harm done, pacified the weeping females, and then we surrounded the villain, told him, each in turn, what we thought of him and demanded an apology!! And got it too, what's more! Then I conducted the mother and child to the hospital. (It was really nothing, but the smallest hurt is apt to go septic here) Now one keeps a pretty strict eye on the future conduct of the villain.

(At intervals, Mabel went back to Uden Camp to visit the people she knew there.)

They are town people with no knowledge of the country – Don't think that the S.O.F. Unit with their campings and picnics at weekends are doing nothing thereby. They take the boys scouting over moors and woods, teach them to make fires, carefully! (and will get them sleeping out before long – when the authorities are educated to it!)

Mr. Wallis is a naturalist, and if ever there was a place for nature study and a time for testing all our theories of its educative nature this is it. They teach the girls to swim in the lakes; they've made a canoe in the camp workrooms. They organise large picnics for camp authorities etc and the scouts do the work for them! Last night we arrived to find an empty S.O.F. hut (save for Mr. Wells and a gramophone he was mending) – and a note to come out to the lake to a picnic for the singing class. We were a bit late (trams late – full of soldiers – weekend leave I think) and the picnic was just ending. We could hear them singing Flemish songs away across the moor, and then met them – about 150 girls trailing away in a long procession towards the Vluchtund, still singing. (It was nice that some of them recognised me for I was only here a fortnight. And there was Chris, looking charming, in the middle of a group of leave taking officials and their wives. (She is now head of the unit, you know.) When they'd all gone we went to a spot among the sand-hills and pines (which they have named 'the Alps'!) and made supper and sang, and talked and then some went back to the camp and four of us slept out. Chris and Miss Livingstone (Flushing unit) and Dorothy Cuss and I.

Today is very peaceful. We woke up about 7, with a thin veil of mist drifting through the pines, and C, who is always horribly energetic in the mornings when I am not, got up and made a fire, and we soon had breakfast and came over to the lakes, where the others are to join us for lunch ... in the late afternoon and evening the lakes were like a seaside resort! People came out from the camps – and especially children, and played about and paddled and bathed, wallowing in the shallow (& warm) water like puppies – and shouting and laughing with joy. It really was a jolly scene ... the day before at the picnic they told me they had taken the children out, two at a time for sails – Think of the joy of those kids! 'War Victims Relief' – I should just think so!

Mabel revelled in her work, writing that it was full of joy; she felt that she was able to give some measure of interest and happiness to the life of the refugees and to help some of the lads and the lasses through their broken times, providing hope for the future. Her work included all kinds of things, from attending to defective drainage, to bathing babies and keeping hens. She noted that all dealings with the Belgians had to be in two languages, for however small the group, there were always both French and Flemish speakers. Whatever the difficulties, Mabel always made best advantage of a situation and got fun out of it. For example, she described a trip she and friends took on the rivers and canals of Holland. They went into a café while waiting to board a boat for their return journey to the camp.

By then it was time for tea; and after it, the café keeper, assuring us that the boat <u>never</u> started before 6, started in leisurely fashion towards the quay, and Mr. R said that if we would go on to the boat he would lay in a stock of ham for future use. So on we went. Behold the boat hooted, quite ready to start at 5, and obviously waiting for us. We got on, and assured them in our best Dutch that Mynheer was coming. An excited crowd on the quay looked for him in all directions – the steamer hooted violently, we explained volubly and thought the captain was quite agreeable to wait when before we quite realised what was happening we found ourselves in mid stream!

And the united Dutch of all four was quite inadequate for telling the captain what we really thought of him. After a wild outburst of indignation, we passed among ourselves, to the stage of outbursts of laughter, and celebrated the sad event in limericks and doggerel; but to the crew we kept up the pose of being lonely and deserted females, and it rather 'put the lid on' when one of them, asking me if we had money with us, I replied casually that I wasn't sure, Mynheer had always paid for us! (he had been treasurer, but of course, we had enough) They all assured us many times that he would go by train and meet us in Kampen; and became awfully sympathetic. There was no fire, and a family with many babies in 1st cabin, and it still rained and was getting dark; so the crew (4 of them) invited us into their cabin, where there was a fire, gave us their coffee in a kettle, and bought milk for us – and refused payment! We had a very jolly evening – we exchanged lessons in Dutch and English, and Miss R played the tin whistle. Of course, we left them some of our food and a tip, and when Mr. R met us on Kampen quay, he gave them the cigars he had bought for the captain. We had only been on the quay a few minutes when Mr. R, who had cycled, joined us, so we were once again a united party!

Kings Langley Priory

Mabel eventually arrived back in Britain in March 1917, having escorted freed prisoners on a crossing from Rotterdam to Hull. She had shown true dedication to her work in Holland; she had enlivened the company wherever she was, and after she left, received many letters, updating her on events and saying how much they missed her. She was particularly interested in the progress of the Scout Troop, and sent money back to help fund their activities.

Soon after her return, there was bad news from the front. Alasdair Geddes had been killed in action in April 1917, at the age of 26 years. Mabel had loved Alasdair like a brother. She talked of his great personal charm, and how well he was liked everywhere. Alasdair had led a full and unusual life. He had been educated at home according to his father's progressive views on education, experiencing many practical apprenticeships; for instance, at age 14, he had spent three weeks working with the fishermen at St. Abbs, on the east coast of Scotland. He worked with builders, with shepherds in the Highlands and on Joseph Fels' experimental farm at Maylands in Essex. (Joseph Fels was a Jewish-American soap millionaire who was an admirer of Geddes and a close friend of the family; he was then looking into the possibility of starting a Zionist settlement in Central America.) With his sister, Norah, he worked in the laboratory of Professor Arthur Thomson, at Millport, and at the age of 18, joined an expedition to Prince Charles Foreland, Spitsbergen, to assist its leader, Dr W. S. Bruce in mapping the island. Alasdair was also talented as an actor and a dancer, had a poetic sense, and enjoyed making solo journeys, cycling or walking. He never took any examinations (which his father called paper blinkers), but despite this, became a top student and won a Vans Dunlop scholarship. In September 1914, he left for India with his father, with the intention of studying the botany of the Himalaya. The war brought them back. Returning by way of Montpellier in 1915, he realised that he had no option but to pursue the war to its end, despite his horror of violence. He remained in France, becoming an observer in a kite balloon. The excellence and certainty of his observations impressed his commanders. He was very quickly made Captain and Commander (the youngest in his service); he received the Military Cross of Great Britain and the Cross of the Legion of Honour of France. Mabel later paid tribute to Alasdair by using an article he wrote while at Montpellier in 1912-13 as an appendix to her thesis.

As the war drew to an end, Mabel, like many others, felt an even greater mission to deliver education that would change the world and prevent descent into such chaos again. She was deeply saddened by what she had seen, and by the distorted values and political systems that had caused it. 'A Society that has driven us to the Great War is far from acceptable,' she stated, 'and its methods of education are far from perfect. It is only by courageous admission of these imperfections, and in trying other methods in favour of children, that we will work more effectively towards the building of a more stable society of the future.'

A week after her return from Holland, she took up a post at Kings Langley Priory, a progressive school in Southern England. The school had formerly been known as Coombe Hill School, founded by Miss Clark at Cromer many years before. Later, she was joined by Miss Cross, and in 1910, the two bought the remains of a ruined Dominican Priory, used as a cottage and stable. They carefully conserved and rebuilt them as school buildings and the school became a mixed sex boarding school, where there were no servants, and all the domestic work was done by the teachers and the pupils. Mabel judged the school they ran to be one of the most interesting in the world.

Mabel first got to know Miss Cross at the congress held by the Regional Association in 1914. She was then asked to go to Kings Langley to inspire the children with the desire to study their environment. Mabel was very busy in Edinburgh at the time, but managed a visit in March 1915. First she had asked the children to show her their countryside, and they had taken her on a walk to a high point, where the view looked over into the next valley. The following day, she held a conference in the school, which all the pupils, staff and some of the neighbours attended. There were about 35 children, between the ages of six and seventeen. She explained the moral and social foundations of the survey and its ideal goal. She then shared out the work among the children, gave some advice, and was forced to return to Edinburgh. She felt the children understood well what they were being asked to do and entered into the work with the spirit of pioneers. She was intrigued to see how they would manage, returning a few weeks later, and from time to time until 1917. After that, she spent the next eight or so years at the school, until she went to Montpellier to help run the Collège des Ecossais and write her doctoral thesis. The children were very enthusiastic, and Mabel felt they achieved some wonderful results, with the older pupils organising the younger ones.

When Mabel joined the school full time, the survey work became a more structured part of the life of the school. Wrote her father to Patrick Geddes in India after her return from Holland: 'Now as to that lassie – she is doing good work for education – yes – I hope she will keep her health and the ability to keep at it and to live by it – the most disquieting thing about Mabel is a readiness (for arguments sake probably) to 'talk pacifist' and even hint that there is something to be said for the Bosche! Of course, we all know that, but it won't bear discussion at present, and I don't think Mabel is always perfectly discreet – Don't tell her that I said this.' At this time he was thinking of sending his son, little Pat, to Kings Langley, believing it would suit him perfectly, even though he had trouble persuading his wife.

In her doctoral thesis, Mabel gave a full account of daily life there:

> At Kings Langley, the occupations furnished by the environment play an integral part in the curriculum. They are neither added on nor imposed by the creation of special conditions, because they are judged to be good and interesting in themselves. It is evident that to give the experience of the whole section of the valley, one needs an ideal environment chosen intentionally, and not one that is found anywhere; otherwise, the experiences would be somewhat artificial. The critique made by Faguet of the methods of J.J. Rousseau is truly applicable here. To teach a virtue by an event which shows the necessity or the use of it is fine. But to invent and contrive this event, using pretence, is simply tricking the child, who is never duped, and this is a weakness that should be disdained.
>
> The Priory gives its pupils all the experiences that its environment makes possible. It is situated in agricultural countryside, especially good for fruit growing. The gardens (of approximately 4 hectares) are partly used for growing vegetables and flowers (the regime is vegetarian) and there are also orchards of

cherries, apples, pears, plums, walnuts and hazels. There is also space for organised games and for pasture. We have not invented occupations, but have tried to use the land as well as possible, as the nature of the region indicated.

There are two gardeners to help with the gardening and the raising of animals, and a neighbour who comes each day to help with the cleaning of the premises. Apart from that, there are no domestic staff; all the work of the community is done by the children and by the teachers. The 35 children are aged between 6 and 18 years, and the resident teachers are not many, and although teachers come from outside to help, they cannot make a great contribution to the domestic work.

The resulting regime is not an easy one. In fact, it is full of difficulties and problems. This is not quite an earthly paradise that we invite you to enter! But the Priory is a fascinating place, and well worth the trouble of the courageous directors to organise it.

In the house, the cooking is done by a teacher with the assistance of two or three children. They have certain responsibilities for a few weeks, then change their role. The table is laid and the dishes are served to each child by other 'servers', and others still, in their turn, clear the table and do the washing up.

Each morning the house is cleaned. Everyone makes their bed, and the older ones help the smallest. Each bedroom is under the direction of a pupil who has sufficient experience, or of a teacher, assisted by a small group of younger children, who must be employed to the best of their abilities. The place is swept and dusted, the parquet floor is polished with cloths, and intellectual work commences in a house that is perfectly clean and in as good order as possible. This takes up one hour, from 8 to 9 in the morning.

From 9 to 12 o'clock, the children follow the curriculum we have discussed. But from midday until one o'clock, everyone once again does practical tasks. At present, most of the tasks are done in the open air. The children look after the animals, which are quite numerous. There are many goats (18, I believe, at the moment, but it is the spring!), ponies, pigs, two dogs, many cats, chickens, ducks and pigeons, bees and also among these, some personal favourites include a tortoise, an aquarium with fish and frogs, silkworms, etc. and in this way the children certainly learn how to look after animals.

In each season, they harvest the fruits; they shell the nuts, dig up the potatoes and artichokes, gather and cut the wood for the fire. In this work, even the small ones can contribute by doing something towards the communal well being, without becoming too bored or tired. For it is always necessary to assure that the tasks are regulated according to the health and strength of the children, and not only this; it works best to allocate tasks according to preferences. Certainly, it is necessary for the chores to be done. The circumstances of the environment impose their own strict discipline, and this resembles the discipline that the earth has always imposed upon man. 'You will eat your bread by the sweat of your brow.' In such an environment, it is possible to give children the sense of the reality of work, and also the necessity to fit in with the circumstances and needs of the whole community; while at the same time, guarding them against being truly unhappy or suffering.

Certainly, this is a happy community, and the children have excellent health as a result. One is always struck by the beauty and vitality of the children; and if delicate children are introduced, they most certainly become robust if they stay long enough in the environment.

We return to the account of a normal day, full of events. After dinner, the children start lessons again, from 2.15 until 4 o'clock. Then there are organised games, and after this, an hour of study. Supper is at 6 o'clock, followed by optional study for the older children, but the bedtime routine is started immediately for the younger ones. (Everyone has a hot bath in the evening and a cold one in the morning.)

Work in the garden is carried on throughout the year, with the haymaking and the harvesting of fruit in the summer. The children also carry out their special chores, such as: fill the lamps, carry the grain and oats from the mill, rake the cinders, clean the windows etc. Everyone, both boys and girls, mends their clothes, cleans their shoes, and has special work or 'offices'. Some of these are changed every fifteen days; others, needing more experience, are continued over a longer time. Sometimes it is possible to choose the office; but often, depending upon circumstances, it is necessary to accept what has been imposed. The amount of responsibility, or self-government, that it is possible to give to the children, is also variable. If the older ones are mature and experienced enough, one cannot do better than leave them with as much initiative as possible. But if it happens (and this does happen, from time to time, in a small school of this nature) that many of the older children leave at once, and only younger children remain in the highest class, then it is necessary that much more of the practical work falls upon the teachers. We have, today, many remarkable pedagogues who speak with force and emotion of the liberty of the child. I make allusion to A.S. Neill, for example, and Professor James Shelley. This last, at least, affirms that to give true liberty to a child, is not to leave them to their own devices and free from any constraints, but to help them understand the 'tyranny of nature, to the conquest of which one can attach the true education of the human race'.

One cannot *give* freedom; it is necessary to struggle to acquire it, and this conquest, for the child, by the child, is the problem we find at the basis of the reconstruction of nations. Another difficulty that springs to mind is that of finding teachers prepared to help with such experiences. These are the very difficulties we mentioned at the start; finding people liberated enough from their own education to study the environment outside school. One comes up against the same difficulty, but even greater, when it is necessary to find 'intellectuals' prepared to do practical work in their environment. Not everyone will accept looking after the goats, cleaning the stables, digging the ground, or picking apples; and then immediately afterwards, delivering lessons in mathematics or history. Furthermore, few understand the connection between the raising of goats or growing of apples and history, and can show this connection to the pupils, or help them find it themselves.

There are many schools who do a similar kind of work. I have mentioned the details of the one I know the best, and that seems to me the most advanced, the school that can bypass all artifice in its methods.

In the classes, often in the open air, still more practical work is done. The little ones make pots with clay that they have dug up in the garden, they dig hollows in the chalk with the flints that they have found and broken; water is put in these holes, and it is boiled with flints heated in the fire, and the results are identical to those found in the fields. They do primitive pastimes, such as making fabrics with grass. We procured some rabbit skins, and made some clothes out of them, sewed them with bone needles, and dressed up in them together with ornaments, flints, bows and arrows. The older ones made less primitive things, such as wooden or metal utensils, clothes made on a loom, and some attractive embroidery ... The work done in the workshop often consists of repairs to school furniture, or the making of something that is really needed, such as a hive.

(Mabel described in detail her teaching methods.)

The smaller children, aged between five and ten years old, worked as a class, and with the help of their teacher and myself, created a model of the village, in the same way as my class in Edinburgh made a model of the castle. Then we went on outings to search for wells. One can never be sure what will be the special ingredient capable of capturing the imagination of younger children. For a time, the wells provided us with this service. Each time we went out, they demanded that we search for wells, a new one if possible, or if not, one that we had already seen. Often the wells were closed and were not visible. It did not matter! They stayed on top, shivering, on the slab that hid the well. In this chalk country, there used to be a lot of wells, but now nearly everyone has water from a reservoir and the wells are closed. When it was possible we researched the depth. When the farmer could not tell us their depth, we sounded for it. On many occasions, we used a rope or piece of string that we had brought with us, and measured the depth approximately. There was also the extreme joy (rarely permitted!) to throw stones down, trying to count the seconds while listening for the sound.

The wells of the village were between 20 and 30 metres in depth: those which were near to us, on the hill, were about 63 metres deep or even more. We found identical results on the other side of the valley; on the bank of the river, there were no wells at all. This was preparation for later understanding the difficult question of water level in the chalk.

Wherever possible, Mabel encouraged the children to be explorers and to make their own documents, rather than simply research in libraries:

We gathered and created a large number of documents, and among them, there was hardly anything done in my hand. I directed the efforts of the children and gave plenty of suggestions, but I almost never touched their work;

the reason for this was that I often found that their method was better than my own! ... As time went on, I used more and more graphical surveys that had already been done. Here is a clear example showing how the exploration of the wells by the first small children was important, especially as not long afterwards, nearly all the wells were covered over and the small houses that guarded them completely disappeared, and it was no longer possible to find the depth. So, in my lessons in local geology with the children today, I use the maps and diagrams of the wells, done by their friends and predecessors in 1917 to establish the depth.

To help with the work of the middle level classes at school and those of the older ones, it was also necessary to get hold of maps. For this reason, I ordered from the Ordnance Survey special prints for us to use, with the valley in the middle of the map (scale 1: 10,560), whereas on the official maps, this was on the right of the section. Afterwards we found that we did not do much research to the east of our valley: it was too far and only rarely that the children walked there, be it by themselves or as part of a class. But we often looked at the other side, and it was therefore necessary that we should have it on our map. As a result, I bought the maps with the largest scale (1: 21,534) and the smallest (1: 63, 360) as well as geological maps.

... This term 'region' is very elastic and difficult to define. For a school, we can consider it as a part of our countryside that exerts an influence on our everyday life. For our youngest children, this may be the extreme limit that the weakest can reach on foot; and this distance may not always stay the same from one year to the next. It is still always limited by other aspects of the curriculum, even in a private school like ours, which can use time quite flexibly. For the youngest, it is therefore the distance, there and back, that we could cover in an hour, and it is also necessary to include in this hour the time needed to prepare to go out and to return to the following class, and after one considers that some time must be reserved for the work which is after all the aim of the walk, one can see that there remains very little time for the whole undertaking.

For the older ones, the radius extends much further, because of being able to (as I mentioned earlier) do the outings by bicycle; and we chose a more extended area to do a less detailed study. This was done using the map of

1: 63,360, and was solely a geographical study, but made more interesting by longer outings that were organised from time to time. The children worked out from the maps the relief of the land, counting the contour lines; the villages and principal railway lines, the churches and the parish and county boundaries, the woods, the parks and the houses. The area in which we did these studies was big enough to include a part of the chalk cliffs, 16 kilometres north of us, and the confluence of our river Gade with the Colne, a more important river 12 kilometres to the south. It goes without saying that there were parts of our maps which we never saw; but it was necessary to do this study to understand our geographical situation and the relations between our bridges and rivers with the general system.

At the start we encountered some inevitable difficulties, at the time of the departure of our first pupils. But after 1917, thanks to my regular presence and the help of the other teachers, the work became better organised, and the Survey found its place in the normal programme. The work became less individual, and more of a whole class affair, and with this a better developed integration became possible. For instance, it is easy for two boys to do a piece of work on the canal, its traffic, the system of locks, connections with other canals and water courses beyond England etc., and to gain a great deal of satisfaction and information for themselves; but the other children know almost nothing of it, being involved in other things. However, they talked a great deal together about their work, and we also tried hard from time to time, in the small conferences that we held, to get them to explain their work to their peers. Often, at the end of term, we organised a small exhibition of the work that had been done. But when an aspect of the environment became the subject of study of a whole class, we achieved more progress.

It is impossible to give a full description of the diverse fortunes and developments of our Survey over ten years, so I will talk only of the present, trying to indicate how it currently operates using several examples. Over the course of several years, the Survey gained a place on the timetable of each class; in general, one hour per week. At the start, the main part of our work was with the older pupils, but now we realise that the most important work is that done with the youngest. Also, as with Valentine Bell, we used our Survey methodology in lessons that were not actually given that name. If I only called one hour per week 'Survey', that would be of little importance, for I used the methods more and more in all my classes; the Survey was absorbed into the general work of the school. In effect, we have come a long way in practising the assertion that, rather than adding to subjects that already fill the timetable, we have found a way of unifying them.

I will describe the classes from the lowest to the highest, in the three main levels in the school.

The smallest children worked in a room which was formerly a barn (17th Century) and which had a wall in common with the doorman's house of the Priory. We could still trace the wall in the arch of the doorway. Here, then, were very obvious points of departure for history, and from time to time we introduced them with classes of small children. We would tell of the monastic life in general, look at the ideals of the friars, read of St. Dominic and his good friend St. Francis; search for pictures to show what their clothes looked like; try to imagine the Dominicans with their black and white robes, passing under this doorway, working in our garden. We made a model of the Priory just as it is now, and compared it with that of a monastery in the Middle Ages in full activity, built by the older pupils (in this case, a model of St. Albans).

But these were the occupations of the winter or the days of bad weather. At the beginning, the first thing with the little ones was to go walking around. All around the village (500 metres) and into the countryside, as far as possible, and in every possible direction, we walked, not looking for anything in particular to begin with. We went to the canal (one kilometre, perhaps) looking at the barges and the things that they carried; searched for animals in our aquarium; and with each generation of pupils, I tried to organise visits to the mill next to the canal. This was previously a water mill, and the big paddle wheel existed just like in the past, the date when it was replaced by a turbine of great interest to the older boys. How long had the mill been working for? We found that in 1066, there were two at Chiltern Langley (at the service of the church and the lord, probably – later, no doubt, for the King and the Prior).

We went to the parish church and each year, I arranged with the grave digger to go up into the tower. This allowed us not only to get a good view of the village, but also to see the bells. This was a great adventure for the little ones, to climb the spiral stairs in the dark; passing through the bell workings and then up a ladder and through a trap door to the roof; I hoped so much that it would give them a taste for adventure!

We went also to a little wood, to the wells where they had searched previously for gravel and chalk; and we noticed that in our garden we also had red clay, with which it was possible to make models.

Later, I will explain how we used these little excursions and these general explorations to start the study of geography and history. The little ones, and myself also, I confess, found great pleasure in the study of prehistory which we built up over many years, and from which I found points of departure for many ideas and more detailed studies, when the little ones were more advanced in school.

In the middle classes, the Survey done in class is more precise. We choose a subject of study, and follow it much further. For example, with many classes I did an in-depth study of the little parish church, in too detailed a fashion to mention here.

Once, we studied this church every week for nearly a year. It was a Gothic church and of considerable interest. It contained the tomb of Edward of Langley, Duke of York and founder of the league of the Yorkist Kings of the White Rose. He was buried, with his wife, Isabelle of Castille, in the church of the Priory, and when this was destroyed, the royal tomb was conserved and placed in the village church. We found there also two 15th Century statues, made in a very interesting way, which were useful for studying the costumes. Several figures in yellow copper were also useful for helping us with our work. The children made a scale plan of the church. Then, each one was put in charge of studying one of its aspects: the doors, the stained-glass windows, the tombs in the interior and those in the surrounding cemetery, the pulpit, the baptismal fonts, the inscriptions, the signs under the porch, the tower and the bells and so on. They took notes, did drawings, drew up plans, tried to find historical references; and all this work, methodically classified, was stuck onto large pieces of brown paper, similar in size to most of the documents, and kept in a folder.

I tried to include the teaching of theory alongside these outings (above all, when the weather did not allow us to go out), taking as a subject the history of the role of the church in the parish, previously and today, and in the life of the community; and specially the church in the Middle Ages, the point of departure for schools, theatre, fairs and many other things. We also, wherever possible, used any literature connected with it.

The Priory itself was the focus of a piece of work. We compared the remains of our home (unfortunately very sparse) with those of other monasteries that were better preserved, and in particular with the large abbey of St. Albans. This was approximately 9 kilometres away, and we went there on foot every year, and even more often when we could, for it is a very rich source of interesting studies. We studied monastic life in some detail, including the function of the monastery, the daily occupations of the monks, the function of the convent, and the work of the nuns. We read again part of *The Chronicles of Jocelyn of Brakelond, The White Company* and *The Last Abbot of Glastonbury.* These things led us to general observations about towns in the Middle Ages, with their markets, their castles, their fairs, their guilds, their religious and civil ceremonies. To better understand the old towns, we used Dutch maps by the old geographer Blaeu, and other plans of old towns. On many occasions, we acted out the life of a Priory.

The castle, which has so few remains that there are even arguments about its location, helped also in the lessons, applying so well to the history of England. Built by Henry III, favourite residence of Edward I and II, it was a place of local and general interest. The lost tombs, buried without doubt in our garden, contained the ashes of the oldest son of the Black Prince, who died in France at the age of 12 years, and was brought back to Langley, and also Piers Gaveston, who was notorious and exasperating, but also very interesting, and favoured by Edward III. Each time we found a bone in the garden, whatever it was, we always asked ourselves, 'Is this Piers Gaveston?'

Sometimes, with the middle classes, we did studies of the crops. We made maps of these from 1916 up to the present.

In the natural science lessons, we studied geology and botany, and these led to the study of elementary science, a little like the methods of George Morris.

The most advanced classes still made, just like at the beginning, individual studies, and this was done easily, after having followed the general studies of the little ones and of the middle school. The individual studies were very varied.

The nearby industries always provide a great deal of interest. Certain pupils did excellent pieces of work on the paper mills, the brush mills and the other factories that are found on the edge of the Royal Junction Canal. For two years, a group of girls made a study of each farm in the area. They drew the buildings, made maps of the limits of each farm, gave the numbers of farm workers, the animals, and everything that was of interest, and they mounted it and kept it in their personal collection. Two boys did an excavation of the foundations of the church, which we had just discovered (with great pleasure) in the orchard.

Another good example of the work of the older students was the study of the gravel quarry in the valley, close to the canal, where extraction began many years ago. Apparatus was installed there to extract and sort the stones, and during the excavation which preceded the establishment of the site, some curious facts were discovered regarding the ancient river bed, for example peat beds, and chalk rolled into little balls by the water. The bones of a deer were found in the peat. Here was something very interesting for my young people!

We made many visits and followed the progress of these sites, with the good-hearted assistance of the workers and the director. It is very rare that teachers, in attempting to find useful experiences for their pupils, do not find all the help they could wish for on the part of the workers, who act as their teachers.

One day, a 13-year-old boy asked me if he could try to do a study of the water adduction pipes and the central heating in the school. I consented readily, but I was hardly able to help him. I am neither an engineer nor a plumber. This pupil worked constantly on his own Survey during the next two terms. He followed all the pipes, including the placement of each basin and tank, looking at the methods of filling and emptying the baths and the radiators. He put it all into a diagram that was so expertly done and so clear that it could have been done by an architect. It so happened that later on the Principal needed to consult engineers about the heating, and she sent them this plan. In returning it, they complimented her on its excellence, having no idea that this was the work of a child.

It is most certainly possible for the pupils, by following their individual interests, to surpass the knowledge and ability of their teachers, as happened with my pupil and his pipes; but the teacher loses neither his authority nor the respect he is due, on the contrary. On the other hand, once the first enthusiasm is passed, the character of each of the children stands out. Some work always with application and interest; some start well, but never finish their piece of work, or stop working or mess about if left alone for very long; there are others who cannot seem to initiate a piece of work by themselves and to whom it is always necessary to make suggestions or even give them an explicit project without allowing them to choose, and afterwards it is necessary to insist all the while that they pursue it to the end. Others know how to gather their information, and do it quickly and competently, but cannot force themselves to do the comparatively more painful task of committing themselves to paper, and at the end do not produce work that compares with that of their peers; others start many different projects if they are allowed to do so, and they always have the illusion that their work is finished, when there is still a long way to go! Others still, although they are amiable and industrious, and work with interest and enthusiasm, have such a lack of dexterity and such poor technique, and are so untidy, that their contribution is not at all pleasing to their peers, who do not want their beautiful pages spoilt by such disorder!

Each child, then, has his own difficulties, and at each step one sees more clearly their true character.

Mabel described how she taught the children to map read, a skill that she believed was of crucial importance:

I have already described how, with the smallest children, we walked around a great deal in the environment of the Priory. When I began to talk about geography to these little ones, I asked them, on their return from one of these outings, to draw a plan from memory. A plan is rarely exact on the first attempt. They therefore took some paper and a pencil with then, and from the starting point, drew a line representing the path. Having arrived at the garden gate, I asked them whether they should make their line turn right or left. I made sure all the plans were correct before going any further. We continued in the same way, drawing all the sections of the journey, and the plan grew larger and larger.

One very quickly found differences between the children, differences that had nothing to do with age. (I had, on average, about a dozen children, aged from six to twelve years). Very early on, I no longer said 'right or left'; but I asked them from which side we never saw the sun. That is north. And the south, that is where we always see the sun through the open doors when we have breakfast in the barn. I told them to make an arrow to the north, and to always turn their paper in the same direction when making the plan. Most of them understood this easily.

Having arrived at this stage, we then left our papers at home and walked. The maps, without a scale, but becoming more and more correct and extended, were drawn up later, during a free hour or a study hour, or sometimes, if it rained, in the geography hour.

But a little later, when we could not do our geography lessons outside anymore, I told them stories with a geographical theme. I described other countries, or I talked to them of notable events happening in the world, even though this did not have any connection with our map-making. I used for this the short poems of R.L. Stevenson, 'Travel' for example; expeditions to Mount Everest, the discovery of Tutankhamen's tomb in Egypt, and the travels that I had recently made myself. I also gave them the concepts of different formations: volcanoes, glaciers, coral banks, using models and many diagrams.

But I return to the more structured lessons. Sometimes, if the children had difficulties in orienting themselves and in making reasonably correct plans, I had them make them in the Grange itself, indicating the entrance hall, the furniture etc. Nearly always, in attempting to introduce houses, trees, etc., they drew them in elevation, like in Middle Age maps. I did not hurry at all to correct this, but all the same, it would need correcting sooner or later, and it is much easier to explain that this is a plan, by imagining that the walls had been completely removed in a room, and that we look at it from high up in an aeroplane.

I had not the least wish to hasten this initial stage of learning. I regard it as of great importance. Sometimes the smallest ones passed many years in the Grange, and at the end of two years perhaps they had done nothing more in geography than get to know the region better and better, making little sketches of it from memory.

But then, it is necessary to introduce the idea of scale.

'Look, Graham, you have made the path very long for the route that leads to the village. Do you think that's right?'

'No, but it takes a long time to go to the village.'

'What shall we do then?'

'We need to measure it.'

And in fact, to begin with, we measured it using the same method as I used with my little class in Edinburgh, by counting the steps of everyone, and taking the average; but later, it became evident that this did not give results that were sufficiently satisfying, and I gave them a measure of fifty feet, used to measure the playground. With this, we measured the village, to the great amusement of the inhabitants!

These visits to take measurements got the children (now aged eight to ten years) used to the need for precision, and also were good for getting everyone to take their part in the work, and this taught them not to be dependent on someone else for their notes or measurements etc. The first efforts to make maps to scale are always difficult. Usually, we start in the Grange, on a rainy day, one step represented by 2cm, more or less, and we reduce this scale more and more. But at the end, we construct a single map of the whole village. Often it is coloured in and very well made, and the Surveyors are very proud of it!

Here we find ourselves at an important turning point in their geographical development. Until now, they have not looked at a map (that is to say, in class). I give them, like in Edinburgh, one with a very large scale (1:2,534). They read it without difficulty, and we have some very lively moments, comparing it to the one that the children have constructed, and in following our walks on the official maps.

But then, supposing we need to use a map to follow our route, it would be inconvenient to carry such a big map outside. And we would find ourselves very quickly on the extreme of the land marked on the map! What to do then? The children already knew, from experience, that for drawing a larger area of ground on their paper, it was necessary to draw a smaller scale. It was not difficult for them to understand the map of 1:10, 560 that I gave them. We had many copies of this and we practised a kind of sport. I marked a point on the map in pencil, and gave it to a child, and he or she had to take us exactly to that spot.

Questions then presented themselves. It was not simply lines for paths and blocks for houses. They discovered all the other signs found on maps, and asked for explanations. I never had to wait for long before someone asked me the significance of the interrupted lines. Sometimes I had to reply that I would explain later if most of the children were not advanced enough to understand. But often I said:

'Let's go, then, and search for this line.'

And then we went to the indicated point. We found nothing, of course, because it was a contour line! That was something quite difficult to understand, the representation of relief, the representation of a real and exact idea by an imaginary sign, something that it is impossible to see, like we see paths and houses. Here was a difficulty that was also found later when trying to give explanations of the poles, the equator and the meridians. I did not make do with the easy explanation of the geography books that this is simply an imaginary line. It is, in fact, an extremely precise reality, and certainly less imaginary than many lines. All the same, one cannot see it.

My poor children had many things to understand, and I confess that I did not know how to help them in a completely satisfactory way. We searched for another place where we might be able to find this mysterious line. Again, nothing at all! They asked, is it a hedge? Is it a path? Has something disappeared? But I told them that we would try to find one of these lines. We did it (luckily, the contour line of 400 feet crossed the common – uncultivated land – and I tried to do this work in winter, when one could walk across the fields without difficulty). At last, someone noticed that we were walking without going up or down.

Then I searched for a little hollow, with a steep slope, and arranged my children from high to low, so that it seemed that they were at an equal distance from each other, and I told them to walk around the hollow without going up or down. After this, I made them construct maps of this basin, and mark the paths walked by each of the children. This was quite difficult, and my true wish was to see my class on a real mountain.

I cannot say that everyone understood straight away exactly what a contour line was. But we continued with our work.

There still remained one important obstacle to overcome. The map of 1:10,560 was still too big; it was necessary to be able to reduce it in order to carry it on expeditions further afield that the children now wished to make. I made them construct maps from memory, indicating the village around Kings Langley. They knew well Chipperfield to the west, and to the east Bedmonde and Abbots Langley, and of the other neighbouring villages, but what about after that? They had to jump from that which they had seen and experienced, to considerations of what they could not see. Further away from Abbots Langley, (at the top of a plateau at the other side of our valley) could be seen another valley with a river, where the town of St. Albans can be found. If we followed the route to the north, we would arrive at the limit of the chalk, at Tring. I gave them the map of 1:63,360 and soon afterwards that of 1:126,720, which is much clearer and nicer to look at. But at this stage, they were ready to pass from the Grange to the middle division of the school, and to start the study of the general geography of the British Isles.

I hoped that these children would always remember that a map is a representation in miniature of real land, and I felt sure that they would understand them better than the majority of adults. How to find a particular place is not of such importance; one can always consult an atlas, but knowing how to read an Ordnance Survey map, or similar, with ease and intelligence, is another matter. It can be a real matter of life and death, as was found by many during the war, or during excursions to the mountains. This skill seems to me something of great importance, and not something that should ever be left to chance, to the choice of children, or left out completely ... One should add that I always find difficulties with children who have missed a step, or who arrive at the school too late to be able to follow this course of initiation, which I have just given in detail.

After this, we study the British Isles in a fairly detailed way, continuing with the regions of the Chilterns to the Thames, and extending this study further and further, constructing sketch maps for each portion. It usually takes two years before this study is finished.

And then, I start immediately, on the whole world: 'Our planet' as the children say. This is a very difficult subject, no matter how it is treated. How many of us truly understand the changes of day and night with the seasons, or can visualise real polar conditions? And why teach these things if they are not well taught, or forgotten straight away? This would be a waste of time, a uselessness, in the same category as dead languages, poorly integrated and forgotten, which I have earlier attacked. It does not seem to me that this is of better value, simply because it is 'scientific' and 'modern'.

On the other hand, I do not see at all how it is possible with the methods of the 'free schools', how most average children would arrive by themselves at an understanding of these astronomical facts. If one truly believes that children should always follow 'projects' chosen by themselves; if it is really true, as Miss Goodlander says, that the teacher must 'never dominate the situation' but *wait* for the arousal of interest, it seems to me that we will be waiting a long time before the children start to manifest an interest in the polar axis!

But the differences between the days really are a matter of daily experience. We can urge children to notice these changes, following the days or the seasons, the rising and the setting of the sun with respect to the horizon. We can follow the changes in the length of shadows of some objects (a nail mounted on a plank, for example) or the height of the sun at midday. After all, we find practical methods to help with the explanations given in the modern geography text books, and intelligent teachers make their own apparatus to achieve this.

After this course, always difficult enough, I repeat it, and having done a fairly rapid survey of the surface of our planet, I give a course in 'Exploration' – the history of discoveries and the increase in the knowledge of the world, from the Phoenicians up to the expeditions to Mount Everest and Amundsen with his plane in the arctic. After that, it is probably our continent, Europe, which demands the greatest part of our attention, but in reality, we are free to choose the part of the earth upon which to commence more advanced studies.'

History was always a particular passion of Mabel's and here she described how she taught it at Kings Langley:

Everywhere, we find indications of prehistory. I will return to this point on the use of prehistory in the second part of this work, because it is of principal importance; but in regard to this issue, it is certain that in the countries of Europe, precise relics of our ancestors are to be found everywhere; and even if we find nothing, it is certain that they are there. At Saffron Walden, we found Paleolithic and Neolithic flints; at Kings Langley, no Paleolithic ones, but there are some in the museums of St. Albans and Watford (and we always hope to find some in the gravel pits). But Neolithic flints are everywhere in the fields, and also potboilers, stones once used for heating. Everywhere today, we find collections of flints in the museums, not always of the same beauty and value of those of Périgueux, for example, but sufficient, and items of importance and extreme value when they are part of and used for the education of our children.

With the little ones at Kings Langley, I read a story from the Old Stone Age, and because of the name of our hero, we always called these lessons 'Ab'. (*The Story of Ab*, by Stanley Waterloo) I cannot say whether this book is exact as regards all the facts, but it is very well written, and of an adventurous spirit, and the children like it a lot. This served as a starting point for many discussions and a great deal of work. At this stage, the inexactitudes are of less importance than the spirit of the book. These can be corrected later.

I searched long and in vain for a comparable story to introduce us to Neolithic times, and also to the Bronze Age. Recently, I found *Dwifa's Curse* (Robert Scott, 1921), and the author lent me the manuscript of another book: *The Luck of the Lakesman.* The story by Rudyard Kipling: *The Knife and the Naked Chalk* has an excellent spirit, but is too inexact archeologically. Nonetheless, I always make use of it, and we have transformed it into a play, which has given us a lot of pleasure.

But here we find ourselves in the domain of the use of literature.

We studied the Bronze Age and the Iron Age in the middle classes. There is an exceptional collection of bronze objects in the museum at St. Albans, but most of the children had seen them in the British Museum. Wherever possible, I used the catalogues from the museum with pictures, descriptions of excavations – the *crannogs* at Glastonbury, for example. In England, we have recently received some very useful books to reconstruct these times.

But it is precisely in the two epochs preceding the Roman Conquest, and that which followed it, that we have the largest gaps in our relics of the past. We do not often find metal instruments, and we do not have any Neolithic terracing near to us. But we have other kinds of heritage. Many of our legends, many of our fairy stories, our mythologies, date from these epochs of bronze and iron. The gods and the Celtic heroes belong to Great Britain more than those of the Greeks, and I would like to make them better known to all.

We have other vestiges of pre-Roman ages in some place names, and above all, in the names of rivers (Avon, for example).

Roman times have left their traces everywhere. If we have neither documents nor buildings, nor place names, never are we far from a road constructed by those famous engineers. It is even more difficult, as mentioned earlier, to find traces of the barbarian invasions. But all indications suggest that they were very chaotic.

Next come the following epochs. It hardly seems possible to find all the history of humanity together in one place. We have not, at Kings Langley, the prehistoric drawings of Eyzies. In northern Scotland, there are no Roman remains. In England, there are no Greek temples. But the history that is of true importance to children is the comprehension of the passage of human events, which traverse their environment like a great river, leaving traces that we can still find. We cannot walk but in the direction that our ancestors made roads; we are the products of the past. Our bodies, themselves, as well as our environment, are determined by a past that has never died.'

In an article written in 1920 for *The Herald of the Star*, the journal of the Order of the Star in the East, published by those inspired by the philosophy of Krishnamurti, Mabel wrote of her work:

Yet the true test of this method is not here, but remains to be seen. Are these children growing into keen observers and great lovers of their own home regions? Will they determine to be 'citizens of no mean city' wherever their city may be? Will they throw their energy and weight into the constructive work that shall in the future, build up a fairer civilisation of peace than the world has yet known? We can only hope that it will be so, and work on in hope, yet remembering that whatever method of education we use, whatever path we tread to seek Utopia,

> '... if ye scour not well
> Red rust shall grow upon God's great bell,
> And grass in the streets of God.'

Entering Olympus

Mabel lived a full and busy life during her years at Kings Langley, making many deep and enduring friendships. During this time, she published articles and leaflets on the Regional Survey and its use for education, occupational education and exploration of the environment. She taught Survey classes all over Britain, and was well known in Town Planning circles. Yet it was during this time that her climbing career began to flourish, and somehow she found time to return to Cumbria and to the mountains whenever she could. She continued to climb with Millican Dalton; at this point she had no other climbing partner, and it did not occur to her to seek one, although, as always, she walked and scrambled alone whenever possible.

While working at Kings Langley, Mabel began going to Epping Forest at weekends to join Millican Dalton and others in the pleasant pastime of 'Tree Boling.' Here, the great beech trunks provided cracks, chimneys, cols and face climbs. They named them, repeated the favourites, and made new ascents. Mabel mentioned that one of the very few scars she carried was a tiny mark on one finger, the result of an Epping Forest tree climb. Millican was then the only man allowed to light fires in the forest; there were happy tea and coffee parties, where they sang songs and discussed the chances of the early Everest expeditions. Occasionally, they went to his hut, which was later burnt down, and with it many photographs and early volumes of the Fell and Rock Journals. Millican's only comment was that, as many letters had been destroyed, he would not have to trouble about answering them.

In 1919, Mabel remembered going up Walla Crag and Mouse Ghyll with Millican. At the exit from the latter she was very tired and had to come on the rope. She commented that only twice again, in a 'fairly long innings', did she remember doing that, and in both cases it was anticipated. At about that time, her brother Arnold married Madge Owen at Rosthwaite Church in Borrowdale, on September 16th 1919. He was later to run the Oddfellows Arms at Caldbeck for 26 years, and would live only a stone's throw from Mabel most of his life. The night before the wedding, she and Madge camped out at High Lodore.

Next morning, what might have been a climbing party set out for

Rosthwaite. Millican acted as best man, in complete climbing costume, boots and rope and all, his only concessions being a pair of stockings; and when the bridal party emerged he at once sat down and removed them. He cooked the wedding breakfast – a chicken boiled in a billy can – in the (then disused) slate caves, and we spent a happy day climbing in and around the quarries.

Later, Mabel wrote a poem in which she refers to this day:

BORROWDALE

Blow, winds in Borrowdale
And rains down fall –
The voices of the waters and the wild birds call.

Black rocks of Borrowdale
And frost-split slate,
Floods in the valley when the beck's in spate.

Dark tarns and moorland where
The mist wreaths form,
And sun follows thunder on the edge of the storm.

'Neath birches of Borrowdale
The wee mosses bide,
And soft is the bedding there for bridegroom and bride.

Blow, winds of Borrowdale.
And snow down fall;
I would come to Borrowdale the last time of all.

From my heart in Borrowdale
The rowan trees shall grow:
I shall be undying in the earth I know.

M.M.B.

In 1921, Millican took a small party, including Mabel, to Taylor's Force. His famous blue bicycle got most of the kit there. They found a cache of tinned goods, deeply hidden in the grass and boulders, obviously long forgotten by its owner; the labels departed, the tins rusted, but the contents in perfect condition. As Millican was a vegetarian, most of the spoils fell to the rest of the party. That was the summer when Mabel began to expand her climbing partnerships; they visited Dove's Nest again; they did Eagle's Nest Chimney and Needle Ridge, and Mabel's first lead, Kern Knotts Chimney. Mabel was delighted. On another glorious day, they did the Needle, Kern Knotts Buttress, and Eagle's Nest Direct, with Ralph Mayson. Mayson's family owned a photographic business in Keswick, and it was he who had produced advertising literature and a series of picture postcards to promote Millican's services.

It was at this time that they first talked about proposing Mabel for membership of the Fell and Rock Club. 'It seemed incredible luck to me, she commented. (Do today's postulants get such a thrill out of it, she wondered?)' That same season, joined by Coward from Keswick, they did a climb now called Black Crag Buttress, but then Troutdale Buttress, and on another day had some fun on the Ennerdale Face of Gable.

'For the first (and most certainly the last) time,' said Mabel, 'I was inveigled into doing that detestable affair called Smugglers' Chimney. Dalton, very knowing about it, kindly gave the lead to Coward. Then he went round to the top, and sat there making sarcastic remarks about how long we took, and 'Snugglers' Chimney, while we fought and gasped in what should really be called 'Strugglers' Chimney. Years later, when helping with notes for the Gable Guide, I flatly refused to accompany A. Wood-Johnson into the thing, and sat below making notes of 'pitches' and listening with grim pleasure to his howls of agony. At one point he reported himself to be upside down. (Incidentally, I wonder if my measurements were accurate; anyone care to check up?)' As for membership of the Fell and Rock Climbing Club, Mabel wrote: 'With great nervousness, I entered Olympus; in other words, climbed Moss Ghyll with H.B.Lyon, H.P.Cain and Dr. Burnett; and that fear passed away with other ghosts of girlhood.'

At last, Mabel saw herself as a fully-fledged climber, and was accepted as such.

The Spare Rib Approach to Climbing

It should be pointed out that, historically, there have been a number of barriers for women climbers, creating an experience psychologically quite different to that of their male counterparts. In the early days of rock climbing, men were the doorkeepers to the sport; if women got a chance to participate at all, it was usually through fathers, brothers, husbands or male friends. A further factor was the restrictive clothing they were obliged to wear; before the Great War they had to climb in long, heavy skirts, and not until afterwards was it acceptable for them to be seen on the crags in breeches. Even then, one dare not appear in public in climbing attire. Wrote Dorothy Pilley, in her book *Climbing Days*: 'One had really done something drastic by becoming a climber ... And it wasn't smiled on either – not with the smiles you like to see. In those days, even up in the Lakes, a girl couldn't walk about a village in climbing clothes without hard stares from the women and sniggers from the louts.' On one occasion in the 1920s, she was ordered to change into a skirt for dinner by the manageress of the Sligachan Hotel. Besides considering the routes they planned to do, women climbers also had to be aware of the impression they made, and what effect this might have on their reputation and future possibilities. They had to remain 'feminine' too. Perhaps the view expressed at an FRCC dinner was representative of the times: 'A man hates a mannish woman, but when a girl equals him at his favourite sport and yet retains her womanliness, he readily admits her claim to a place on the rope.'

Not surprisingly, even well established women climbers had complex attitudes. For instance, Dorothy Pilley stated: 'No sensible woman will imagine that she has the strength of a first-class man. But she need not lack judgement and the capacity to limit her enterprise to her powers.' From the hindsight of the 21st Century, one could easily make facetious comments about weight-training; but Dorothy's remark suggests an acceptance that participation was allowed as long as women knew their place and were not too ambitious. Social tradition dictated that heroic feats in climbing, and other aspects of life, could only be achieved through the sort of intensive male bonding so encouraged by clubs. Between the wars, however, attitudes began to change.

The first two women's climbing clubs in Britain were established because the doors of men's clubs were closed to them. These were the Ladies' Alpine Club and the Ladies' Scottish Climbing Club, both founded in 1907. The FRCC, established in 1906, was open to women from the outset, although they were heavily outnumbered. The Great War, however, led to a broadening of horizons for women, and in 1921 a climber called Pat Kelly decided to establish the Pinnacle Club, a mountaineering club exclusively for women. Pat, who was the wife of another leading climber, H.M. Kelly, was one of the best climbers in Britain at the time. She said: 'Perhaps we got tired of being taken in hand by men climbers, kind and helpful though they might be, perhaps we sympathised with the would-be climbing woman who had no man friend to take her in tow ... As in other walks of life, women wanted to find their own feet: it was very splendid for some women always to be able to borrow crutches in the shape of a man's help, and a man's rope, but it is even better if we have feet of our own and can climb some things as well as a man climber.' Pat liked best to solo climbs. 'Solitary climbing was a passion of Pat's,' wrote her friend, Dorothy Pilley. 'She enjoyed it for the peculiar heightened consciousness it gives, and she was so complete a mistress of the craft that with her even very difficult solitary climbs were perfectly justified.'

Other women also shared the idea that a rock-climbing club for women would give them the chance to climb independently of men, so developing better leadership and general mountaineering skills. Many were adamant that this was not a feminist gesture. Dorothy wrote: 'It was a rooted sense that training in the fullest responsibilities of leadership in all its aspects is one of the most valuable things that climbing has to offer, and that women could hardly get such training unless they climbed by themselves. A women's club would make such climbing seem normal, would collect those who shared this aspiration, would help them to form real climbing *ropes* as distinguished from strings of people who happened to be climbing together.'

Sadly, Pat was killed when descending on Tryfan on April 17th, 1922, when she was at the height of her powers. Nobody saw what happened to her – she was found pitched headlong on the ground on the west side of Tryfan, with a climbing shoe missing. The other climbing boot was not found until six months later. She had been trying out a pair of boots with new nails, and must have tripped on loose rock. The full truth was kept hidden for 60 years; in his diaries of the time, H.M. Kelly did not refer to the accident. He simply recorded 'Bangor', where his wife was in hospital.

Despite this tragedy, the Pinnacle Club continued to flourish. Perhaps to hammer home this spirit of independence, or as small acts of rebellion, members called each other by their surnames, and smoking was popular. The Pinnacle Club always had close contacts with the FRCC, with many original Pinnacle members having dual membership. Pat Kelly had written: 'We are glad to have the sympathy and help of our big brother, the F. & R.C.C. I say Brother, but that is not quite enough; to some of us the Lakeland club is more like a Wise Parent, – shall we say Father and Mother in one?' It seems that the climbing establishment did indeed have a paternal 'spare rib' approach to women's climbing and the formation of the Pinnacle Club. Wrote R.S.T. Chorley, editor of the FRCC Journal: 'To the Pinnacle Club, members of our own club will extend a particularly hearty welcome, for it is very much bone of our bone and flesh of our flesh.'

When Mabel began roped climbing, at the age of twenty-seven, she did not have the right to vote; yet she refused to be restricted by constructs of women's place in society. She had gained her love of the fells independently, and once she found her way into the climbing world, little was going to hold her back. She had skill, confidence and strength of character; outwardly, she made no attempt to challenge existing beliefs but simply got on with the activity of climbing. She found herself partners of suitable ability, regardless of gender, age, race or class, and boldly went where few others dared to go. She climbed blithely past the limiting beliefs of her time, and her attitudes and achievements were to encourage women climbers of future generations to follow suit.

A Continental Holiday

Mabel's next exploit was a visit to the Austrian Alps. Some years before, while at the Epping camp, Mabel and Millican had discussed the idea of a continental holiday. In August 1922, she collected a large party together, and they set off for the Tyrol. At this time, postwar Europe was still undergoing reconstruction, and foreign travel was cheap due to the strength of sterling against foreign currencies. Mabel did all the organisation and paperwork, sorting out tickets, passports and money exchanges; Millican, in his turn, 'dealt patiently with a company ranging from middle-aged women to small boys, and taught many of us all we ever learned about negotiating glaciers and snowfields.' The party initially included, among many others: Miss Cross, from Kings Langley, Gertrude Walmsley (an ex-Saffron Walden student) and Mabel's 14-year-old brother, Pat.

Mabel wrote long letters to her father from 'Camp Schlieffstein', near Mayerhofen in the Zillerthal, 'on a site where loveliness and novelty had to make up for the fact that not one square yard of it was flat'. 'The journey went off successfully,' she said. 'We could hardly believe that we accomplished it, and that not one of the 30 people or their 90 pieces of baggage were missing when we finally unloaded off the mules here on Thursday night!' The night before they left, she had stayed up late finishing a botany paper with Miss Gibson, another member of the party. The journey lasted three days. They first took a crossing to Ostend, then spent the rest of the day travelling through Belgium, which now looked 'wonderfully prosperous and industrious'. Next was an unplanned change in Cologne at midnight, where there were problems with a German family occupying their reserved carriage. 'It's open – we come in,' they said. She replied, 'That's the policy that didn't work, isn't it?' and wondered if it hit home! Finally they arrived in Munich, and later came up the 'heavenly valley' to Mayerhofen, where the luggage went in little carts and pack mules, while they walked the eight miles to the camp site. Mabel was entranced by the flowers, and sent a packet of roots back to Miss Glaister, her childhood mentor, in the hope that she might see them again one day.

Over the first few days, she and her companions went up to visit various climbing huts, where rates were cheap at 1/- for a bed and two meals. While away, she wrote to her father: 'A small boy has arrived, called Franz, whom I 'ordered' from Vienna, to share (Pat's) tent – and I hope, teach him German: only Franz speaks very good English, having been a year in Godalming with Mr. Mallory the Everest Climber!' This little boy was Franz Knefel (later changed to Nevel), who had arrived from the English Kinderheim orphanage in Vienna. He deserves a chapter of his own.

Mabel and her party enjoyed camping at Schlieffstein, although they were amazed at how every patch of land flat enough to lie on was cultivated, making the camping somewhat uncomfortable. She took great interest in her surroundings – how crops were grown, how the Austrian families – papas and fat mamas and little girls with their rucksacks, loved to go on walking tours. There were few English in the valley, and she remarked that they created quite a sensation.

Mabel's first experience on a glacier was an attempt to climb the Loffler. They did not get all the way up it, but Mabel relished the experience. Soon afterwards, they went to a folk festival near Mayerhofen, where all the men and maidens wore lovely costumes and did local Tyrolean dances, and there were many singing and drinking huts made from newly felled fir trees. In typical Mabel fashion, the English then held their own festival at their camp; two girls did a play, and they had a campfire and songs and dances of their own. Many of the local young men came along and brought a concertina, so they had more Tyrolean songs and dances again. The men asked Mabel's party to go to the neighbouring Gasthof afterwards, under the pretext of being able to dance better on the floor. Mabel commented 'They enjoyed themselves immensely, and could easily have become too attentive!'

Soon, she went up with Miss Hirst to meet Millican Dalton, Miss Hamilton (an old friend of Patrick Geddes) and Gertrude Walmsley at the Furstschagelhaus, with the intention of crossing the Schönbichlerhorn to the Berliner or Alpenrose Huts in the next valley. Mabel wrote to her father: 'We got off the track a bit, got onto a ridge, and went along it – too far to our left as it turned out. We got up a thing, which was not the Schönbichlerhorn, but the Talggen Knopf, 3203 metres. It was made of the rottenest rock we had ever struck, but not otherwise difficult.' They met adverse conditions on the way down, with wind and hail, and did not consult map and compass as they should have done. As a result, they started down the wrong side. The three novices were roped, with Dalton in front and Mabel at the back, sometimes on the rope and sometimes not.

> At one point, one of them said to me, didn't I think they might unrope for speed? I said better not – and a few minutes later a large rock came away in the hands of Gertrude Walmsley and carried her down a steep slope. She was brought up all right, but had hurt her leg a bit, which delayed us of course. The result was we couldn't get right down in daylight! That was the night on which it chose to snow and we were some 7000 feet up the mountain!! It sounds rather an awful experience, but in point of fact it really wasn't. They were a most sporting lot. We had half an inch of candle in a lantern, food & cigarettes – & we sang & told stories & huddled close for warmth. Luckily there was no wind. The customary thunderstorm arrived, with most curious effects. As a rule we all kept under a mackintosh, but once when we all got out to rearrange ourselves, all our hair was electrified! Gertrude stood up against the sky and had a veritable halo, every hair with a spark of light on it. Some of us slept a bit & we went on again as soon as the dawn came, in a wonderful white world. I wish any of us had taken a photograph, but you may imagine we were cold enough & dreaming of beds & coffee! All very cheery & good tempered though. The dawn came behind a great peak, with glorious colour, which we memorised to enjoy later. On the way down we met flocks of sheep. Tame wasn't the word for it – they simply mobbed us, baaing & pushing! At 7 a.m. we arrived at the Alpenrose Hütte, where the dear folk had us in dry beds in no time & brought cups of tea into which they put spirit, without asking us – & later when we made a list of what we had eaten & drunk (to help in the perfectly awful reckoning in thousands of krönen) crossed it off firmly! They seemed amused at us & the way we took it all. We took off all our clothes, & were prisoners at their mercy! Had a very nice day, mostly asleep, & came back to camp in the evening. Nobody is a penny the worse, & even Gertrude has only a bruise on her leg, & is game to go anywhere again tomorrow ...

Mabel included details of this incident in her obituary to Millican Dalton:

> His passion for making tea and coffee in all sorts of queer places was more than useful, but on one occasion when his brew would have been more than welcome than manna from heaven, I think the apparatus was missing! This was when five of us – four women and Millican – got caught in a blizzard and benighted high up at glacier level above the Alpenrose, and spent a very uncomfortable night out in the snow. A violent thunderstorm added excitement to the situation, the lightning striking our ice-axes, while drops of water on our hair shone strangely, so that for once at least we wore halos. Perhaps we deserved them, for though drenched to the skin before we gave up the attempt to go down, and all very cold, we sang songs and told stories through the long night, and nobody 'woke up dead'.
>
> When the light came, heralded by a glorious sunrise, Millican led us down to the Alpenrose Hütte. I remember the strange spectacle of him defending himself with an ice-axe from a mob of sheep ... Millican went up again later for the rope which we had left because it was impossible to coil it, both we and the rope being far too stiff. In the evening (for we had spent the day in bed) he led us down to camp, a white handkerchief round one ankle, and a lighted cigarette helping us to follow in the dark.

This adventure did not discourage the explorers one bit. 'We are just back from the most gorgeous expedition I have ever had,' Mabel wrote soon afterwards.

> On Friday, a selection of us set off again up the valley. Dalton, Gertrude Walmsley (nothing daunted by a rather stiff leg!) & two who came for a week – Dr Thomas (a lady) and Mrs Venables. We got up to the Grawand Hütte, & none of us feeling very energetic, stayed the night there. Gertrude & I wandered into the kitchen in the evening, where the host was playing a sort of zither. A woman came in who could speak English & talked a lot. She told us among other things that some of us were supposed to be on unemployment pay, living in Austria because it was cheaper!! They were all so friendly. We are all greeted with the jolliest smiles & of hails (Gruss Gott – i.e. Greetings in the name of God is the common salutation) all up and down the valley. Next day, Dalton went up to the place where we stuck on Wed to find a lost rope; & the other four went to the Schwarz See; a tiny lake about 8000 feet up. On return-

ing to the Alpenrose where we had booked rooms, they found two other friends, Wallie and Lottie Camelus. Dr Thomas and Mrs Venables had to go down again, but the next day, the others fixed to go up the Schwarzenstein, following a party of English boys ... It was glorious. None of the climbing was very difficult, except for a steepish snow slope which troubled Lottie who is small & fat! It was a long 6 hours climb up, mostly over pure white snowfields; with a clear atmosphere & cloudless blue sky, almost indigo overhead. The top, 11,500 ft or so, is the Italian frontier ... we spent a long time there, & actually made a fire & some coffee (some waste wood). We looked into Italy & Switzerland, far away, & away over the Tyrol. I never saw such a view in my life, & one might never see again I think. We went down the other side to the Greizer Hütte in the Fententhal. Much steeper, & over a glacier – Poor Lottie had a stiff time! I was last on the rope, behind her, & got her down by letting her slide like a sack in all the steep places, the length of her rope, & then coming down & coiling it as I went! She was wet!!! Anyway, we arrived back in camp about 8.30 p.m., tired & hungry & awfully pleased with ourselves.'

On 21st August, Mabel wrote home to say that Pat had left that day in the charge of Harry, who was female. They went to Innsbruck for a night, and then on to Oberammergau, where they had tickets for a performance. When they arrived back in London, Harry was to 'post' Pat back on the train to Carlisle and telegraph his father. 'I fear he is rather grubby,' wrote Mabel, 'in spite of immersions in the river; but no doubt H will wash him somewhere on the way home! And he looked quite respectable in the grey suit. It is as well that he has got it for the journey, for his greens are pretty far on in life by now. His little companion, Franz, is still here – & I may take him to Vienna myself at the end of the week –'

Soon after this, the Americans Lewis Mumford and his wife Sophia arrived in camp. Mumford was an ardent admirer of Patrick Geddes, and was then at an early stage of his distinguished career as a sociological writer. He had corresponded with Geddes since 1913, and in 1923 arranged a lecture tour for him in the United States; he was to call his own son, born in 1925, Geddes Mumford. Sadly, 19 year-old Geddes Mumford was killed in combat in Italy in 1944; his father wrote a book about his life entitled 'Green Memories.' In that book there is a picture of the young Geddes visiting Troutbeck in the Lake District, in 1928, when perhaps Mabel met the family once again.

The final expedition involved Gladys Mayer, a German student from Leipzig called Reps, Franz, Millican Dalton, the Mumfords, Miss Hamilton, and Mabel. The Mumfords were not equipped for climbing and it was misty, so they did not embark on the planned route, but went on to the Alpenrose for the night, and in the afternoon played about on the Horn Kees, the glacier near the Berliner Hütte. Reps, Franz and Mabel were on a separate rope, and together they went a bit further, and had some adventures in crossing the glacier and finding the way off in the mist, having missed the easiest place for crossing the moraine at the first shot. Reps then dropped his ice-axe down a crevasse, and Mabel retrieved it (not a deep one, but quite amusing, she commented).

The next day everyone (except the Mumfords, who had to return to Mayerhofen) went over the Schönbichlerhorn, and this time found an easy path over the summit, with a glorious view from the top. Millican found wood, lit a fire and made coffee and tea, which was dispensed to various tourists who came past. Next they descended to the Furtschagelhaus in the late afternoon. Reps and Mabel became ambitious – it seemed their one chance to do a decent climb – and after some discussion they hired a guide to take them up the Hochfeiler next day. This is the highest mountain of the Zillerthal, at 11,600 feet, and said Mabel, 'reckoned as stiff'. The guide was Alfonse Holhager, the 'master of the Furstschagel', who had worked there for 22 years. He charged £1 English money for the job, and told them that once they had done it, they would not say it was too much. 'Wherewith I agree heartily,' said Mabel later. 'It was my one extravagance anyway – so far!' She found him an excellent guide. At 2.20 a.m. he roused them, with coffee and rolls. They set off at 3.30 a.m. on a clear starlit morning, he carrying a lantern. After an hour, they stopped to put crampons on, the first time for Mabel. The dawn was marvellous, with a morning alpenglow coming on to the snowy glacier. Unfortunately, the last page or pages of Mabel's letter home are missing, but we know that she enjoyed the route enormously, made all the more satisfying because of a challenge.

After taking Franz back to Vienna, where she spent three days, those left in the group crossed the Brenner Pass to Italy for a look at the Dolomites. There Mabel met up with Millican again, and being the only two climbers left, had a small taste of the wonderful quality of the rock – she forgot where. Millican was tired by then and they left him at Tre Croce to make contact with a friend, while most of the party set off for home and the new school term. Mabel had agreed to go camping with some of her friends in the Kibbo Kift, a new movement which combined outdoor life with ancient ritual.

Mabel never managed to climb in the Alps again. On her only visit in 1922, she limited her plans to routes that could be achieved with those much less able than herself. Had she continued with alpine mountaineering and gained more experience, she could doubtless have achieved some very hard routes. But Mabel was content to stay on home ground, and it was here that she concentrated her efforts.

Franz Nevel

Franz was born in 1911 near Vienna. In those years, this was an unstable region of shifting borders and politics, where at different times one could be in Czechoslovakia, Bohemia, or Moravia. He was the illegitimate son of an army officer with an ailing wife, and the governess who looked after his daughters. He refused to acknowledge the child, and because the mother was unable to care for him, he was placed with varying foster parents and homes and orphanages. There his mother would visit him on Sundays to take him to church, where he would have to spend hours kneeling and praying. As his widow, Marianne Nevel commented, 'It rather spoiled his relationship with her and didn't do much for his religion either.'

The years of famine during and after the Great War stayed most vivid in Franz's young mind – he talked of how people sold all their possessions to barter for food on the black market and from farmers, and the suffering was appalling. Franz himself was never quite sure how he first arrived in Britain; somehow he was passed along a 'humanist' chain after the war, possibly as part of a famine relief programme. There he was given a placement with the Mallory family. Franz was a few years older than their own children, and he flourished in his new environment. He was a lively and endearing boy, full of interest in the world around him, and able to make the most of the opportunities that befell him. Marianne wrote: 'This opened up a whole new world for Franz. The Mallorys were wonderfully kind to him and for the first time in life he was part of a family and had siblings (although the girls probably regarded this newcomer with mixed feelings). He soon hero-worshipped George, and later kept a diary and all the paper clippings he could lay his hands on of the fatal expedition.'

Having spent a year with the Mallory family, little Franz must have relished the chance to join an English party in the Tyrol, especially the chance to be companion to a boy of similar age. At that time, George Mallory was away on an Everest expedition, and the two boys must have talked excitedly about it. 'He is a very delightful child,' wrote Mabel. 'Most helpful around camp and rather worried by Pat's untidyness in the tent, I gather! They hoisted a flag in camp yesterday. I was told that it was of combined British and Austrian colours, but as it was made of paper it had already dissolved into a rag by the time I saw it!' The two boys became totally absorbed in an Austro-English Climbing Club, of which they were the committee members.

When Pat returned to England, Franz stayed on, and took a full part in the rest of the expedition. Mabel took him back to Vienna, together with her friend, Miss Hamilton. She had become attached to the little boy, and could see very little future for him in a children's home in Vienna. She began to wonder if there was not a way to bring Franz back to Britain; she discussed this with her friends, and the Mallory family must have been consulted too. Soon after her return, an application was made to the Children's Hospitality (After-Care) Committee (Registered under the War Charities' Act, 1916). The object of this body was 'to provide such after-care as may be necessary for Children in Central Europe who have been repatriated after staying in this country'. On 5th December, 1922, Mabel received a letter from Isaac Goss, the Honorary Treasurer and Secretary of the Vienna Sub-Committee. He wrote:

'Franz Knefel.

Upon receiving your letter with regard to the above boy I had a talk with the Home Office people. They tell me that there may have been some slight delay owing to the fact that your application went to the Foreign Office, but the matter is now in order, is in hand, and you may expect to hear from them in the next few days.

It is very interesting to hear of your plan, I saw Franz last July, he is a nice boy and I feel sure you will find what you are doing to be worth while in the long run ... '

The next day, Mabel received a letter from the Aliens Branch of the Home Office:

'Dear Madam,

With reference to your letter of the 25th November regarding Franz KNEFEL, I beg to inform you that before facilities can be granted for his journey to this country I must ask you to forward to me a letter from his parents, agreeing to his coming to you, and also to give me an undertaking that you will be responsible for his maintenance while in this country, and for his return to Vienna if called upon to repatriate him.

I should add that if he is allowed to come to this country his admission will be subject to his satisfying the Medical Inspector at the port of arrival that there is no medical objection to his being allowed to land. Great care should, therefore be taken to ensure that before he starts he is in good health ... '

On January 17th 1923, Mabel's friend, Miss Hamilton, received a letter from a Mary Houghton of the Children's Hospitality (After-Care) Committee, who was the representative in Vienna. She wrote that she was 'interested in what happens to any of the children in our big family ... I believe that Miss Levin is hoping to send Franz over to you as soon as possible, but it is not easy at this time of year to find someone going over, with whom he can travel. It does seem splendid that you should take him under your wing again, for there seems no chance of his ever having a happy home-life here.'

After lengthy correspondence with various bodies, Mabel and her friends finally received the necessary agreement to bring him over to England. They made themselves jointly responsible for his education and his wellbeing. Mrs Fraser-Davies, Mabel's good friend from her Saffron Walden days, also became closely involved with Franz's wellbeing and maintenance. Marianne recounted: 'He arrived in 1923 with a label round his neck giving his destination. His mother had seen him off at the station (in Vienna, I think), giving him a photograph of herself showing a beautiful young woman and inscribed with many blessings. One can only guess at the heartache!

I did try to find out from Franz what he felt on this voyage, was he frightened or apprehensive? But he didn't think he was, after all he was quite used to being moved around fairly frequently and this journey was much more promising and exciting than any transfer before.'

Franz's godson, Julian White, referred to this experience during Franz's funeral address in 1993. 'However friendly the smiles on the faces of those who had made this possible and no doubt welcomed him – again just picture, if you can, the reality of life at that moment for that boy of 10 or so. The bewilderment, the clacking of foreign tongues, the fear, the confusion, the giant adults who surrounded him.' Franz immediately attended Kings Langley Priory, where Mabel was able to keep watch over him. He stayed there for two years. Well versed in survival tactics by then, one result was that he became the leader of his hungry school friends on an occasional raid of the school pantry or of a neighbouring orchard! Pat Barker was also a pupil at the school for a time. Said his son, Tim: 'This was altogether an "advanced school" and I don't think my father actually thought much of it! He finished his schooling at Appleby Grammar School.'

During the school holidays, Franz took part in the mountaineering and camping holidays organised by Mabel and friends, particularly the regular Seathwaite camps. He kept an album of photographs, showing him and Pat and other boys cooking and fishing and generally having fun around camp. 'Franz had some wonderful times camping and climbing with Mabel and her climbing friends,' said Marianne. 'He particularly remembered being very ill on one occasion and not being able to join the party on any climbing expedition, but lying in the tent in his sleeping bag in a delirious state. It was later diagnosed as pneumonia and left one of his lungs scarred. This wasn't discovered until long afterwards when he had to have a medical examination for an insurance cover.'

In November 1923, Mabel received a letter from Miss Levin of the English Kinderheim in Vienna, which read as follows:

'Dear Miss Barker,

I am writing to ask you whether you would be kind enough to see that Franz Knefel's mother has regular news of him. I understand you do not wish him to have any intimate relations with his mother. Considering how much he dislikes her, I do not think you need have any fears. She will never have any influence over him. On the other hand, she is absolutely justified in insisting in having news of him at regular intervals. The boy has not been legally adopted by his English friends; the mother is his legal guardian, and is the only person, except his guardian, who has any control over him. Her request is therefore absolutely in order, and you can only put yourself in the wrong by overlooking it. I am continually having complaints made to me, so I do hope you will see that a postcard is sent regularly.'

Meanwhile, Franz had a busy life in England. He kept closely in touch with the Mallory family and followed the progress of the 1924 expedition. He always remembered the excitement of packing up for expeditions, and at some point, was given one of George's Everest expedition tents, which he used for camping. (This later became one of the exhibits in the Rheged Exhibition). On March 8th 1924, he received a letter from George Mallory, addressed Anchor Line, T.S.S. California:

'My dear Franz,

I never wrote to thank you for a very nice letter you sent me in the Xmas holidays. I was so busy for a long time that I really didn't write any friendly letters till I came on board ship; but I haven't forgotten you.

I am having a very nice voyage. It has been beautiful weather since we got about as far south as Lisbon, 2 days from Liverpool. The Mediterranean has been perfectly smooth until to-day with light breezes & plenty of sunshine. Three of my companions for Mt. Everest, Irvine, Beetham & Hazard are all on board & very nice men. I particularly like Irvine who is splendidly built and rode two years in the Oxford boat.

A great many passengers are going to Egypt & will be getting off at Port Said tomorrow; they belong to a Cook's Tour, if you know what that means, & will have six days in Egypt, which doesn't seem long after going so far; but then they have had a very gay time on the way, with plenty of dancing, the deck made gay with coloured lights and flags; no doubt some of the young girls will come back engaged to be married, & then quite a lot of people will be happy, themselves & especially their mamas, some of their papas & brothers; & quite a number of people that have nothing to do with them will be excited to hear that Mr. A is going to marry that pretty girl Miss X; & that will give them something to talk about & they will be pleased too.

The people on the Cook's Tour are all Scotch; though foreigners from the English point of view so that one feels their country to be a foreign country. They use the same words as we English do; only they make them sound quite different and *you* wouldn't understand their language at all. English people however can quite easily get to understand it when they have learnt the trick. You may have noticed that English people have a strange way of dealing with the letter *h*. Some people say *h*ot & others 'ot & so on – and some say ache (meaning a pain) & others *h*ache (pronounced hake, the name of a fish) so that if one tells you that he has a bad ache or a bad hache, you have to consider whether he is a fisherman or a fishmonger before you can know what he means. Now the Scotch way is this: - wherever the English have one *h* they put in another & make *h*hot; if a word begins without an *h* they put one in the middle; if a double consonant comes in the middle they try if they can to turn both into *h* (thus letter may become le*hh*er or at least let*h*er); and anyway one Scotch *h* = 2 English *h*s in pronunciation. It is dreadful to think how we shall lose our *h*s when all the Scotch get off at Port Said.

On the 19th we shall reach Bombay; & three days in the train from there will bring us to Darjeeling where we shall find General Bruce & the others; at least I hope they won't have started without us. From the plains of India we shall go up 7000 ft to Darjeeling in a lovely little railway which goes first through tropical jungle & then goes winding up & up through the hills; everywhere the hill sides are very steep; there are wonderful trees & flowering shrubs. Up near Darjeeling we shall find pink & white magnolias in flower & also on many of the houses a lovely creeper Solanum jasminoides, which grows at Westbrook outside the drawing room window – but at Darjeeling it grows bigger and flowers more abundantly.

We shall have four or five days at Darjeeling; not less I hope, for it is a very attractive place with its wonderful views across the deep valleys - & then we shall be on the march through Sikhim with our ponies and mules & boxes & the fat general dripping with perspiration.

I expect you will get someone to help you read this letter; be sure that you choose a Scotchman and ask him to read the le*hh*er.

Your affectionate, George Mallory'

Franz must have been devastated when his hero failed to return to tell him all about his adventures. He remained very close to Ruth Mallory, and she took great pains to ensure that Franz was happy and later arranged for him to go to Rendcomb College near Cirencester, where he had a wonderful time and made some lifelong friends. Franz was not academically oriented; his childhood experiences must have disrupted his early education and added to that, there were the difficulties of learning in a new language. However, his abilities at craftwork began to develop, and he had a wonderful woodwork teacher who was inspired by the Cotswold Craftsmen.

Franz's mother and father did eventually get married, when his father's first wife died. His mother tried hard to get him back, but Franz was sixteen or thereabouts by then, had become very anglicised and did not want to go back. He was also advised not to do so, not least by Ruth Mallory, who considered his mother to be very unstable and unfit. He did, however, remain in touch with his mother all his life and used to send her parcels of clothing. At one time, much later, after he was married, he made efforts to bring her to England to live with them, but by then she was living in a home in Czechoslovakia, where she suffered from religious mania and other mental problems.

Franz changed his surname to Nevel, and after leaving school, entered a traineeship at the Waldorf Hotel in London. In order to augment their frugal pay, he and a schoolfriend used to make pieces of furniture, and this little enterprise soon took up more time than he had to spare. Pat Barker would visit him there from time to time and take him to the Speedway. Strongly influenced by the work of William Morris, and bored with hotel management, where prospects seemed very slow and unpromising, Franz decided to go into partnership with his friend and furniture-making became his full-time career. He established a firm named Betula Ltd, which survived and prospered until World War Two severely disrupted production, and many of the skilled employees had to leave. On special occasions, such as weddings, Mabel would give her friends gifts of craft objects made at Betula. Franz's godson remembered visiting the workshops, with their 'marvellous, evocative smell of the wood, so lovely polished and brown.' Here there is surely a resonance with Mabel's theories about the fundamental occupations, including that of woodsman, and the importance of working with the hands.

Marianne met Franz in 1950 when she came to London for a year, as many Swiss girls did in those days. By the time the year was up, Franz had proposed and they were married in Switzerland in 1952. Marianne remembered going to visit Mabel at Friar Row when they were holidaying in Cumberland at the beginning of the marriage. She remembered a lively and friendly lady who had some very interesting plants, including an orange or grapefruit grown from a pip. Theirs was a long and fruitful marriage, and four children quickly followed. However, the early happy years were shadowed in 1964 by the death of their son Nicky, at nine years old, who drowned in Coniston Water, whilst the family was on holiday there. They had visited Mabel's nephew and wife, Lindsay and Mina Barker, only the day before. Nicky had been excited at the promise of coming back the next day to talk to Lindsay, who worked in the RAF, about his great interest, aeroplanes.

After this sad event, the woodwork business stumbled too, due to fighting off cheap imports and the craze for plastic. But Franz managed to pick up his stride again, and with great courage and determination the family moved house and the business was re-established at Ayot Green in Hertfordshire, where it later continued under the stewardship of his son, Vince.

Marianne commented that Franz remembered Mabel and kept in touch with her all his life. He always spoke of her with admiration and gratitude. He was a very kind man; the hardships of his early life made him very sympathetic to other people's problems. He always wanted to help people – sometimes not very wisely. She often thought that he should write his life story, but said that he was too busy living and enjoying his six grandchildren, and hated having to sit at his desk.

Godson Julian White, the son of one of Franz's schoolfriends from Rendcomb, talked of his later days at his funeral. By 1980, when Franz was 69, Marianne was trying to slow down his insistent pace, and in the early days of a rather halfhearted retirement, they returned to his beloved Cotswolds to live, in some style, in a house that was perfect for entertaining. Julian remembered how, one sunny afternoon, Franz drew the children aside and took them to look out of the window. Then he led them out onto the lawn, claiming that it had been raining. They all knew it couldn't have been. But it had rained little packets of sweets all over the lawn, and the little girls' faces were full of amazement and excitement as they ran to collect the treasure. This was what Franz specialised in, he said – marvellous, simple fun.

'It may be well to end just there,' said Julian, 'with a picture of children having fun, because Franz always managed to – fishing, bicycle rides, camp fires and climbing trees, right up to his 80th birthday. With a boy, and later a man, who suffered what I am sure were many hardships in life, but who I never heard complain – he always managed to smile, adapt, and quietly carry on, with fortitude, with optimism, right to the end. A survivor. With a man who had a great love of nature, not just of mountains, walks, his honey bees, gardens and flowers, the great outdoors, woods – but above all, people. That brown and polished wood-smelling man. A man who carried always that childlike sense of fun. Simple fun which created pleasure for all of us who knew him – as children and adults alike.'

Climbing with Frankland

After her continental holiday, Mabel returned to Kings Langley Priory and her usual busy schedule, which now included attempts to bring young Franz over to Britain. Whenever possible, she went to the hills and climbed. As a fully-fledged member of the Fell and Rock Climbing Club, and with some Alpine experience behind her, she had now gained in confidence. Although she kept diaries of her climbing exploits, these sadly did not survive. Among her climbing companions of the time were H. B. Lyon, Dr Arthur Wakefield and H. P. Cain. Lyon was an active member of the Fell and Rock who came from Kendal. In 1923, he put up the first climb in White Ghyll, White Ghyll Chimney. On August 12th that year, he set out to do the first ascent of Bracket and Slab on Gimmer. 'I was able to commandeer a strong party,' he wrote, 'including Miss M.M. Barker, Herbert, Cain and Wilton. Only Herbert and Miss Barker, being of slighter build than the others, followed up the Chimney, which is certainly not to be recommended as a pleasant afternoon's recreation.' The previous week, on 5th August, Lyon, Cain and Barker, accompanied by T. R. Burnett had done a new variation on Moss Ghyll Grooves. Lyon later served in the Indian Army, and spent most of his life in India. Arthur Wakefield was also from Kendal, and a formidable fell runner. In 1920 and 1921, he seconded George Bower, one of the leading climbers of the day, on several new ascents on Gimmer. He was a member of the 1922 Everest Expedition, but was badly affected by altitude.

Cain was a committee member of the Fell and Rock, and it was he who, in 1919, had suggested, 'Let's buy a fell,' as a memorial to members who had not returned from the Great War. This idea was unanimously accepted at the AGM. A deal was finally struck with Mr. H.W. Walker of Seascale, who agreed to sell, for £400, a vast acreage of the high ground on all sides of the Sty Head Pass, embracing twelve fells, with Great Gable at the centre. The money was quickly raised by club members, and the title deeds were handed over to the National Trust, and in effect to the nation. Dr Howard Somervell of Ambleside, who took part in the Everest expeditions of 1922 and 1924, proposed a bronze tablet inscribed with the names of the twenty club members who had been lost in the war, to be set on the summit of Great Gable. On June 8th, 1924, about 500 people assembled on the summit of Great Gable. The hills were swirling in cloud, and the rain was cold and driving. The club President, Dr Wakefield, spoke briefly and unveiled the memorial. Geoffrey Winthrop Young, who had lost a leg in the Great War, made the following tribute:

'Upon this mountain we are met today to dedicate this space of hills to freedom. Upon this rock are set the names of men – our brothers and our comrades upon these cliffs – who held with us, that there is no freedom of the soil where the spirit of man is in bondage; and who surrendered their part in the fellowship of hill and wind and sunshine, that the freedom of this land, the freedom of our spirit, should endure ...

By this symbol we affirm a two-fold trust: That which hills only can give to their children, the disciplining of strength in freedom, the freeing of the spirit through generous service, these free hills shall give again, and for all time. The memory of all that these children of hills have given, service, and inspiration, fulfilled, and perpetual, this free heart of our hills shall guard.'

Godfrey Solly then read Psalm 121, 'I will lift up mine eyes unto the hills ... '; Cain read the inscription on the tablet, saying that it was for 'the use and enjoyment of the people of our land for all time'. Two buglers sounded the Last Post. For Winthrop Young, it had been the hardest and longest walk he had done since the loss of his leg, and he struggled to get to the summit. Later, in writing about the ceremony, he said: 'As I spoke the words, well as I knew them, the emotion of their meaning welled up through them, and it held me like an inspiration; for once I felt like I was speaking to the mountains, in those terms in which they had spoken all my mountaineering life to me.'

It was in the summer of the previous year that Mabel first met Claude Frankland. He was a headmaster at Sweet Street School in Leeds, married with two children. He had learned to climb on the local crags at Almscliff and Ilkley, regularly walking the nine mile journey each way. 'It is the cleanest, healthiest, cheapest, rarest, most natural form of recreation that any man can pursue,' he said. At Almscliff, Frankland reigned supreme. His routes included Whisky Crack, Traditional Climb and Central Route, but without doubt his finest climb was Frankland's Green Crack, put up in 1920, when he was forty two years old, and then the hardest single unprotected pitch in the country. Today it is still considered one the top gritstone classics. By 1927, Central Route and Frankland's Green Crack had still not been led by anyone else. As a result, Frankland was held in awe by all the young climbers of the day. One of his favourite sayings was 'The difficulties are only mental.' Another was 'No advance without security.' Fergus Graham said of him 'His was the finest climbing I had ever seen, and a wonderful object lesson. He would choose a hold carefully, and once it was found he just stuck to it until he passed on to the next. There was none of the nervous paddling with the toe, or taking a handhold, letting it go, trying another, etc. It was just slow, smooth and inexorable movement.' Geoffrey Winthrop Young wrote about seeing him climb: 'Soon after the war I was invited to watch C.D. Frankland on his Almscliff verticals and overhangs, and I had the satisfaction of seeing him illustrate fully for the first time continuous movement up severe rock, with its rhythmic fluctuations and grace.'

Back from the war in 1918, after serving with the West Riding Field Ambulance in France, Frankland wrote: 'A feeling of wonder arises as to whether the old recreations will ever appeal again so keenly as before.' All the old climbs he had done now seemed hard. 'Had the armchair epoch arrived? ... Was one too old at forty plus?' But of course, all the old enthusiasm soon came back, and he regained his form. He even found age worked to his advantage. 'The old climber goes more slowly but more surely than the young shaver ... Increased skill more than compensates for their failing of strength with advancing years ... Age knows its power. Youth does not know its weaknesses.'

Frankland was a member of the Yorkshire Ramblers' Club and a keen caver too. He was involved in the exploration of many caves in Yorkshire, and made many first descents, including parts of the Gaping Ghyll system. In 1920, Frankland decided to undertake a course of solo climbing in the Lake District. This decision was taken only after a great deal of soul searching and influenced by the poor belaying techniques of the time. Safety methods were minimal in the 1920s, and the technique of belaying was in its infancy, used only when natural rock features could be exploited. It was because protection techniques were so limited that Frankland preferred to solo many routes, claiming that he knew he was capable of leading them successfully, and that to take anyone else with him would be to expose them to unnecessary risk. The hemp ropes were heavy and difficult to manage, especially in wet weather. Frankland wrote about this issue in an article entitled *In the Tracks of the Rubbermen*, published in the Yorkshire Ramblers' Club Journal of 1921. He said: 'On the climbs for which I desire to qualify, the rope is declared to be more dangerous than useful. Anchorage is often lacking. The pitches are very long and there would be no question of either shoulder or rope. It would be playing strictly according to the rules of the game if I tried the climbs myself, before inviting others to trust their safety to my leadership. Companions capable of leading are few. I came to the conclusion that I must climb alone.' Following on from this, there was a reluctance to publicise new routes because he was worried that less competent climbers would be tempted to try them, with possible fatal consequences. For example, he made the first ascent of Pulpit Corner but did not record it, regarding it as 'unjustifiable'. During this period, the use of rubber-soled shoes generated a great deal of interest. Frankland was a convert, and while some thought that the use of rubber soles was cheating and meant that the climber did not develop a good technique, he thought that climbs became safer and easier when using them.

Frankland's wife, Kitty, was somewhat bemused by his climbing exploits. She tolerated them, but was not altogether happy about it. Frankland confessed that he a habit of 'stealthily climbing up to his bedroom window by way of corbel and bay or even stealing up the corner of his dwelling, where the stonework is suitable.' In an unpublished manuscript, entitled *The Finished Product*, Frankland humorously gave us the picture. 'My wife, a level headed woman, put down the Daily Mail with impatience. I waited.

'I have just read another article on rock climbing,' she said.

'No!' I replied, knowing her views on this subject.

'Yes,' she contradicted. 'I've been reading them for years. How is it they never pass on beyond the raw material to the finished product?'

I began thinking of the technical difficulties.

'How long have you been climbing?' was the next question fired at my head.

Regretfully I admitted twenty two years.

'Then get a move on.'

Frankland then wrote of his solo ascent of Botterill's Slab, finishing with the statement: 'Exposed climbing is continued to the end and the most difficult slab sweeps down from the feet of an exultant victor.

My wife read the above with a frown. 'Is it true?' she asked.

'Every word.'

'And do ladies go in for this?'

'They have started recently.'

'Fools.'

My wife is a very level headed woman.'

During this period, Frankland climbed long routes on Pillar Rock and Scafell, and was soon ready to break through the psychological barrier of Central Buttress, first climbed by Herford, Sansom and Holland in 1914, and still not yet repeated. C.F. Holland warned all prospective climbers that it was 'The most arduous ascent in the Lake District; unexampled exposure; combined tactics and rope engineering essential at one point; not less than three climbers. Rubbers; the difficulties met are so great that the expedition ranks among the world's hardest. And it is possible only under practically perfect conditions.'

On 20th August, 1921, Frankland set off with Bentley Beetham, a schoolteacher at Barnard Castle School in County Durham, to make an attempt on Central Buttress. Beetham was also a strong mountaineer, and later was to join the 1924 Everest Expedition and to play a major part in the opening up of Borrowdale as an important climbing area. (Frankland and Beetham are said to have first noticed its climbing potential on walking back from Wasdale one wet day in 1922, to get the train from Keswick; they did the first recorded climb on Shepherd's Crag, Brown Slabs Arête.) Sansom and Herford had gained access to the Oval from the lower part of Botterill's Slab, but Frankland and Beetham instead climbed the steep rib of rock which is now the accepted start to Central Buttress, and took a good look at the Flake. 'Beetham thought it would go and said so. I did neither,' said Frankland. They threaded a rope and started attacking the two bulges preceding the overhang. 'By the time I had reached two holds, which are designed to be well-known by reason of their rarity, the left one on the edge of the Flake and the right one on the wall itself, I had begun thoroughly to enjoy myself. The rock was sound and the climbing simple. It is true that it was extremely strenuous going, but it was just as hard to remain still, and there was always the splendid flat top of the tall narrow chock to justify any slight 'overdraft' on reserves. As soon as I could, I hitched one rope across the top and dropped my arms to rest. While threading the other rope on the Flake side of the jammed block I found a short, blackened fragment of old rope, firmly wedged. It is still there, its suggestion of mythical legend perhaps accentuated by the harsh croaking of ravens, wheeling over Mickledore.'

Frankland 'set about' the overhang and tried to lead straight through, but struggled for at least half an hour before admitting defeat. After lunch on the Oval, they tried different tactics; Beetham climbed up the threaded chockstone, tied himself on, and Frankland then used him as a launching platform. Within five minutes, and by using Beetham's head and shoulders as holds, Frankland was able to turn the overhang and reach the finishing holds on the top of the Flake. Frankland described the experience of pulling over the top: 'The fingers curled over and hooked the sharp crest. Then, with feelings unbecoming of expression to a man who has reached my side of middle age, I enjoyed the luxury of lusty hauling, which was sheer joy with such a hold and such space below to spur one's efforts ... one of our friends was crawling at this moment carefully along the knife-edge of the crest of the Flake when we met literally face to face. The situation was ludicrously unexpected, and the exclamation 'They're up!' was accepted as an intimation of surprise, and a quaint form of congratulation.' The two friends were Bower and Kelly, who also had designs on the climb, but were taking the precaution of prospecting downwards before doing so. The foursome then joined forces and finished the climb together.

No wonder, then, that Frankland had a fierce reputation, and Mabel was thrilled to have the chance to climb with him. 'I think it was Lyon (or the late Dr Wakefield) who introduced me to Frankland,' she wrote in December 1958, at the behest of writer Ethel Mannin. 'I was camping at Seathwaite, and he came and camped near us. I had been on my first climb with the Fell and Rock. We did Moss Ghyll – got off the route and did a new variant. I think the party was H.B. Lyon, Cain, Wakefield and me. One of them said, 'Go and see Frankland and tell him you are worth taking out'! Very nervous and daring, I did so. He said, 'I've only once climbed with a woman, and she came off'! I thought, but did not say, 'We'll see about that!'

We asked him to supper – we were using the old barn and had a kettle slung from a beam. He asked 'Who put that up?' I said I did – He replied, 'You've got a long reach' – and to my surprise and joy, turned up a few days later and asked me to go to Gimmer. I went, and that was that.'

Frankland also told the story in his unpublished notebooks, while reminiscing about Skye: 'Come the war and then the call to the Alps, not indeed to me but to my companions, and all thoughts of merry parties in Skye or even Cumberland began to fail, until one day in Seathwaite, a climber approached our tent. Well, you know what Yorkshiremen are and ... two days later we mended our ways a little by toiling over to Gimmer with the new acquaintance who was to spend the night in Mickleden.

It's a long way and it was very hot. I was enjoying a sharp attack of what was either lumbago or anno domini but we climbed all day, up and down Gimmer in the hot sun and before we struggled back all the weary way to Seathwaite (where Hilton did a sprint to catch the milk at eleven), I had realised that the climber had justified her claim to that title.'

In 1959, Mabel wrote down more details of this climbing partnership.

> You have asked me to give reminisces of the late C.D. Frankland, saying that I 'climbed with him a great deal.' In fact, it was only for a short time – during 1924-6 – and then for short periods during the summer holidays. Moreover, as I was always in charge of a camping party, mainly students and children, it was only on rare occasions that I had the great pleasure and rare privilege of climbing with him only.
>
> I first met him in 1923, in circumstances which I have given in my first letter to you. I think it was on Aug 11th that he and his camp companion, Hilton, came to our camp and asked if I would like to come to Gimmer with them – I have a small photograph taken that day. I think we did Kern Knotts Crack a few days later.
>
> In a letter which I have lost or destroyed he said, 'I could see you were not much stretched on the Gimmer day.'

The two climbers corresponded with each other over the course of the following year. They must also have followed with fascination the unfolding events on Everest. Both knew a number of the mountaineers involved, including Beetham, Somervell and Mallory. Mabel must surely have tried to console the young Franz when it became known that his hero was lost, along with Irvine, on June 8th, 1924.

Of Frankland, Mabel wrote:

I must have sent him a p.c. in July 1924, for I have a letter, dated 28th, it which he says it makes the holidays seem sublimely real and near since we smoked your cigarettes and drank your coffee at the Seathwaite camp. I have had two adventurous spells among the hills, one of them in Eskdale where we did a new route near Bower's Esk Buttress; and another at Gaping Ghyll. It seems ages since last August ... I have resigned myself to a quiet, not to say dull, lawn tennis holiday.

He then remarked that I had evidently undertaken to look after four children, and ends 'Can you get anybody to take the responsibility for the four? Would you then be free to do a week's climbing? And would you care to if you could?'

Would I care to! We seem to have corresponded further about it, for C.D.F. arrived at the Seathwaite camp on Aug 8th. My party of students, friends and the four children, were fell walkers, but not climbers. He led most of them up Needle Ridge that same day.

The following day we did Gillercombe Buttress, and the day after the Cat Walk on Kern Knotts and Sansom's Buttress (where is it?) My father had joined us, so I had to pretend it was dead easy!

On Monday 11th, we reversed the Girdle Traverse of Scawfell in 2.5 hours. We went to Buttermere for a ridge walk and got in the Oxford and Cambridge Buttress; and on the 13th to the 15th were on Pillar (I have a good snap of him on the North West). On Saturday 16th C.D.F. left us. Someone had nicknamed him 'The Colonel' and the name stuck.

On the 18th he wrote congratulating himself on escaping the very wet weather which followed, and went on – 'I have dug out from the shelves all the information I could gather about the climbs enjoyed so much with you over the last week. With regard to the Girdle Traverse I find I was wrong in describing the ascent of the Oval as one of the unclimbables. As to the West Wall climb, and the Nook and Wall climb, I maintain that we did the former, or at any rate the severe pitch of the latter. Kelly's earlier description in the 1921 journal refers to an impossible groove passed on the right by a traverse or corner, a wall and a 'glacis'. In the Y.R.C. Journal of 1906-7, F. Botterill described the first ascent of the N.W. Pillar. The second picture is of some interest. It shows at any rate the lower part of the difficult face above the cairned buttress rather well. I see that the Guide to Pillar assesses its difficulties more highly than it does those of Walker's Gully ... I see in this morning's paper that Beetham leaves Calcutta on the 21st. I wonder if we can get him to Almscliff for the weekend when you will be here ... '

I give this extract to show the attention with which he studied the detail of climbs. He once told me that he used to visualise a difficult move, and go over it in bed at night! He also refused to try a climb by a rope from above, but tackled its problems as they came, never making a move he could not reverse. (Personally, I seldom remembered details of climbs, and if I read up a description afterwards had great difficulty in believing that I had ever done it!)

In 1925, Mabel's article on these events was published in the Fell and Rock Journal, entitled 'On Scawfell'.

August, 1924, was a wet month, almost as wet as August, 1923, but once again we spent it in camp at Seathwaite. My camping comrades, who had narrowly escaped drowning by the swollen Derwent, and squashing by a fallen tree, insisted upon returning there and nowhere else. One of them was on honeymoon, and wanted to ensure a thorough initiation for her husband, and so had to have her way; and perhaps I didn't take much persuading anyway. But more than chaff for their love of water, or congratulations on their grit are due to my cheery fellow campers, for whatever happens to them, it is I who am sure to get all the best going out of camping in Borrowdale.

That August, 1924, for example, while we sat at the foot of the swollen Sour Milk Ghyll, C.D. Frankland came and stayed at Seathwaite Farm for a week. That week was fine, all except one day, on which we stayed in camp to receive all his families, none of whom turned up; but all mine did. It simply poured. I believe they think I arranged it on purpose!

He suggested one day, rather casually, that we should go and do the Girdle Traverse on Scawfell. I was thrilled at the idea, but somewhat dubious of bringing it off. All I knew of it then was that it was reputed to take about six hours, and included Botterill's Slab (which had been pointed out to me as 'a foul place'!) However, I had never climbed till I had had enough, and the chance of so long on the rocks!

'Which end shall we begin?' said I innocently, as we wandered through Hollow Stones.

'O, the Mickledore end, I think,' said my partner. I did not know that this was not the usual proceeding, and that it was even doubtful whether a complete reversal had ever been made. We were nearer it, and it was convenient for the lunch pool on Mickledore, and chimed with my own inclinations.

Not having done all of the Girdle Traverse the usual way, I can offer no very definite opinion as to respective merits and difficulties, but one thing was obvious. Taking it our way, the descent of Botterill's Slab comes almost at once, very early on the climb and before one has 'got going.' It has to be tackled in cold blood, and it remains a vivid memory of one of the thinnest bits of climbing I ever did. No muscular effort is required, nor any particularly long reach, so it is theoretically possible for anyone – and just possible. The upper part, where it is climbed on the edge, is not so bad; but these holds fade away, and one has to traverse on to the face of the slab. Here I have the impression of a long, long pause. In retrospect I seem to stand for the greater part of the afternoon on the ample security of a half inch ledge, wishing I had brought a pocket lens with which to look for a handhold; assured by my optimistic partner that there was a foothold somewhere beneath me; wondering if suction could be applied to the rock. Reluctantly, I had just said that I didn't see what to do with it, but come on the rope, when I tried something – have no idea what – and with immense astonishment and relief found my right foot in the hold. The rest was easy; but C.D.F.'s descent of that slab, as watched from the belay at the foot of it was probably one of the most beautiful bits of balance climbing ever seen.

After that it was mostly pure joy. I am a poor hand at writing up a climb, for I fail to remember detail, and when asked how I liked so and so, am generally driven to reply vaguely that I suppose it went, while trying in vain to remember what my questioner is talking about, and being at the same time seized with a horrible suspicion that I never really did that climb at all, but got off it on to some alternative and far inferior route. If a description is available I then read it to see what we are supposed to have done. The result is unconvincing, and I am inexorably driven to the conclusion that I haven't done a single decent climb in the Lake District! Or would be, but that there were such vivid and purple moments. One cannot very well get 'off the climb' on Botterill's Slab or the Flake Crack!

Anyway, I did read up the previous accounts of the Girdle Traverse, and the Guide (when it came) with great interest, and must surely have missed out large portions of that climb. (And as this is being written by the Mediterranean, I cannot get them up again now). But I remember the traverse from the Fives Court very clearly, for it went well that day; and the thrill of reaching Hopkinson's Cairn for the first time, and looking from it into Deep Ghyll is unforgettable.

It began to rain slightly while we were on the Pinnacle Wall above Deep Ghyll, and my partner betrayed some anxiety, and hurried a little. Now I thought that the traverse continued round the West Wall (and why not?), and when asked the time, replied tranquilly that it was 4-20 (we had started from Mickledore at 2-0 precisely). 'Hasn't your watch stopped?' said he. 'Good heavens, we'll be on the top of the Pinnacle in ten minutes!' We were. I believe he would have suggested the Central Buttress then and there but for the rain; also we wanted to go to Wasdale to vindicate the character of my blameless watch.

Frankland also wrote about the Girdle Traverse, although it was never published. His account reads as follows:

'Jill is just a plain schoolma'am. In her school the youngsters lead a kind of Robinson Crusoe life, not only doing such schooling as is considered suitable to modern kiddies but actually running the establishment, the only servant being the gardener, hay making and the usual farm work, forming part of the curriculum of this. It is no sitting down job to be a school ma'am there.

Jack realised in very early youth the vast physical and muscular superiority of his sex. About the mental he was less cocksure. Whether it was Jack or Jill who had the brainwave is not revealed. Probably neither of them knows.

One of the longest and most interesting methods of making hill climbing an adventure, with ample opportunity of repeating the traditional catastrophe and the sovereign remedies, is to be found by a simple adaptation of the Girdle Traverse of Scafell.

The brilliant idea was conceived of starting at the wrong end of the Girdle, that is at Mickledore, climbing across the grain and concluding the journey on top of the Scafell Pinnacle. This would include such choice bits as the descent of Botterill's Slab and the ascent of pitches where those who designed the Traverse, descended with a double rope.

It was 2 o'clock when they started up Keswick Brothers' Climb making for the top of Botterill's Slab. It was a bright sunny day. The little party was sheltered form the wind. The outer edge of the slab was dry but the inner chimney down which Jill rapidly descended was, as usual pretty wet, and when Jack joined his leader in the narrow cave, the wet moss struck cold through his clothes.

From the stance the smooth pale slab sweeps steeply downward, apparently to the distant foot of the crag, and it is no light matter to ask anyone to step out along the inch wide crevice with negligible hand holds, towards the climbable outer edge.

Jill did not know the way and was relieved to see the two ample shelves immediately beyond the edge and slipped carefully down to the first. The two ways of reaching the second niche were known to Jack. The outer edge meant leaning boldly back to the left outside the chute and taking long steps downwards. The face method requires strong nerves, fingers and toes, as the exposure is extreme and the holds almost inadequate.

It is perhaps natural that Jill should choose the delicate face and thereby make Jack decide to use the less refined outer edge. As far as this, the difficulties had been largely mental. The holds, difficult to see below, always appeared farther off than they really were. But at this part of the Slab, the warning, issued by the most skilful of rock climbers, came to mind: 'It (the Slab) stands in a class by itself ... We once again emphasise the extreme severity of Botterill's Slab under the best of conditions' and Jack, securely jammed into his little corner, watched with mingled admiration and surprise, the calm deliberation with which Jill stood gracefully poised on invisible holds while she surveyed imperturbably, the appalling downward prospect from the centre of the vast rock wall.

The rope was a hindrance rather than a help, for the position was one of such nice balance that the least pull would have proved upsetting ... For 60ft the leader has no adequate resting place, but must advance on holds which in several places are barely sufficient.

However, in spite of these difficulties, the lonely figure could be seen slowly to descend, moving a little to the middle of the face and then back gradually to the edge. For some distance the peculiar whitish grey colour, entirely camouflaged the tiny ledges which are sunk into the surface, but when the ledges could be seen, once more progress became rapid.

At last, grass was reached and throwing a double hitch over the happily placed rock pin in the corner, Jack was called upon to come on. The eighty foot rope was not quite run out, but it was found distinctly embarrassing and decided at once the question of delicate face work with this handicap, in favour of the strong pull against the outer edge.

The pull of the heavy climbing rope actually gave additional security to the movement down to the second niche, where Fred Botterill once sat, and, kicking his heels, enjoyed the view. Then, prompted by his leader, and making the most of the braking his rough clothes made possible, Jack 'came tumbling after'.

Although a narrow ledge is almost in reach from the foot of the Slab and leads completely across the thrice climbed Central Buttress, it is necessary to descend twenty feet before a feasible climb up to the broader part of the ledge, the Oval, can be attempted. In descending this pitch during the original traverse a doubled rope was used although it was said to be unnecessary. Such luxuries were not for a party reversing the climb and the greasy pitch was attacked with respect, but the Oval was quickly gained by lusty hauling, on holds which seemed enormous by contrast with what had gone before.

Jill would have liked a trip up the Flake Crack, but Jack was now constant to the original idea. The party walked round the western corner of the Buttress and Jill led the way across a stiff traverse into the third pitch of Moss Ghyll above, and avoiding a steep grass gully.

The twenty foot wall to Tennis Court Ledge and the fifteen foot crack to the Fives Court were old friends whose acquaintance was gladly renewed.

The traverse across Pisgah was as charming as ever and the chimney on the far side proved easier down than up. Jill was not very familiar with the geography of the crag and Jack took great delight in pointing out the easy way up into Steep Ghyll and out upon the Pinnacle Face; the crevasse at the foot of Slingsby's popular chimney, which they intended to descend later in the day if all went well, the Slab routes and finally the start of the comparatively recent traverse to Hopkinson's Cairn from thirty feet down the chimney on the far side of the crevasse.

Hopkinson's Cairn masks the outer edge of a very remote platform. The situation is surely unique and the ledge almost inaccessible. A dozen people could stroll about on it in comfort, but not with eyes closed.

The mists were closing round and on three sides the party peered down into swirling vapour. Jack led off up the back wall of Hopkinson's and Tribe's Route. But left it and turned off to the right at the top of the first pitch.' Frankland ended this version here, and carried on with another version in his notebook. He concluded: 'The climb was done safely and enjoyably. The rain mattered little. I was anticipating a little, just a little fuss at the top: mutual congratulations perhaps, even a handshake; such things have been known. But no! I was to be denied. It takes two to make a cheer.

Instead of the glad look, 'Where next?'

'We've finished!'

'Finished?' in consternation.

'Yes,' rather dully.

'Oh. I thought we had all the way round there to go,' pointing to the West Wall.

'No. What made you think that?'

'Well, you said it would take 4 ½ hours. We started at two and its only 4.30; that's two and a half hours.'

It was not until we had verified the time at the Hotel, that we could believe a lady could reverse the Girdle traverse in so short a time. The impossible had been done when Sansom and Herford made the first traverse. They pronounced the route exceptionally severe and now it had become a short afternoon's gentle exercise for a lady.'

Skye 1924 and 1925

After their success on the Girdle Traverse, Frankland wrote to Mabel on September 8th, asking her to his home in Leeds for a weekend 'to sample Almscliff.' However, before doing so, Mabel and her old friend, Gertrude Walmsley, managed to snatch a weekend in Skye, scouting for campsites. Despite mist and rain, they promptly made for Scavaig and Loch Coruisk. Mabel wrote about this experience in a YRC Journal article entitled *Camp at Loch Coruisk*.

> In the late summer of 1924, after an August spent in dogged enjoyment in camp at Seathwaite, a too trustful comrade came with me on a rapid reconnaissance of the west coast of Scotland, in the course of which we managed to get a week-end in Skye. Armed with a Bartholomew half-inch map which we thought could be trusted, and with a compass which we thought, from Coolin tradition, could not, we went straight to Sligachan and over the pass to Glen Brittle, and the following day, unable to see the Coolins, but fiercely determined to see Coruisk, we went right round the coast by the longest possible route, and made Loch Coruisk about 5.30 p.m. We tried to follow a track along the loch and over the Coolins. The track was not there, the mist was, so were the Coolins, for we felt them. I am not going to detail that adventure; sufficient to say that we spent the six hours of utter dark somewhere on the south side between Bidein and Mhadaidh, carried on in the very grey dawn, and by the aid of our most trusty and commendable compass got down, with the proverbial luck of lunatics, into Coire na Creiche by Tairnlear, reached the farm, ate an enormous meal, and walked back to Portree that same day. Anyhow the point is that we saw Coruisk, and for a year dreams and schemes for a camp there ran through our minds, coloured our correspondence, affected all our intercourse with our fellow campers, and gradually took shape.

She also described the experience in 'The Third Round, or Ridge-Walking in Skye' published in the Fell and Rock Journal of 1926.

> We never saw the Black Coolins, but ... we crossed them, going round (very far round) by coast to Scavaig, along the south side of Loch Coruisk, through a river in flood, and, armed with an unreliable half inch map and no knowledge, started up in the dusk, wet to our skins and with all the food eaten,

> to look for a track marked bold and clear by the perfidious Bartholomew. Of course we spent most of the hours of dark on a rocky ledge somewhere near Bidein, but with the first daylight we got safely down (still in the thick mist) into Coire Tairneilear, and back to Glen Brittle and Mrs. MacRea, whose anxiety was converted into faith in our luck which nothing has yet shaken. That was our first round with the Coolins, and they won hands down. They wreaked their will on us that night, and wove strange enchantments from which we shall never recover.

Frankland later wrote: 'My next visit to Skye was due to an escapade it was no less – on the part of this lady, Miss Barker. She and Miss Walmsley arrived, during a snap visit to Skye, in Scavaig at 5.30 p.m. Taking the tracks marked on the Bartholomew too literally, they proceeded up the valley above Coir' Uisg and were naturally impounded, spent the night on a narrow ledge and received their baptism of mist, rain cold and darkness. Mist found them descending with a camera strap doing duty as a rope. They had breakfast, a wash and brush up at Glen Brittle House, and set off to walk to Portree the same day. Instead of being satisfied with their experiences, they hankered after adventures and that is where I came in.'

Soon after her Skye escapade, Mabel managed to visit Frankland in Leeds, on October 10th. She had two days on the grit, and 'got a charming snap of him resting. He encouraged me up a perfectly awful pitch, saying ' – couldn't do it, and – came off'! On the 28th October, he wrote about Skye, and the advantages of June over August – also: 'Beetham wants to photograph the Central Buttress in summer: you had better do it then, and be in the picture ... '

Mabel pursued the question of Skye, and on November 19th Frankland wrote that he had forwarded the summer photograph album. There was some question as to whether he could take leave of absence from family duties the following summer. He wrote, 'I gathered that you are up to the eyes in it until you also may neglect a thousand duties, and waste in delicious day dreams (of Skye and other Celestial Cities) the precious hours away ... do you think that Rhudunan Post Office will open its hospitable portals to the Barnstormers of Seathwaite? However, and Well! Well! I remind myself of a foreign language phrase book:-

Q. Are you going with us?

A. Yes I am. I am not.

You must realise that you are positively wickedly alluring! Witness this – 'during which time we will (sic) most assuredly 'sneak over' to Scavaig - & climb Blaven? & go up Coire Ghrundda? & down Garbh a Coire? The questions arise of themselves, all difficulties forgotten ...

We are now climbing in boots at Almscliff, a regular school, nine of us last Sunday ... I had extreme finger fatigue, a sort of local exhaustion for the first time for many years. What is it a sign of? Decrepitude?'

On December 12th, Mabel received an invitation to climb on the gritstone again, a note about a hut in Scavaig, and 'Last Sunday I fell off a climb with great gusto and a bump. A man who saw you in the Lakes last summer, and looks sideways at our little climb suggested the seriousness of it at 400 ft. I agreed cheerfully.' Mabel did go to Leeds on the way home from Kings Langley, but it was the end of term and she was too tired to do anything decent. They went to the Cow and Calf Rocks.

In January 1925, Frankland continued their correspondence. 'I have heard from Beetham again. I am asking him to stay with me when he lectures on Everest. I am going to try and fix him up for Easter at Ogwen, where I am already booked with our own club for the meet. If necessary I won't go to the meet. (There seems to have been some feeling about a member called Brown whom we had met in the summer.)' On February 6th he wrote again: 'I have duly consigned the Brown letter to the muddy flames. I couldn't read it! The penmanship was so finicky, wasn't it? Yes! I know Slingsby's Chimney on Pillar. That was the way Field took us just 25 years ago, after the N. Climb. Mrs Benson, you & I came down the easy way. It's a club meet at Easter. This fact seems to have scared off Beetham ... I am trying to get him to come on for a day or two after the others have departed ... ' On the 25th he wrote about a loan of slides, sent by his daughter Mary for a lecture at Kings Langley. By this time, Beetham had stayed with Frankland for the lecture and a day at Almscliff. In April, he acknowledged the return of the slides and mentioned Mabel's impending departure for the Dordogne. On April 26th he wrote – 'Begrudgingly, N. Wales offers good climbing. The good routes are over-crowded.' While there, he saw an accident on Lliwedd, and made a new route up West Peak, calling it Ashtree Climb.

In May he wrote further about the Skye programme – 'Beetham claimed me for his summer holiday either in the Alps or elsewhere. I have put your suggestions briefly before him, and still hover in some doubt.' Then in July – 'Sorry to have been so long undecided. I have finally decided to take intimate advice & go where I long to be – May I join your merry party with permission? When do you go? You are the organising genius. Two boys who you met at Almscliff are motorcycling to Skye & hope to be taken into the brood. They delight in camps, & will bring all their own kit, but they are setting off on the 22nd.

I shall myself be an awful case if you have me. I am writing B. breaking the news gently that he must come, or else go to the Alps with another crowd. I should feel more comfortable about going if you could give me a rough estimate of what it will cost. My holiday starts on July 24th and ends September 1st. I take it that you will put in a day or so at our crag, & so put me into the way of it. Please thank camp for so kindly pressing me to do what I want to do-'

Mabel took up the story:

> As a matter of fact he would have liked very much to go to the Alps – he had never been – but told me that he simply could not afford it. I think Beetham did not believe this, & never forgave him. But he always spoke of B. with the greatest kindness and affection, & we never mentioned the break in their companionship – of which I was only too conscious.
>
> We met in Carlisle on July 31st. C.D.F. then travelled to Skye in Gertrude Walmsley's Austin 7, & I on my small Excelsior motorbike 'Little Amy'. We camped on the way at Glen Dochart (near Crianlarich) & Broadford & arrived at Glen Brittle on August 2nd. The party was joined there by H.V. Hughes. We sent a joint p.c. to H.P. Cain, who had advised on the route. Frankland's contribution was 'B- midges!'

In *Camp at Loch Coruisk*, Mabel wrote:

> Our base camp we made at Glen Brittle with Mrs. MacRae, ever kindly and thoughtful, and an empty cottage as an ultimate refuge in time of storm. And well so for us! The storms were not unbearable, though we had two of three pretty tough gales to weather, but the large crate of provisions ordered

from Glasgow was three days late, owing to a misunderstanding (and then only retrieved by a heroine who motored over those appalling roads to seek it when she might have been in Coire Lagan), and for those three days we were fed by Mrs. MacRae. However it arrived, we fed wisely and *very* well, and planned for the Coruisk expedition.

Next day we went to Coire Lagan. C.D.F. had been there eleven years before, and seemed very happy, saying 'This is what we came for.' We took G.W. up the Cioch. The following day, I think that H.V.H., C.D.F. and I did Great Wall Gully, a first ascent of a pretty stiff thing on Sgumain, which in the new guide is called Frankland's Gully.

Frankland contributed his own account in an unpublished article about Skye: 'In 1925, I was again happy to be invited to join a party of nature lovers, this time being botanists all. To a layman like me, it is astounding how many different varieties of wild flowers can be passed unseen in a place like Skye. After my first visit I felt that the flora was very simple, being mainly goose grass and that the rocks were the things to study and admire. (His first visit had been with two keen geologists, Charlesworth and Brown.) Now I am a sadder and wiser man. My wisdom does not yet amount to a knowledge of flowers; it is limited to a knowledge of my supreme ignorance of a very fascinating study.

The pretty specimens that I collected turned out to be examples of a family maligned under the name 'lousewort'. In Scavaig the insectivorous plants, especially sundew, are really prosperous. Miss Barker poked one in the ribs and drew off a string of sticky stuff. More strength to their secretions! White heather seemed particularly abundant. I never found any myself but set down the good fortune that attended our enterprises, to the numerous presentation sprigs which passed among us.

Among other pieces of luck was the finding of an unclimbed gully on Sgumain on Tuesday August 4th. Like many another great gully, it looked small as we hunted in the mist for Collie's Route up Alasdair. We did not find this route, being in the Sgumain Stone Shoot, but we descended near it when all the mist had been driven off by the hot sunshine. All we wanted to do was to reach the ridge of Alasdair and our new gully seemed as likely a way as any, so we put on the rope.

We could make nothing of the first pitch direct. Long, clear, crystal streamlets flowed from the ends of hanging vegetation of some beauty (but of little utility from our point of view) beneath the overhang. A vague traverse from the right followed with extreme diffidence. As on the easy traverse of the North East on Pillar and Jones's Deep Ghyll-Pinnacle climb, a short movement left meant a considerable increase in height above scree level. Then the small triangular stance at which we aimed was somewhat inadequate. Round the sharp corner on the left, a sloping shelf was almost out of reach and in boots at least, the next two feet up implied considerable confidence in one's cobler (sic). Worst of all, when the sloping ledge could be reached the crack which should have presented itself at the back was the merest suspicion of conformity with the ordinary rules of rock erosion.

So now reliance had to be transferred from the cobler's (sic) care to the manicurist's neglect. Personally I was happy with long nails. My friends, when they were at that place, each required a little help, which speaks well for their tidy habits.

Then it dawned upon us what a complete change had come over our fortunes. An hour or so before, we had been moving about, cold, damp and lost on wet scree. Now we were earnestly engaged; an exciting pitch below us and sport lying before us in a long steep gully running up into the mist, alongside a huge vertical wall on the right. A clean gully and a true gully. We persevered and finally became impounded in what was evidently the top pitch. It was a worthy fellow and can probably be climbed straight up by the overhanging crack. The chockstone at the top appeared to me too big to be surmounted that way. The interest is confined to the left wall looking up and even that is somewhat sheer. The general movement was like that at the Collie Step, with the difficulty concentrated in rejoining the gully at the top.

Again my comrades demanded a little encouragement from the rope, very probably because they had followed my way, rather that the crack direct, a method preferred by Miss Barker. Anyhow it was a fine pitch and brought us to a very airy, narrow ridge, where after 30ft of good climbing we built a little cairn, admired the scenery and named the place Big Wall Gully. *(The original name)* There is now a cairn at the bottom also.

Another piece of luck was the happy dispersal of the mist which enabled us to locate the climb, ascend Alasdair and descend Abraham's Route, in the very teeth of a barrage of gnats.'

Mabel later related how this climb was done:

... on the second day out after seven months off the rocks, and at the end of a rather weary time. The direct attack on the gully looked wet and uninviting, so we climbed a pinnacle alongside, and traversed back into it. On the way we encountered a mantelshelf. C.D.F. led up to it: I tried to follow. H.V. Hughes, who was third, could only see my boots from his stance. He says he went to sleep, woke up again, and they were still there. However, they are not there now, nor is he, so we all got up somehow in the end, but it was not a star performance, except for the leader. Higher on the same climb there is a pitch leading by a thin but delightful traverse out of a cave, and then back at a higher level over a very narrow ledge, rather like the 'Cat Walk' on Kern Knotts, only going to the right instead of left. I needed just rather more than moral support from the rope there: yet I am sure the climb would go either by that or the alternate route taken by C.D.F., or perhaps straight from the cave. It is certainly a splendid climb, easily the best we did in Skye, where for the greater part of the time we ridge-walked ecstatically, unencumbered by rope ...

We took a party up Sgurr nan Gillean, & on the 6th the whole party went to Coruisk by the coast, & carried some supplies. On the 8th we went there again with designs on the Ridge Walk. We tried it on the 10th, Frankland, Hughes and I, in wind & mist – a hopeless effort.. ... The first move towards it (Coruisk) was a reconnaissance in force, by the coast, but not by our laborious and long route of the year before. By keeping well up near the openings into Coire Lagan and Coire Ghrundda, and high also on Garsbheinn, we got a view of Loch Coruisk in about four hours. There some of the party waited, while the four strongest, carrying rucksacks full of food, went down to the loch, found the hut as we had left it, observed good store of drift wood, cached the food, bathed in river or sea according to choice (water f. and s. at our Scavaig Inn!), and got back to the others (and tea) in about two hours.

Mabel also described this in her Fell and Rock article:

So August 1925 saw us back again, ten in number this time, camping in Glen Brittle, and with the intention of organising a flying camp by Loch Coruisk and the Scavaig River, in the most fascinating camping site G.W. and I had ever seen. Unfortunately four of our party had to leave Skye in five days, and five more pledged to rejoin them in Borrowdale at the end of a fortnight. This limited the choice of days for the excursion, but all wanted to see Coruisk, and this gave rise to the project of a one-day reconnaissance, on which we should dump food. This we carried out on August 6th, and found to our satisfaction that the corrugated iron and concrete hut by Loch Scavaig was still in the condition in which G.W. and I had seen it the year before, neither too 'sore decayed' nor yet repaired – in fact, most uninviting as to comfort, but weather-proof enough to make it unnecessary to carry tents. We noted plenty of drift wood, and made our cache, but this dumping of stores being an eleventh-hour brain wave as the party was starting we made no list of what we took, with results that might therefore be expected, e.g. everyone thought that someone else had taken the tea!'

By this time however the camp at Coruisk had a purpose; it had become the pivot on which a bolder scheme depended. H.V. Hughes suggested that some of us should try the great Coolin main ridge walk in one day, the party including the first female; to which she added the rider that if we did it from our camp by Loch Scavaig, so working from a base on the concave side of the crescent, it might be just possible to get round and back to our starting point the same day; and we should be the first of any sort to do that.

But we realised from the start that success was doubtful without a more detailed knowledge of the ridge than any of us possessed, and that all we were likely to gain this year was experience. Another question was that of the route off Sgurr na h-Uamha, supposing we ever got there, and of whether, when down into Harta Coire, we should go east and join the Sligachan-Coruisk 'track', or cross the low col out of Harta direct to the south, and keep parallel to the Druimran-Ramh for most of its length. Obviously the question of this last lap for a tired party and in failing light needed careful consideration, and none of us had been over any of the ground, nor was there time to explore it thoroughly.

In *Camp at Loch Coruisk*, Mabel wrote:

So far well. A few days later we set out again, six humans and a dog, carrying more food, bedding, and a minimum of camp tackle. That was a glorious day, one of those precious days revealing a beauty indescribable and unforgettable, jewels set in that golden August of 1925. We went up the shoulder of Sgurr Dearg, and had a sample of ridge-walking, arduous enough when all carried heavy packs. We had no rope either, for we had preferred to take out its weight in food, and the plucky little 'low-geared' Sealyham asked and got a friendly lift now and then. By the summit cairn some of the party rested for an hour after lunch while the more active or less tired got up the Inaccessible Pinnacle most ways (Long and Short routes, up and down: South Crack: Pigott's Climb, and some uncharted scrambling). Then we made the Banachdich Gap, and plunged down the screes on the Coruisk side. It was a fairly long descent, though cheered by finds of much white heather, and it seemed a long two miles down the side of Loch Coruisk for all its loveliness; and we were glad to make the hut, and to find our cache safe. Near it are the fragments of another structure of which practically nothing is left but a concrete floor and a chimney. There we made a fire and welcome supper, Gertrude and Margaret promptly taking charge of that department with crushing efficiency. The other four tackled the uninviting floor of the hut, which was simply a jumble of concrete blocks and timbers, with a low wall dividing it into two, lengthways. We moved a few blocks, and packed it with bracken and heather, and when the groundsheets and sleeping bags were in place, a small fire lit inside to drive out the midges, and our possessions were arranged all over the place, it began to look like home. Some of the family tried sleeping out: the others reflected that we were in Skye – and turned in. They were awakened later to the tune of rain on the corrugated iron roof, while the imprudent ones made a perilous traverse round the prudent to the inferior sleeping places kindly reserved for them.

After climbing on the Inaccessible Pinnacle that day, they had made a cache of scones and apples and water at its foot '– a fair advantage to take of our being there, surely for we had not gone on purpose to make it!'

The next day, Sunday August 9th was wet.

The three victims were perhaps not sorry (well, one wasn't) to have a day's easy going after the trek of the day before, but the delay made the food problem acute, especially on the bread and meat side, for we had only been able to carry enough for three days generous rations, and we had to be fed more, not less than usual. The idea that the supporting party, or a portion of it, should make a return journey by coast was abandoned in favour of a relief expedition to Camasunary for 'as many as will'. It was carried through with signal success by H.V.H., M.M.B., and 'Brown Badger.' They also did some useful scouting on the Uamha-Coruisk route question, and decided against trying to make the Sligachan track.

Claude also wrote his own account of that day: 'Food was found to be scanty and a foraging expedition to Camasunary was organised. This meant crossing the river, then in spate. An elderly member, whose name I should hate to divulge, carrying a boot in each hand for greater comfort afterwards, tried a short cut just above the rapids by which the Scavaig River runs into the bay, and the subsequent proceedings of the foraging party interested him no more. He spent the remainder of that day between blankets, trying to prevent contact with his tender abrasions, with all his available clothing hanging on a line. How it was that he arrived on the further bank still carrying a boot in either hand, is unexplained.'

Mabel gave more details in her article for the YRC Journal:

So the morning was wet, and the long excursion planned for one full day at Scavaig was impossible. To ensure another day with comfort more food was necessary, - *not* bully beef (of which we had cached a 7-lb tin, nor raisins and chocolate, our staple for walking on, but bread and meal. Also by some strange error we had forgotten the tea. What is camp without tea? A relief expedition was arranged, not going all the five hours back to Glen Brittle but to Camasunary, where we understood there was a keeper's cottage. Now strictly speaking we could hardly ask the keeper to help us to camp at Coruisk; more-over it was the Sabbath. However it was a case of try that or give up our extra day, so all the discretion, tact and information discoverable in the party was canvassed. Now there is a certain song about a certain party that once 'Came to Camasunary,' so we simply collected – and used all the information given in the said song. (H. has an amazing memory for doggerel!)

ɑabel, 2½ years old, 1888

Henry Lindsay Barker, Mabel & Arnold

ɑabel Barker in her middle years

Mabel & Roc at Friar Row in 1947

Above: Sunnyside, Mabel's birthplace

Left: Mabel's mother, Mary Barker

Mabel's first evening gown

Above:
L to R, Frank Barker, Aunt Kate & Arnold Barker (the aunt left Mabel some money in her will: this helped Mabel start her school at Friar Row)

Mabel playing the part of Morgan le Fai in 1911

George Morris

At Elisabethdorp Camp, Holland, in June 1916. Mabel third from right

Dr Wakefield, Sept. 1924

Group at Almscliff, Oct. 1924

Mabel on Akerman's Cornerr, Almscliff

Patrick Geddes (centre bearded figure) with HRH the Maharajah of Indore

Franz Nevel & goose 1926

Jack Carswell

4th ascent of CB, Scafell,
& first female ascent,
August 1925.

Upper fig. Claude Frankland
lower fig. Mabel Barker

Claude Frankland at Almscliff

On the Girdle Traverse of Doe Crag, 1930. Tony Musgrave, Nancy Ridyard and Mabel Barker (inset).

Camp in Borrowdale, Whitsun 1927. Mabel & Fred Power

Mabel & party, Barngates Dinner Party, Nov. 29th 1930

Kibbo Kift: camp & rituals 1924

Building the F & R hut Brackenclose, 1938

Millican Dalton, Joan Brown & Mabel at Grange, Borrowdale

St Martin's School from Leeds, evacuated to Friar Row in 1939

First attempt on Inaccessible Gully, Dovedale.

Ernest Wood Johnson and Mabel

Mabel on Dovedale Slabs

Setting off to Seathwaite, 1931. Mabel on her Excelsior motorbike

Friar Row

Joan Brown on Gillercomb Buttress

Honister road above Seatoller in 1931

Mabel Barker & Claude Frankland after their traverse (1st female) of the Cuillin Ridge Gertrude Walmsley on right.

Mr & Mrs MacRae with daughter Nancy outside Glenbrittle House

The Wood-Johnsons at Middle Row in 1927

In the Zillerthal, 1922 – setting out to explore

The shelf on Cioch Direct

Mabel skating on Derwent Water, 1929

Mabel & her 'children' in July 1930

Dramatisation of 'The Jungle Book'

Edith Wood-Johnson visits Mabel's school at Friar Row, Easter 1928. (The children have been shaking mats.)

The party on the Hornkees glacier. Millican Dalton left; Mabel 2nd left

The badly crevassed Hochfeiler glacier

We set out from the hut six strong, not to mention the dog, but the rain had fallen and the Scavaig River risen. The foraging party of three found the stepping-stones by feeling for them, and found the crossing quite sufficiently exciting. Margaret and Gertrude decided to get supper ready, aided by Patch (who, in point of fact, very promptly produced a rat as her contribution to the food question: now whence a rat in such a place?) Frankland found a patent crossing of his own lower down, fell in with great thoroughness, damaged his ankles, and came near to the supreme tragedy of losing his boots, which he had taken off! He clung to them at the risk of his life, struggled to the farther shore, and after a short interval presented himself to the provision-seekers clad in a wet minimum. However they said that dignity, tact and discretion were needed on this job, and sent him back (and he must have spent the day in bed, or continuing to bathe).

Two hours' easy going brought us to Camasunary, and nobody could have been kinder to the most deserving than Mr. and Mrs. Anderson were to us. We returned by another route, crossing the Sligachan track to Coruisk and giving us a view to the east of the Druim nan Ramh; and so returned to the shanty and the rest of the family, well pleased with the day's work, and with time for a bathe before an early supper. ... (The story is taken up in 'The Third Round, or Ridge-Walking in Skye' in the F & R J.) The command of the supporting party was kindly but firmly taken by G.W., and the Dauntless Three found themselves fed and put to bed early, with the whole course of action for the morning planned out, even to the position of the matches. 4 a.m. on Monday 10th found a section of the party awake – whom the others no doubt cursed heartily. It was *not* a bright morning, and no joyous shouts were heard as we crawled reluctantly from our blankets. It was cloudy but not raining; impossible to foretell the kind of day in that grey dawning, and this being our last chance we decided to do what we could. We left the Scavaig Inn at 5.30 a.m., H.V.H. being 'Chief of Staff,' armed with map, compass and aneroid. He and C.D.F. also carried in turns the rucksack with our (useless) rubbers and extra sweaters, while M.M.B. carried the food, a diminishing load. We carried no rope but a length of clothes-line for lowering rucksacks.

H.V.H. led up the N.E. ridge of Gars-bheinn, and at about 2,000 feet we got into thick mist which never lifted for a second all day. There was also a strong wind blowing, and it was evident that our chances of success were almost nil. Still, we made fairly good time to begin with, and were on the summit by 7 a.m. Then the trouble began. None of us had been there before, and we could only see a few yards ahead. Gars-bheinn has three summit cairns; the red-line map which Hughes carried showed three ridges meeting there, and the compass was not very definite in its advice. We did take the right line, but became uncertain, and decided to explore in the opposite direction. When it was quite certain that we were going down the south-west ridge, we retraced our steps, and took the main ridge with more confidence, but the whole manoeuvre had lost us time.

Thereafter Hughes kept the direction splendidly, and we maintained a steady but not very speedy pace. The wind was troublesome, and it was not often possible to get on the leeward side of the ridge. One kept hoping it would drop, hoping that the mist would rise, hoping for a fine afternoon (O yes, it *was* raining by now!), and hope died hard. We made Sgurr Bhig and Sgurr nan Eag, and enjoyed the Caisteal a Garbh-Choire, which came upon us suddenly out of the mist, and then surprised us by the ease with which it's A.P. walls were scaled. Then came Sgurr Dubh an Da Bheinn, and the next excitement was the Thearlaich-Dubh Gap. Here our clothes-line came into play, and that not only for the rucksacks. It was not very long, and it is perhaps as well that no serious call was made upon it, but with the rocks all wet, our hands numb with cold, and a route unknown to two-thirds of the party, and remembered from 11 years ago by the remainder, I for one was glad enough to pretend there was a rope for a moment. (Its east side is rather like the Tennis Court wall, only one traverses more to the right in descending, and if both were dry, the Gap is probably easier).

Then we made a slip and did not rectify it. We had intended to include Alasdair, but in the mist H.V.H. led straight off onto the Thearlaich instead, and taking this now as a trial trip, we were well content to carry on. The only other bit of stiffish climbing that I can remember is King's Chimney, which C.D.F. led into and up very quickly. Considering that he had not been there for eleven years, that nobody could see more than a few yards ahead, and that the mist condensing on his glasses gave continual trouble, it was a creditable performance, even for him. There is rather a nice traverse out of it to the right. I remember it because there the mica glass, about which I had swanked, came out of my watch (which was time-keeping for the party) and went tinkling down the rocks, and the watch had to retire to a match-box.

We were ticking off our pips happily now, warmed up and going strong. After Mhic Choinnich, we noticed a cairn marking the pass from Coire Ruadha to Coire Lagan. Then came some very loose and steep stuff. At first we took it for the Inaccessible, but found it was the east side of An Stac. It might be selected as typical of the worst Coolin rock, for its basalt dykes are repulsively loose and rotten. The Inaccessible came in sight at last however, just after H.V.H. had asked me to take the lead for a little. 'With pleasure,' said I cheerily, but the pleasure and speed diminished perceptibly on the short side, and just when we were all on it the rain, which had been playing with us so far, began to come down for all its worth. 'Perhaps it will clear after this,' we said with incurable hope, as we lunched off our cached apples, with wan smiles at the water bottle. Not it! The gods of the Coolins had far other treatment in store for us.

We felt pretty hopeful as we set off again, making as we fondly believed, for the Banachdich Gap. But things looked very queer and unfamiliar in that dense mist and pouring rain. Presently, C.D.F. was far below us. He was certainly on the Coruisk side, but none of us were then quite sure of that. We, it seems, must have been on a false ridge. He (rightly) thought we could not join him by following it, and came back to join us at the summit. The compass began to go mad. Re-united, we all tried to follow it into the gap, but not a bit of it. We must have been quite close to it, for we went back and had the matter out with Sgurr Dearg on a day when we could see, but there was no finding it then. Probably the gods of the Coolins just lifted it. All three got separated this time, and I experienced the sensations of a hen with two chickens that would run about. I think it was seven times in all that we were back on the summit cairn, it and the Inaccessible the only stable things left in a grey and unreal world; while the compass justified all the hard things that have been said about the unreliability of its kind in the Coolins. Perhaps it was not really necessary to find the Gap. We might have worked across Coire Banachdich and struck the ridge further on; but the ridge flattens out queerly here, and the Gap is an unmistakable landmark with an upright pole in it; and after a while we abandoned hope even of a shorter round by the Druim nan Ramh, and desired only to find that Gap in order to get through it and down to Coruisk before dark.

The tighter things got, the livelier was C.D.F. He began making short excursions on his own again, dashing off at incredible speed, while exhorting his amused party to 'Keep together, it's more sociable!' We tried his route under the false ridge, and got a good long way down on the Coruisk side (we hoped, and almost believed), by way of a very respectably thin traverse and another rotten dyke. It might have been a sporting descent in clear weather and with a rope, but as things were it was 'unjustifiable,' and we retraced our steps. Any controversy as to the way we had come was soon settled. C.D.F.'s rapid manoeuvres with dimmed sight had resulted in his wearing through the tips of his fingers on the gabbro, and we followed gory tracks. Perhaps this blood-offering appeased the gods, for now H.V.H. suggested that we gave up hunting the Banachdich Gap, and returned over An Stac to see if the Coire Lagan one was where we had left it some hours before. The mist was so thick that the question of being benighted had to be taken into consideration. For my own part I hadn't any intention of giving in to the Coolins to that extent. If we couldn't get down one way we could go another, but I *did* want to return to our family in the hut, and not go down to Glen Brittle.

We now tried the Coire Ruadha side of the Pinnacle, lured there by the red-line map; didn't like it, and came back. Summit cairn again! Then we tried to go round An Stac on the Lagan side, and funked that too in the mist and gloom; so we came back for the last time, and went right over the darned thing. I got 'the fright of my life' when a large rock came out in my hands (one should not use both hands on a block of basalt!). I just didn't come off, and it just didn't squash Hughes, who was following. C.D.F. was climbing at a terrific rate, leaving bloody marks like a paper chase. I dared not try to hurry any more, but crept gingerly down the rotten dykes of An Stac, cheered by his lusty shout announcing that the Lagan Gap had not been tampered with.

Gladly then we plunged down the screes of Coire Ruadha. They seemed even longer than they were two days before, but we got out of the mist at last. We were too wet and cold to pause long anywhere, but were all good for hours more of going. And in the hut they had a great welcome and supper ready for us, bless them! Probably they were more disappointed than we were, for we had had a great day, were tired but not played out, and knew that we could depend on the Coolins being there next year, and also on a support party that can wait 17 hours and be neither irritable nor unduly anxious when its wanderers fail to turn up before the light fades. So that was the end of the first chapter, and it might be called 'Defeat with Honour.' The Coolins had won again.

'We were as wet and tired as well could be,' wrote Mabel in her YRC article, 'but 'It's the best day I've ever had' said one. Well it was a sporting and happy failure. Meanwhile the others again had a good day of more restricted walking and plenty of bathing. Never was there such a place for bathing. Anyone who can swim at all can do it happily in the warm salt water of Loch Scavaig when the tide is full. You can get into the rush of the Scavaig River and go down its water-chute, and play in the yellow sea-tangle like a seal.'

Frankland's journal entry was somewhat shorter: 'August 10th: 'Ridge in vile weather. Garsbhein to Sgurr Dearg but failed to find Banachdich Ridge although we searched for 3hrs in worsening weather. Found the Lagan Bealach by traversing An Stac in storm. Down to Coruisk just before dark. A terrible day.'

'Tuesday 11th was glorious again,' wrote Mabel. 'Coruisk and the Coolins showed us their grand beauty bathed in sunlight, and the salt lochs and little islands were all smiling and sparkling. Perhaps the Lordly Ones had tried our mettle, and found us not unworthy to walk their hills, and will allow us to go again. Anyway all our wet things dried nicely, and we evacuated the hut and ate up everything in a last grand meal. Regretfully, and hopefully, we left Loch Scavaig ... ' That last night at Coruisk, however, there was a storm, and the next day they returned to Glen Brittle and spent the day drying out in the empty cottage. They did manage a ridge walk on the 13th and saw some lovely Brocken Spectres. (Mabel managed to photograph them, but then mislaid or lent the 1925 album). On the 14th August, they all left for Seathwaite, repeating the camps en route.

Central Buttress

Once back in Seathwaite, they lost no time. That evening, they climbed Raven Crag Gully, and the very next day, headed straight off for Central Buttress. As Mabel wrote in her account in the FRCC Journal:

> So when on August 17th of this year we returned from a fortnight in Skye, splendidly fit and in beautiful weather, we suggested to the camp in general that we might as well go to Scawfell next day; the Corridor Route always made a good expedition, and some new friends had joined us who were anxious to see some climbing. The day was fine, and we set off in a leisurely mood, which persisted through lunch in Hollow Stones. But this late start was partly a strategic move in order to give the rocks time to dry (for the morning had been misty) and about 2 o'clock we went right on to the climb.
>
> The first ascent of the Central Buttress of Scawfell was made in 1914 by S.W. Herford and G.S. Sansom, C.F. Holland, C.G. Crawford and D.G. Murray, and having been pronounced 'unjustifiable' was again climbed in 1921 by C.D. Frankland and B. Beetham. A third ascent was made in 1923 by A.S. Pigott, Morley Wood and J.B. Meldrum; so ours was the fourth ascent and Frankland is thus the only man who has been up twice. It was this, of course, which made it possible for us to climb it as we did, straight through without loss of time or undue expenditure of energy, and with very great enjoyment.
>
> The rocks were dry, but not in perfect condition according to C.D.F., because of the amount of lichen which has grown on them since his last visit; but I cannot blame the lichen for the fact that during the first part of the climb I felt decidedly scared. No doubt I would have climbed better and more confidently had we done something by way of prelude, for most of us probably take a little time to get warmed up, and this was again like meeting Botterill's Slab early in the Traverse; but my nervousness was partly due to my respect for the climb. It seemed a sort of impertinence to approach the Flake Crack at all – and I had dreamed of it for a year!
>
> Up the rib to the Oval was just good stiff face climbing with small holds which did not always appear when one first called for them. C.D.F. seemed

to walk up lightly with a jest about their insufficiency, and I crawled after, endorsing it heartily.

We had an 80 foot rope (which proved ample) and he ran most of it out on this section. When I joined him near the foot of the Flake he seemed wrapped in meditation. There was the question of the wretched thread belay. We both knew it wouldn't be wanted, but of course it had to go on. He got up a short pitch, and I came right along to the foot of the Crack, where there is a good enough stance, narrow but quite sufficient. The left hand and arm can go right into the crack, but there is nothing to hold there, and there is nothing for the right hand. It is a position where the second can wait comfortably for any length of time in reason, but cannot safeguard the party. If the leader came off during the difficult business of climbing up to the chock stone and putting the loops of rope over it the second could not possibly save either of them. We therefore wasted – no, spent – about twenty minutes of precious time and temper, he trying to induce a loop of rope to pass behind a small chock stone near him, while I tried to see it, and then to catch it with the left hand and pull it through. Coils of rope seemed to be fed into the crack, while nothing happened so far as I could see! At last it appeared; I pulled it through and put my left arm through it. Meanwhile, however, there was time to examine the crack near me and I think that there is a very small chock stone, far in and pretty low down, which might serve for a belay if it can be reached and if a rope will go round it. If so, it would be a great simplification and help at this part of the climb.

The loop belay settled, however, C.D.F. led up the crack, and passed three loops over the chock stone and under himself. I pulled on each loop to his direction, but not quite to his satisfaction, for the rope sagged a little, and he said the ropes were lower than on his former ascent. He then called to me to come up as quickly as I could. I did so, but by this time was too excited to climb decently, and scrambled up in an untidy fashion, remarking as I arrived that I was tired. It was a thoroughly commonplace observation, meaning nothing, but was bad psychology, for I fear it alarmed my partner. But after the long wait and this short struggle, the next few moments of tense excitement and rapid action passed quickly, and I do not really know what happened; except that I got onto and over my partner and off his head as quickly as possible. He says he felt for my foot to hold it if necessary, but could not find it, and I do not know where it went. Probably, being slimmer than former climbers, I got farther into the crack, and chimneyed it. I faced out, and think there was a small hold far up on the inside wall. Almost at once I felt the top of the Flake with the left hand. 'I've got it!' I said, thrilled with the realisation that the thing was virtually done, and there was probably not a happier woman living at that moment!

There is a good belay a few feet along the Flake. I pulled in the slack as the loops were taken off the chock stone, and C.D.F. came up very quickly on a tight rope. We looked at the traverse in front of us. It is a marvellous situation, and it is difficult now to believe that I have been there.

'Beetham walked along and coiled the rope,' said C.D.F. 'Well, I'm going to walk along it,' I said, and did so, but with the utmost caution, and with both hands on the wall; and then saw to it that as C.D.F. followed there wasn't any loose rope for him to coil! Another upright piece of Flake follows ('dead easy') and another broader edge, still to the left and leading into a collection of broken rocks easily visible from below. Here C.D.F. took the lead again, and just then we heard voices and came within sight of two men on Keswick Brothers, who asked with some interest what we were on.

'Central Buttress: just got up the Flake,' said my partner, with careful indifference, and just as his second appeared. There are moments when it is rather good fun to be a woman. Probably no lady in history was ever so sure of creating a mild sensation by the mere fact of being where she was.

The traverses to the right again, and especially the second one, are undoubtedly very thin indeed. Its poor handholds and sloping footholds are just about the limit. There is nothing to put one's weight on, and the only method is a slow and careful change of balance. Nor must the climber take any risk of a slip, for though the stances are good, the belays are poor. The climb is by no means over when the famous Flake is conquered.

But after the second traverse it is relatively easy, and my memory of its detail is vague.

There was a nice slabby wall presenting no special difficulty, and the climb finishes among several small slabs where I lost my partner's trail, so that we chose different ones. We forgot to look at the time, but our patient support party watching from Hollow Stones, say it was just 2½ hours till they saw us on the sky line, and we joined them again in three hours exactly, having come down from Moss Ghyll (without help from Professor Collie, as we think, but is there only one Step?)

I was told later that there had been some criticism and talk of risk taken on this climb, and I would like to say here that no risk whatever was taken by either climber. All the rules of the game were most carefully and conscientiously observed, and had there been any risk at any moment I should surely know it. I can also say quite honestly that at no point did I find myself having any serious difficulty with the climbing. Whatever he may say about it, I know very well who was the real leader at every point. Frankland found the route, carried through the difficult matter of engineering the loops over the chock stone, gave calm and clear directions, and took all responsibility. What remained for me was a very real sense of co-operation (absent in some measure from the stiffest slabs and traverses which can be done alone, for I do not think that the Flake Crack is possible for the safest solo climber), and a perfectly splendid climb throughout, compelling respect for it, and giving no excuse for carelessness or relaxed attention at any point. Yet nowhere was there very much call upon my very small reserve of muscular strength, nor had I ever the feeling that my power was taxed to the uttermost, and the pitch unjustifiable without the moral support of the rope.

In *The Central Buttress of Scafell*, Graham Wilson (the editor) writes of the inevitable male outcry at Frankland's irresponsibility in allowing Mabel to climb the crack unaided, but the facts indicate that this was 'mere prejudice rather than sound judgement'. This was perhaps typical of the general attitude of the time, but characteristically, Mabel gave it little thought and simply got on with what she was good at.

The next day, still rearing to go, the group set out again. Frankland took 'as many as will' of the novices up the Needle, where they encountered Dennis Murray, who had been in on the first ascent of CB and had sat on the Oval for three hours holding ropes. Mabel and Frankland also climbed Tricouni Rib, which was a first ascent, and did several other climbs in the area. On the 20th, they took Gertrude Walmsley up Moss Ghyll. C.D.F. said he was going to take a rucksack of concrete up, and repair the damage done to the Lake District (Collie Step).

In a YRC article of 1927, entitled *Some Severes,* Mabel wrote: 'I have had much more trouble on humbler climbs. There's that top pitch of Walker's Gully for example! We did it some days later, and all went merrily, with the consequent lack of detailed memory. At the top pitch we belayed carefully, both in the cave and on the wall, where a loop was duly threaded, but not used, for both climbed it by the backing-up method. This is recommended for tall climbers if I remember rightly, but being 5 feet 4 inches I found myself 'stretched' rather literally! The rope, or a knob of rock, or both stuck into my back and hurt: it demanded real hard work, such as I hate, and in short, I was glad to get out of it!'

The following days were wet, but they walked to Grange, had a day on Pillar (North Climb via hand traverse) and one on Scawfell, where there was a thunderstorm. They visited both Pillar and Scawfell again, and also the Ennerdale face of Gable, and then C.D.F. left on the 27th August. In her YRC article, Mabel wrote of the days they spent together:

> For most severes dry rock and rubbers seem almost essential for one to get the whole joy out of it, to raise a good face climb (which I love more than any gully or chimney) to the full ecstasy given by speedy movement with a good margin of safety. Therefore we proposed to spend a fine Sunday on the Pinnacle slabs. There was a distant rumble, but we judged that the threat had passed, donned rubbers, and started up the slabs from Deep Ghyll to Hopkinson's Cairn. But it had rained the day before: the slabs were not perfectly dry, and one's steps had to be chosen daintily, and with an avoidance of vegetation. Either I could not see the leader, or did not pay attention, and had not read the book of words, for I am told that I did not negotiate the Gangway according to rule, but walked along it upright, with extreme slowness and caution, and thinking it a pretty thin traverse. We had barely finished Herford's Slab when, without warning, a deluge of rain descended. Soaked in a few

moments, we retreated hastily round the corner by the bit of Girdle Traverse leading into Steep Ghyll. The rope belayed itself maddeningly round every point of rock. I stuck on the corner ledge, wet to the skin, in rubbers, longing for holds which did not exist; while C.D.F. sat in the Crevasse, a waterfall from Slingsby's Chimney pouring down his neck and told me depressing stories about that corner. Again some of my camping comrades had played audience, and when we joined them, not only had the rain stopped, but *they* had sheltered and were quite dry! The rocks were not, nor were we, - camp as quickly as possible, and no more slabs that day.

It was hopelessly wet the last day of that summer's holiday. But what then? It *was* the last day, and could not be wasted. The Ennerdale face of Gable was near, and is nearly always wet anyway – an hour passed in Smugglers' Chimney six years ago has impressed my mind. Engineers' and the Oblique Chimney took some finding in thick mist, but when found we did them thoroughly, in boots, of course. We were not quite wet through in the Engineers', and I enjoyed it; but by the time we got to the Oblique the rain had become heavier and the wind was cold. Soaked through, we went up it and down the Bottle-shaped Pinnacle with a sort of 'Well, *that's* ticked off' feeling, and were caught by the rest of the camp an hour later having tea at the farm (the only time that summer – honest!) Yet it was surely 'a good day of its kind' as a Scotswoman said to us years ago, a party of youngsters setting off to cross from Glen Lyon to Killin in drenching rain. It is good to have done them under bad conditions, good to know oneself not only a fair-weather climber and friend of the fells. You cannot be that if you elect to camp at Seathwaite most Augusts!

Thus, in the summer of 1925, a subtle change came about in the relationship between Mabel and Frankland. Until this point, Frankland's letters were all addressed to 'Miss Barker'; from then on, she became Dr Mabel, and finally Mabel or M.

Montpellier, 1925-6

Mabel left for France in September 1925, to help with running the Collège des Ecossais in Montpellier, a college established by Patrick Geddes. By this time he was seventy one years old, and this was his final planning and building project. In 1924, he had bought a plot of rough hillside, consisting of two acres of limestone heathland called *garrigue*, on which there was a little two-storeyed homestead, the nucleus of the college to be. By 1925 the main building was complete and capable of accommodating twenty students or more. Some of these were from India, where Geddes had lived and worked for many of the preceding years. The college was an unconventional one, and never attained the status that Geddes had hoped for, that of the Cité Universitaire of the future, which he conceived as a galaxy of study centres in each great university town, all sharing fully in the life of the alma mater. Later on, a new building was erected in the college grounds and used for regional ecological research.

It was here that Mabel spent ten months, writing a thesis entitled *L'Utilisation du Milieu Géographique pour l'Education*, or *The Use of the Geographical Environment in Education*, for which she achieved her doctorate. Here she set out her beliefs that the best methods of education consist of putting children in direct contact with all elements of their environment. This was underpinned by a philosophy based on the necessity for human beings to live in harmony with their surroundings, and with each other. 'Learning,' she wrote, 'based on the influence of the place in which life develops, has an inevitable importance for all life forms. Only modern man has believed in arriving at something outside this influence, that which he calls 'Education.' And indeed, he grows up in a curious situation, being educated in a false environment which he has created for himself, but which is nothing more than a barrier to his real surroundings.'

She explained the concept of the Regional Survey, which looked at the geographical, geological, botanical, zoological, economic, historical and prehistorical, literary and artistic aspects of an area, these different points of view integrated by the idea of their sociological unity. She was particularly interested in ways in which the Regional Survey could be adapted towards education. In her historical introduction, she gave a severe critique of the traditional methods of education, pointing out how little they meet the needs of the developing child. 'I find myself in agreement with the belief that is often expressed by modern educators: that the education given in most schools, at least since the industrial revolution, has almost completely lost its sense of reality.' She was particularly bothered by the way in which knowledge was fragmented into different subject areas. She wrote:

> Our school system has sliced our knowledge up into little pieces, and has carefully prevented them from mixing with one another. History is taught separately from geography; mathematics, most of the time, has nothing to do with the sciences; the fine arts never seem to have any correlation with each other; languages each have a separate place as part of the timetable. Children go rapidly from one thing to another ... We naively believe that the accumulation and memorisation of facts found in books, and the power to reproduce these facts on paper, constitutes, by some magical process, knowledge and wisdom, and are somehow useful in life ... I do not wish to discuss such questions in any further depth. My two criticisms: firstly, that the subjects taught in ordinary school are too distant from the realities of life, and secondly, that there is a lamentable lack of integration between them, seem only too evident.
>
> It goes without saying that this state of affairs is the result of unfavourable conditions in the society that has built these schools and established these systems of education. We are trying to retrieve these social conditions at too late a stage.

Mabel believed, however, that a great renaissance in educational thinking was taking place, moving away from the sterile methods that she so objected to. She cited many of the great thinkers who had helped to bring about this renaissance, beginning with Jean-Jacques Rousseau, who first put forward the idea that the natural environment was important in schooling, and the collaboration between J. Arthur Thomson and Patrick Geddes, which resulted in nature study being introduced to the school curriculum in 1900. She gave a list of schools in Britain currently experimenting with the methods she advocated, which included Abbotsholme, Bedales, Oundle College, and of course, Kings Langley Priory. Also cited was relevant work going on in other countries, notably in Belgium, France, Scandinavia and the United States.

Mabel then described in detail some of the experiments that had recently taken place in British schools, starting off with the experiences of a teacher called Valentine Bell, who taught at a school in Lambeth where many of the children were poor or underprivileged. Bell volunteered to take on a class of 56 boys who none of the other staff wanted to teach. He split them into groups, got them started on studies of their environment, and used the results for cross-curricular studies. By the end of the year, not one of the boys had played truant, and the school inspector had congratulated him on the intelligence of the boys in his class. He became a friend of Mabel, and the two agreed that these methods were crucial for giving children an understanding of citizenship, which would eventually lead to environmental improvement. As a Captain in the army, Bell was later to find that his students had improved powers of observation during their army service, and were able to make better use of their skills afterwards. In an article entitled, 'Citizenship through Regional Survey', published in *The Herald of the Star* of July, 1919, he wrote: 'As the result of the terrible crisis through which the world is passing, there is little doubt that an intensive study will be made of Social Science, and it is to the real live citizen that the Survey Method should commend itself as a logical and scientific training for that study. Such a training, I dare suggest, would lead the various classes to understand each other better in peace time, just as the whirlpool of war has thrown them together during the past four years to their better understanding.'

The second part of Mabel's thesis was concerned with our prehistoric foundations; she wanted educationists to acknowledge their importance. Of the processes of human evolution, she wrote:

> We have enough biological knowledge to easily understand the influences that unite an organism to its environment; a fish that does not have water is not a fish – it is a skeleton; plants of the same species do not develop in the same way when they are grown in sand as when they are grown in the marshes, or in the light compared with the dark; a domestic animal does not have the same character as his free and savage ancestor. So, is this not true for human beings?
>
> I do not at all want to say: 'Give me a the perfect environment, and we will certainly become perfect human beings,' but it seems to me that without

question, if one changes the environment one obtains different beings and different social structures.

To illustrate her point, Mabel used the 'Section of the Valley' which represents symbolically a slope on the earth's surface, going from the mountains to the sea. She then elucidated upon the primitive occupations; how on the bare hills, primitive people took to using the earth to make arms and tools; lower down, in the forests, woodsmen were found, who used a different kind of material for arms and habitation – this is the level where fire was first born. At this level, primitive peoples profited most easily from what the earth has to give – fruits, birds and animals. In this way, the people of the forests also became hunters. On the smaller hills and on the steppes, the pastoral peoples developed their way of life. In descending the slope again, the terrain becomes richer and here humans learnt to conserve the life of plants as well as animals and became farmers. Finally, next to the water, the hunter altered his technique to become a fisherman. 'Here then,' wrote Mabel, 'on our section of the valley, are all the primitive occupations of man: Miner, Woodsman, Hunter, Shepherd, Farmer, Fisherman. From the Stone Ages to our own days of such complex civilisation, we do not find any other ways of using the earth but these. The modifications, the combinations, the occupations that we derive from them are infinite, but they always lead us back to these simple and fundamental connections between man and the earth.'

Mabel was convinced by the idea that humans advanced by working with their hands, which forced them into intellectual effort. They made this effort as a result of climate change, which caused them to become carnivores, and, as a result, hunters. She cited O.T. Mason in *Women's Share of Primitive Culture*, who believed that the division of labour dated from the point of invention or discovery of fire, maintaining that the industry and militarism of the world dated from the time when women had to stay near the fire and guard it, while the men went in search of game. Mason proposed that most of the peaceful inventions, the majority of the constructive occupations, were due to the labour of women. Mabel believed that the type of occupation followed by a human being led to the development of different characteristics; that they made progress because of their work, and that if they had done nothing with their hands and brains, they would not have evolved. Her conclusion was that on one hand, the earth determines the occupation of human beings, and that, on the other hand, these occupations determine, in their turn, the social organisation and the characteristics of those that practise them. She felt that this was particularly important for education, and that it was necessary for children to work with their hands to develop their intellect.

In talking of forest dwellers and woodsmen, Mabel touched on a topic that is even more relevant today than when she wrote her thesis in 1925. 'It was those who left the forests who destroyed them,' she said. 'They destroyed the forests everywhere, and without reflection ... Is it really necessary for the human race, as it grows and evolves, to take the forests, to vanquish them and use them for their own needs, like the stones and the beasts? ... But when man takes to dominating his environment, this environment that he has changed, it in its turn dominates him again. And in our days, we have arrived at a time when the disappeared forests take their revenge.' Mabel was well aware of the perils of deforestation and the effects on climate, and in her thesis, made a plea for it to stop: she asked that those who understand the connection between man and forest must look further into the future.

Mabel was concerned about the balance of life in the modern city:

> Until recently, the inhabitants of towns seem to have forgotten the countryside and their dependence on it. Our primitive types came to the city and forgot to go home. The towns grow larger and larger, and the occupations of those who live there become more and more distant from their rustic origins; furthermore, they scorn these origins and the fundamental occupations; the things they make are more and more artificial (that is to say, separated from nature by more degrees of derivation than it is possible to look into here) and more and more ugly and useless. But they continue to make them, because it is necessary to give work to industrial towns; it is necessary to maintain the illusion that the inhabitants of towns can be self-sufficient, and produce things that humanity needs. *It is impossible to produce anything in towns.* It is only possible to transform the products of the countryside. One can raise neither beasts nor plants, nor dig the ground to search for minerals, nor fish, nor replant trees, in these deserts of industrial towns; and one can no longer live a civilised life in

these dirty, ugly environments. And this is a very dangerous state of affairs ... It is necessary to reconnect with the land, discover again the lost traditions, and reinforce the local and regional pride, the love of the countryside so dear to us. The war was made by the great cities, not by the villages, the provincial towns, or by the countryside.

Mabel was influenced by G. Stanley Hall's Theory of Recapitulation, adapting it to suggest that the spirit and character of the child follows the route of our ancestors as they evolved towards civilisation. What the child needs, she thought, is the recapitulation of the experiences of the occupations of primitive man; they need to follow the activities of their ancestors, not just read about them, and her ideal school would provide suitable opportunities to do so. She approved of children doing practical work as a part of life, 'by finding that at the heart of the essential occupations needed to live, true arts and 'crafts' come about by force of circumstance.'

In her thesis, Mabel referred to a number of educational experiments then taking place, including those of Kingsley Fairbridge, A S Neill and Bertrand Russell. Also mentioned was the work of John Hargrave or 'White Fox', who founded Kibbo Kift in 1920. She had a number of personal contacts within this movement, and took part in their camps throughout the 1920s. Mabel had jointly edited a leaflet with Hargrave, entitled 'Discovery', written for The Regional Association and published by Le Play House in 1925. This was included in her thesis as a leaflet called *A la Decouverte*, with the slogan 'If you know how to explore your region, you know how to explore the world.' It suggested questions for teachers to pose as a starting point for environmental studies.

Mabel finished by saying that an essential condition for a future school was that it should be close to the mountains; she was thinking at this point of her own future venture, Friar Row. 'Children who are given access to the most varied surfaces of the earth would have chance to develop most fully the heritage of their ancestors; things hidden in their subconscious, that would probably not be developed in an environment that consists purely of books.' She ended the thesis by giving an account of the short life of Alasdair Geddes, the older son of Patrick Geddes, who died in April 1917, defending his country.

She explained how his unusual education had given him the facility to succeed at everything, including as a soldier; he was the youngest Captain and Commander in the army. He had written an essay about the Civic Survey of Edinburgh during his first stay in Montpellier during 1912-13, and Mabel appended it to her thesis as a tribute to its author.

During her time in France, Mabel took every opportunity to visit prehistoric sites, especially cave dwellings. In 1926, she wrote an article on the Prehistoric Museums of the Dordogne, and the following year, an article on the Cave Men of the Dordogne was published in the Horn Book (III,4), an American educational journal.

Before she left for France, Mabel had organised for work from Kings Langley Priory to be shipped out to the United States for various exhibitions on the subject of progressive education. There was a growing interest in her work in the U.S. and she was invited to teach in America for a year, but turned down the opportunity in view of plans to start her own school in Cumbria. Perhaps her climbing projects also played a part in this decision.

Skye 1926

Mabel was itching to resume her 'third round' with the Coolins, held over from the summer before. She returned to England on July 12th 1926, joined Gertrude Walmsley (chief of the support party) in Devonshire, and drove to Cumberland with her. There, they were joined by C.D.F. and headed straight for Skye, camping near Loch Lomond and Downie Ferry, which they missed. Her FRCC article tells the story:

> I went to France for a 'winter' of indeterminate length: and during nearly a year of the life of a University city near the Mediterranean, the fells and the Coolins seemed further away than their actual distance warranted. But during the whole time our purpose was never allowed to swerve for one moment from Skye for the first fortnight of August. The chief of the support party somehow took command of the whole affair. Whatever happened (and many things seemed possible) she gently and inexorably shepherded her scattered troops towards the Coolins.
>
> But even she couldn't prevent the effects of the Coal Strike. To our disappointment, H.V.H. had to take his holidays in July, before the rest of the party could join him. So he took them – in Skye – and passed on to us the results of his scouting on Sgurr na h-Uamha, and some good advice about the Banachdich Gap.
>
> The fates seemed against us somehow. I lost a lot of kit in a train fire; several more of the party couldn't get there; illness in her family limited G.W. strictly to the fortnight; the Austin 7 and Excelsior 1.5, which transported a section of us, developed frequent minor ailments, so that we lost time and ferries; and the phenomenal good weather broke two days after we reached Glen Brittle. But we did reach it, six strong; and the feel of the rocks is good after a year's exile.

On August 2nd, camp was established near Glen Brittle House. The following day the whole party went to Coruisk by the coast route. Mabel's notes report:

> 'Frankland said casually, 'Let's go back by the Dubh Ridge.' Innocently, I agreed. It was a marvellous excursion, but by the time we came down to Coire

Ghrunnda I felt pretty well played out (it was the first day of climbing after nearly a year in France!): so instead of following a party we saw ahead of us down the Coire, C.D.F. proceeded to lead up over the shoulder it seemed like the last straw! Then followed an interesting bit of psychology. Down at last in Coire Lagan in fading light C.D.F. said 'Are you tired?' 'Yes' I replied. Plaintively he said 'I'm ever so much more tired than you are, and I'm afraid of the dark.' It may have been true, for he was shortsighted, but whether or no, he could have made no better move. When I was ready to sit down and howl, he threw the lead onto me: 'O come on, Colonel, I rather like the dark. We'll be in camp in no time.' And we were in before the other party reached Glen Brittle.'

The next day they went to Coire Lagan, and while having some difficulty on what they hoped was Mallory's Route, found they were being watched by yesterday's party of young men. They introduced themselves as Wood-Johnson and Hennessy. Mabel and C.D.F. replied with Frankland and Barker. 'You're the Central Buttress people,' said the young men. 'We modestly admitted it,' said Mabel. 'They came to supper in camp, and so began another long connection.'

The following day a large party were taken up the Cioch, and the day after that they were on Sgumain and Alasdair. 'On one of these, some of us were playing on Harland's Boulder, and one of the group watching made an interesting observation of our differing technique – George Wood-Johnson looked till he saw what he wanted and grabbed it: I tapped the rock till I got the hold desired: Frankland's fingers never left the rock.'

On 7th August, they did Water Pipe Gully and visited the Fairy Pools. Then, on the 8th, they were ready for further action. 'We inspected the hut and made our cache, and didn't forget the tea. We provisioned ourselves for five days (including the treks). We made some good allies, too, also staying in Glen Brittle; and leaving two of our party (and the Sealyham) in camp there, the four others went to Loch Scavaig on the afternoon of Sunday 8th. The morning had been disgustingly wet, and the weather was anything but promising. C.D.F. and I were left of the climbing party; Gertrude Walmsley and Edith Davies were 'in support.'

Said Frankland of the support party: 'Theirs was an unenviable place in the team, but just as important as ours. They were both school ma'ams. (We were all pedagogues!) You would never have guessed it, had you seen their laughing faces looking up at the Bad Step 'twixt Sgumain and Alastair or when sharing their oilskins with four big boys from Glen Brittle, during a deluge at the Great Stone Shoot. As I saw them from the shelter of a cave that splendid afternoon, exchanging chocolates and things, they were far more like laughing, chattering school kiddies.'

Mabel continued: 'Monday morning was horrid, but they thrust us forth. We went up on Gars-bheinn. Rain – mist – wind.

'We didn't have a second cup of tea,' said C.D.F. The hut looked very nice when we got back to it.

Tuesday was even worse, but G.W. woke up, and woke C.D.F. up. The inspection was brief. We had a delightfully lazy day, and I was very glad of it. Presumably in a last attempt to frustrate us, the Coolins hit me rather hard when coming down on Monday; I skidded on a slab covered by loose scree, and was uncomfortably stiff, and a bit anxious. Certainly it made me slower in climbing – but most virtuously careful!'

Frankland wrote: 'The support party did us well; perhaps too well. We were enjoying our exalted position (figuratively speaking) as shock troops, far too well to go over the top. Then on the last day, the chief cook put down her foot. That did it.'

Mabel described the scene:

> So Wednesday 11th was absolutely the last chance for this year. It didn't look quite so bad at 4 a.m., but then we couldn't really see it.
>
> 'The weather is quite good,' said the heartless Gertrude, 'I can see quite a lot of stars.' So we ate our breakfast and shouldered the rucksack, packed overnight for the third time.
>
> 'Now don't let me see you again until you've done it,' said she. So what choice had we?
>
> We left the hut at 5 a.m., and varied the route up Gars-bheinn by sticking longer to the N.E. ridge. It gave a little more rock-work, and let us in for an unexpected gap, but we were again on the summit for 7-0. Mist – rain – pretty strong wind! (I should like to see the view from Gars-bheinn). It looked depressingly like a repetition of last year. But on the way we had seen Sgurr nan

Gillean clear of mist to the summit, so we hoped that we might walk out of it during the day, which came to pass. Again we carried no rope, but lots of food.

After the Thearlaich-Dubh Gap we were pleased to recognize the small area visible as the head of Alasdair Stone Shoot, which happily we had visited a dew days before. We ran up on to Alasdair (10 a.m.) When back on Thearlaich, the greatest of the Coolins suddenly gave a curt acknowledgement of our visit – loomed out huge, dark and close upon us – then drew the veil again. (*O Midyir, Lugh and Angus Og! O Dana, Mother of the Gods and Men! It is a good omen at last?*)

Thereafter came other breaks, increasing in number and duration, till we actually had glimpses of sunlight on the sea. It was misty on the Inaccessible, but not raining; indeed, drying so fast that we talked about rubbers, but didn't. Sgurr Dearg – 12-40 and time for a rest – but not till we leave that Gap behind us! Down the screes on the Coire Banachdich side we went, followed H.V.H.'s advice as to when to traverse – and behold the mist lifted completely and suddenly as by a miracle, showed us the Gap and the Ridge beyond it, and all the glory of the views to east and west of it, views surely unparalleled anywhere when seen like this; then closed again. (*Thanks, O Midyir, Lugh and Cuchullian! Hard, bright, and beautiful gods who rule her for ever!*) And we settled to lunch and rest with quiet minds.

We had samples of every kind of weather and scene that the Coolins can give. Violent hail-storms were followed by sudden clearances and brilliant sunlight. Once we saw Blaven in bands of colour, not in an arched rainbow, but as though a veil woven from a spectrum were thrown over it. Somewhere about Mhadaidh it kept dry for so long that we changed into rubbers, and enjoyed them exceedingly for about an hour. We rested on Bidean from 4 to 4-30, revelling in the loveliness of Coruisk, our own physical well-being, and the view of Sgurr na h-Uamha, which of course looked rather deceptively near. (As Frankland put it, 'We had tea without tea on Bidean.') But it seemed a long pull up to Bruach na Frithe. I began to feel tired, and we lost time on this section, sheltering from very bad hail storms. A particularly fierce one just after Naismith's Route, left me wet through and horribly cold, and it took all the shoulders available to help me up the nasty little overhang on to Am

> Basteir. But it was the last difficulty, and C.D.F. was going better than when we started. At 8-30 we were on Sgurr nan Gillean, in bright sunlight above a sea of cloud. A sudden rent in it showed the Red Coolins framed in white, and far beyond them, miles and miles of the mainland. But our Ridge remained completely hidden by clouds, and we had to use the compass again to find its direction.
>
> An hour more, and we stood on Sgurr na h-Uamha, the whole landscape clear, and Lochan Dubha and the Scavaig River crimson in the sunset glow.

Wrote Frankland: 'With the low sun behind, the light was perfect. Iridescence finished in the gauzy clouds like a broad belt of rainbow, only lighter. The pearly hues, which are the boast of Skye, the dainty blue peculiar to this coast in the evening light, the varied forms, (was that Ben Nevis over there?) the vigorous lines and the soft distance are all familiar to Skye lovers. Nor are these joys just passing thrills. They live on in the memory still.'

Mabel continued:

> Then came the unrehearsed portion. We returned to the col between Uamha and Sgurr Beag, and thence went down practically due west into Lota Corrie. This route off presents no special difficulties, fortunately, for it was a race with the dark, and we only just won. We were across the Sligachan River, a little above the crags, by 10-15, and in the shadow of the Druim nan Ramh the light was almost gone, six miles from camp. We contoured the west side of Harta Corrie, crossed the low col to the south as planned, and felt some relief and satisfaction when we found the burn running our way. It was nothing then but a steady plug over boggy, but not very difficult ground – a case of keeping on till we got there. We had brought a candle lantern – the property of Gertrude – but when we proposed to use it, somewhere about half-way, found that neither of us knew how to make it stay put! However, it held together with kind treatment, and we kept on, cheered by its gleams and chocolate.

Frankland wrote: 'Lota Coire was new to both of us and what a wild chasm it is, apparently walled in by Druim nan Ramh, Am Basteir, Sgurr nan Gillean and Sgurr na h-Uamha; its gloom that night was profound. A lusty roar rose from the rocky bed of the torrent as we wound our way through the labyrinth. On our right, rose high a black wall, on which five white streams, the head waters of the Lota, hung in snowy contrast. Lonely it was, barren and desolate but lacking the dreary sameness of Ennerdale. The effect was by no means sad. There was a vigour in the stream and energy in every tumbled boulder, which was frankly cheerful. Of all the highland glens I have seen, the one I am longing most to see again is Lota Corrie.'

Mabel continued:

> Gars-bheinn and Sgurr nan Eag suddenly appeared, a dark silhouette against a starry sky, over Lochan Riabhach (Strange! Were we really there this morning?). And so slowly down to Coruisk, and with some mighty bad going too, along its east shore in the dark. Fording the Scavaig River anyhow was good fun, and we crept round to the hut like thieves, betting as to whether the 'support party' was asleep or not. Asleep? At 1 a.m.? Not they! Apparently they had timed our return to the minute, and just got supper hot. Lights, and fire, and hot Bovril before we could speak. Well, we could face them.
>
> We had been out 20 hours, and were quite respectably tired, but by no means done. By 11 a.m. we were all off on the return trek; but our heavy packs did not get carried all the way to Glen Brittle. For when about half-way there, we met a Rescue Party (E. and G. Wood-Johnson and W.G.Hennessy) coming round to pick up the bits; carrying food, too! It gave a sort of expeditionary finishing touch. (And I suspect that some expeditions have not been quite so glad as we were when they got 'found').
>
> I do not think our distance was much greater than the Glen Brittle to Sligachan route of former ridge-walkers. The S.M.C. Guide gives that as 16 miles; ours comes out to about 18. Of course our times won't bear comparison with those of any former conquerors of the Ridge (except perhaps for sections of the actual going while it was fine). But we were not trying to make time-records at all, only to do it in a new way, rather a jolly one, and to enjoy the whole thing, in both of which aims we succeeded beyond all expectations. The time could be improved by anyone in decent weather, but also, I suggest, by doing it 'widdershins'; by getting the six miles of fellwalking to the foot of Uamha done in daylight (and one could start earlier going that way, with a lantern); and perhaps a direct route could be made up the south face of Uamha from Harta Corrie, avoiding our detour to the west. Then all the way after

Bidean one would be getting nearer home, nearer the support party, and their supper, and their welcome. For they hold the key to the Round of the Coolins from Coruisk.'

Said C.D.F. in his notes: 'It was presumptuous on my part to congratulate Miss Barker. The first woman that ever traversed the Black Cuillin in one expedition, was probably harassed by the responsibility of seeing her companion safely back again, and I did have a somewhat narrow squeak. For instead of returning to the col by the same way we had come, following the scratches, I thought to find a quicker way down and was almost too successful. A flat sort of flagstone, about the size of the driving board of a tram, went adrift as I stepped aboard. It was certainly going my way but preferring to walk, I dropped off again, and it disappeared over the edge. Judging from the sounds, it was as well that I did so, for it seemed to have a pretty rough passage on its way down to Lota Corrie.'

The whole party were in Coire Lagan on the 14th and on the 15th August on Sgurr Dearg, and many climbed the Inaccessible. They left next day, camping at Loch Lochy and near the Forth Bridge, and went on to Welton (the home of Mabel's brother) at which point C.D.F left them.

May I Never Say Goodbye to Scavaig

On 24th August, C.D.F. wrote to Mabel with thanks for a 'jolly good holiday.' A few weeks later, he sent her a long letter, referring to the kindness and what he called spoiling by all members of the camp:- 'I'm no saint, nor want to be now or hereafter; but I am sure a bit of a pussy cat. I purr comfortably when I snoodle up, physically and metaphysically, and that is a dangerous thing to do ... Don't you see that next thing I'll be doing is to drop climbing for sheer funk at the risk of dropping literally out of the nest upon rocks cruel and hard: or our sweet young things will realise that they are being made use of by a couple (I include you, please) of climbing cranks for our own ends. For instance, we have not finished with Skye. They have decided that they have (?). May I never say goodbye to Scavaig. I do honestly feel that I love Scavaig for its sunshine even more than its subtler moonshine. We must be first at the complete ridge walk including Blaven and Clach Glas. You and I can do it in dry weather. Rubbers will solve it.

Have you written up the walk yet? ... it might help to keep warm that particular memory if you want to do so ... our editor said we'd been making history. Well, we had ... I've made the mouths of ——— fairly exude with envy when ... I rough drafted the life in the Tin Palace *(the 'Scavaig Inn')* ... I ought to give it up. The Mrs is quite sure, morbidly so, that I shall in the end break my ugly neck. She knows it, and hates to think that she has not been able to make me give it up ... I shall always be glad to see you, and proud to climb and bag peaks with you. But be warned ... (of advancing years) Will you then be leading me like a sheep up the climbs – 'suitable for beginners'? ... This is such utter trash. So unnecessary. I dare you not to destroy it. No I don't but please be merciful ... much I demand in return for the climbing we have been able to do together, but patience and tolerance, beyond even what I have exacted up to now; and so may we yet live very vividly in patches ... until you are perfectly fed up, as you soon will be with letters like this ... I value your regard: I dread the day when I shall lose it. I need as much as you can spare ... '

A little later, Claude wrote to Mabel about her plan, then maturing, to start her own school at Friar Row, and went on '... A young man at the O.D. Ghyll

Hotel got himself presented to me by Benson, and opened his remarks like this: 'I want a few minutes quiet talk with you. You see, I fell out of the overhang of the Flake Crack three weeks ago'!!! ... I trust that we shall have many jolly good climbs together again ... We must do that Esk Buttress, Cam Spout etc etc some day before I'm old (older, I mean).'

On October 14th came a long letter from Claude, chiefly about the journals of the YRC and the FRCC and their delay in appearing –

'I am glad for my sake that you won't be able to afford things next year. We shall then be all aboard the same boat, adrift on the sea of economy, where we shall proceed to camps and live on mixed metaphor. Hooray! No, not in life shall we say goodbye to Scavaig, nor cast away its spell.'

In November, Mabel wrote to him in some depression about the progress of her plans and he wrote back a long letter about bad luck: 'How pathetically we say 'Oh you don't know me yet'! Especially when we reply 'I know him only too well. I've finished and he's never the same man again, except when he is with you. He's different with another friend, and again with another. There's a queer psychological thought for you ... I read your article with great and refreshing pleasure ... When I had first been down Gaping Ghyll all other pots seemed paltry. I was spoiled. After C.B. all other climbs seemed tame. After the Ridge the rest was picnicking, and jolly good picnics too.'

He referred again to Gaping Ghyll, the descent of which was to be one of the excursions at the Leeds Meeting of the British Association in 1927, and which Mabel and others proposed to attend. He referred again also to the chap who fell out of the Flake Crack – 'He faced the wrong way at the top, and fell out as any one would. I am to take him up next year, so you will be needed please, to lead up once more.' Later, he wrote: 'I am glad the Wood-Johnsons are to be in camp and trust you'll still have me ... I can't afford hotel life. I waste too much money on G.G., Wales, Dungeon Ghyll weekends and tennis.'

C.D.F. wrote Mabel many long and speculative letters at this time, some of which were lost. In another, he told about a new passage he found in Gaping Ghyll, beyond the Mud Pot. '... you may judge of the size of the hall, and my delight when I sang out 'Here's a passage, as promising a place as ever was'! for we were exploring under the care of the prince of the pot holes, Roberts.'

In January 1927, he wrote of daydreaming of the Ridge Walk ... 'Did I ever confess to you a sudden spasm I had on Mhic Choinnich that day? The mist, you remember, was thinning out. We had just found Kings Chimney too simple, and were going well – slipping into the stride of the thing and my morning surliness was wearing off – the vapours evaporating if you like – and the tears came! What a silly confession to have to make, and all my subsequent behaviour will give the lie to it. And why? ... In a double sense the sharp emotion was uncalled for. But I could have howled – just for a little moment, mind you. Why? Well, I had a premonition, a strong feeling, that you were going to do the Ridge, and do it well. I cursed myself for hallooing before being out of the wood, counting before hatching and all that, but – I knew it, I knew it. And I revel in that and other happy memories of a great day together, a long day, a full day, a memory collected to last with me as long as life itself ... '

On March 3rd, he said 'I am booked for Easter with the Y.R.C. at Ogwen' and in April, said he was not clear where she was. 'I have six different addresses, and not one of them is Caldbeck'! 'Now, to make you slightly jealous I have just got the loveliest 100ft A.C. line to use at Lliwedd at Easter.' Mabel noted that this was interesting, because he never seemed to have a rope of his own and always used hers. They had done C.B. with her one and only 80ft rope. He said that all his climbing pals were dropping off – getting married and so on. 'I must look round for ... some other complacent Johnny who will play the irresponsible idiot on steep rocks.' He then wrote about a model he was making of the Cuillin Ridge, of which he sent her a photograph when it was finished. In the same letter he commented on the death of H.P. Cain ... 'I sat next to him at the Rucksack dinner. He told me all about his heart, but expressed no fears. It was, as his daughter thought, 'so soon'. Lots of jolly memories spring to mind with Cain amidst.'

'You are very kind,' wrote Claude. 'You ask me to climb with you. I will. There is none better, for we know each other's ways, and you are patient with my whymsies. Are you patient enough and so on to see that I have missed Easter with you by the very least little move? I shall probably fall off with no one to back me up. I keep doing it nowadays through sheer carelessness. At Brimham last Sunday a side handhold snapped off and down I came! But I am getting skilful with frequent practice, and alighted on a twelve inch block as if I meant it. I shall be very cautious in future ... ' There followed a lecture on ropes and the care of them (a friend's rope had broken while he was using it on a tree!). Then came more about the B.A. meeting and Gaping Ghyll, and a promise to try to ensure that Mabel was among the 25 selected members to be taken down. (Mabel and Gertrude Walmsley did in the end go down, but not with Claude.)

In July he wrote to say that he had been in Gaping Ghyll for three days. On Almscliff he had picked a quiet day and was again accosted with those fatal words 'May I have a word with you?'

'I write much more infrequently than I should like. I've had much to say, all about myself as usual, and have refrained with such satisfactory results that I may, I mean that I can, and will, come to the Lakes, pretty well when you think is the best time.'

A postcard on the 7th July said that he was again going to Gaping Ghyll to have a practice stunt for September. The YRC was to camp near G.G. and he suggested that Mabel might join them there, or he would find digs in Leeds. On the 16th he wrote: 'The F & R Journal is far above the usual standard. Don't you think that yours is in good company? Chorley has done us proud. Your article reads well and the pictures and map add flavour. Are you going to drag me up M.G.G.? (*Moss Ghyll Grooves*) Mason's picture of Pillar is wonderful. Might be up to Keswick on Wednesday.'

That was the last letter that Mabel received from Claude. She went to camp at Seathwaite with a party on Friday 29th July, and took a tent over to Wasdale for the FRCC Meet. On Sunday 31st Claude joined her there.

A Happy Ending?

'Shall we call it a happy ending?' wrote Mabel many years later. 'He was never to grow old, or be less than a great leader. He never said goodbye to Scavaig or Borrowdale – that was left for the rest of us - ' Speaking of the death of Mrs Kelly, Claude had once said to her, 'That's how a good climber would be killed.' Mabel took heart from this.

'I have kept many letters written to me as though I had lost a brother indeed, all witnessing to the loss to the climbing world. (I think it was Howard Somervell who once spoke of him to me as probably not only the finest, but the safest climber living) One letter from Harry Scott should be quoted: - 'He was regarded as so absolutely safe that no matter whatever he did, an accident was unimaginable. And now it has come, even to him ... Let us give thanks for the brightness they (the lost) have added to our lives, the joys we might not have known without them ... and finally, when Tony Stoop was killed ... Minor said 'I'm going on climbing right away – if I stop I shall never have the nerve to start again.' I've always believed it sound advice, and hand it on to you ... '

Her father had already said to her, in camp at Seathwaite, 'I suppose you won't stop climbing?' and she had replied – 'No, I can't – it wouldn't be fair to Frankland.' Mabel thought he was pleased.

From one of the party came the words 'To me Great Gable will always be a monument to one of the finest men I ever knew' and from another 'What a very gallant gentleman he was, and how glad you must be to have such wonderful memories, especially of Skye last year ... '

His daughter Mary wrote ' ... I want to thank you for the knowledge that Father was killed through sheer bad luck. I could not believe that anything had happened through his carelessness, or from his attempting something he could not do. I had absolute faith in his skill at climbing, and nobody would be more annoyed than he himself if he had been killed through his own fault ... '

Mabel also received letters from Claude's father, who she went to see, and with whom she corresponded for several years. He had asked for descriptions of the climbs they did together, and for photographs. In one letter he gave a charming anecdote. 'The following may be news to you. Some years ago

I read an article in 'The Strand', written by one of a party of five. They set out to do a climb which was a new discovery, hoping to be the second party to do it. 'About a quarter of a mile away they came into view of the cleft. They had made every preparation for success – rope, grappling hooks and other aids. At that distance they examined the rock with opera glasses, and to quote: 'We saw a little grey-haired man going up alone, like a cat running up a tree.' Of course, it was your friend, Claude.'

C.D.F. had himself written notes for lectures to the Yorkshire Ramblers' Club. It is not known if these lectures ever took place. In them he talked of the philosophy of climbing. 'G.K. Chesterton, as an authority on British games,' he wrote, 'describes them as an escape into a fairyland of happy unreality. In the game of climbing the magic staircase had a way of collapsing at inopportune moments and one may be brought up roughly against very hard facts ... '

After Claude's body was carried down, it was laid out on the snooker table at the Wasdale Inn. Paul, Claude's 20-year-old son, went to Wasdale to identify the body, accompanied by Kitty. A verdict of 'Accidental Death' was returned, the coroner remarking that rock climbing seemed to have a tremendous fascination for people, and that they seemed 'gripped by an urge to conquer.' The family was greatly upset by his comments. By then, it was time to move on with the burial. It was too late to bring the body back to Leeds, so the funeral took place at the small church in Wasdale. Unfortunately, in all the confusion surrounding the death, Claude's brother, Harwood, who was a bank manager in Keswick, was not informed in time. As a result he could not attend the funeral and there was a split between the Leeds and Keswick sides of the family, lasting until 1961. This was a particularly sad outcome, as Claude had been close to his brother and done all his early fellwalking and climbing with him.

Paul, Claude's son, was badly affected by the manner of his father's death. Perhaps the affects were worse because his father had also been absent during the Great War. There were also serious financial problems for the family. John Frankland comments that his own father did not like to talk about Claude's death and certainly did not want his own son to go climbing. 'Look what happened to your grandfather,' he would say. He did not go on holidays to the Lake District until he was much older. 'Youngsters should be taken to the seaside for holidays,' Paul would say.

There have been questions asked over the years as to the nature of the relationship between Mabel and Claude. Was it more than a climbing partnership? But there is no question of any impropriety between the two. Yes, theirs was a deep and intimate friendship, of a different nature to a same-gender partnership; but they were both able to keep it so, and saw each other as brother and sister rather than anything more. If she did not wish to enter into the institution of marriage, Mabel was respectful of the ties and responsibilities entailed.

John Frankland still has his grandfather's somewhat tattered copy of Owen Glynne Jones' *Rock Climbing in the English Lake District*, first published in 1900 at a cost of 20s. Claude obtained his copy soon after Jones' own death through a fall in the Alps. It is full of notes and comments in the margins. On the first page, Claude has outlined in red the author's quotation:

> But ever when he reach'd a hand to climb,
> One, that had loved him from his childhood, caught
> And stay'd him, 'climb not lest thou break thy neck,
> I charge thee by thy love,' and so the boy,
> Sweet mother, neither clomb nor broke his neck,
> But brake his very heart in pining for it,
> And pass'd away.
>
> Gareth and Lynette

Claude's grave is in the little churchyard at Wasdale. Upon its stone are the words: 'Here he lies where he longs to be.'

Friar Row School

After what must have been a heart-rending blow, Mabel continued climbing immediately. By August 6th, she had already taken part in a first ascent of Great Doup Pinnacle with two of the Wood-Johnson brothers, George and Ernest, with whom she had a close friendship.

However, Mabel's energy was now directed into starting her own school, at Friar Row, in Caldbeck. In 1923, her aunt, Kate Morison Barker, had died in Perth, leaving her £3000, a vast sum of money at that time. This was one of the aunts with whom Mabel had gone to live after her mother had died. She was then successful in attracting the support of Mr. Wilkinson of Sebergham Castle, who owned several cottages adjoining the derelict mill in Friar Row. This was a row of very old houses once inhabited by the Farm Friars of Holme Coulton Abbey, and was gifted to her on the condition that she built a school there. Mabel set about renovating and converting the premises into what would form a part day and part boarding school.

The school opened in 1927 on a modest scale, but gradually expanded. Boys as young as five were admitted both to the boarding house and the day school and girls of up to the usual school-leaving age came in on a daily basis. The two Principals were Mabel and her old friend, Gertrude Walmsley, who gave up her job teaching English and handicrafts at West Buckland School for Boys in Devon to come and assist, and who possibly put some money into the venture. In Devon, she had taught R.F. Delderfield, author of *To Serve Them All My Days*. Her elder sister, Sarah, was married to a housemaster there named Taylor, who was apparently the model for Delderfield's character in the book. (Could this be the Taylor referred to in Henry Barker's 1911 letter to Anna Geddes?) Gertrude was supposed to teach mathematics at Friar Row, although the school timetable gave little importance to the subject. Another teacher was a French girl called Yvette, who taught French by using nursery rhymes. A leaflet put out by Mabel at the time said the following:

> The buildings and land of Friar Row, Caldbeck, Cumberland, are in the process of reconstruction, and will be opened in September, 1927, as a co-educational school on modern lines.

Caldbeck has been selected as a village of ancient traditions, deep in the country between the Cumbrian Mountains and the Solway Plain, and affording ample opportunity of exploration and varied occupational experience from hills to sea.

It lies in a sheltered valley on a tributary of the Caldew, and though apparently low-lying is 520 feet above sea-level. The district is notably healthy and invigorating. It is on the border of the Lake District, but its rainfall is less than half that which obtains a few miles to the south.

Friar Row stands in its own gardens and orchard, which slope due south to the Caldew, receiving a great deal of sun. Ninety acres of park and woodland adjoin it, and many miles of open common surround the village. A good water supply, modern sanitation, central heating, and electric light are being installed, and the buildings are being carefully adapted to the requirements of a school of this type (Architect, F.C. Mears, Edinburgh).

Boarders, weekly boarders, and day children can be taken from kindergarten age; and arrangements can be made for holiday board, or for the entire charge of children whose parents are abroad. The possibilities of the environment are such that these 'holiday schools' are likely to be a notable feature of Friar Row.

As it is desired to preserve the atmosphere of a good home, and as the Principals are deeply convinced of the importance of practical work, there will be no distinction between the domestic and academic staff. Staff and children alike will take a share, according to age and aptitude, in the work of the community indoors and out.

School pets will be kept. Private pets *may* be kept, but will be the sole responsibility and charge of their owners.

The school aims at giving an 'Education for Life,' and that by means of living as fully, happily, and healthily as may be. Regional study and occupations will be given prominence in the methods employed, for the Principals believe in the value of real experience as the basis of all education, as apart from mere instruction. They aim at the education of 'Head, Hand and Heart.'

To this end undue stress is not laid upon the 'subjects' of the usual school curriculum. In general, nature study, science, history and geography will be under the direction of Miss Barker, while the kindergarten work, English, handicrafts, music, and housewifery will be under that of Miss Walmsley.

Much care will be given, however, to such subjects as cannot be adequately approached by direct experience, *e.g.*, Languages. There will be a French member of the staff; and full advantage will be taken of the possibilities now afforded by a powerful wireless set. There will be an extensive library.

While no emphasis is laid on preparation for public examinations, pupils can be prepared for entrance to the Universities or Public Schools; but public examinations will not be taken unless definitely desired.

Instruction in religious doctrine of any special type is regarded as the work of parents and clergy rather that of the school. Religious instruction will not appear as a subject on the school time-table, but will be provided by arrangement with neighbouring churches of the various denominations when parents desire it. Attendance at the parish church of St. Kentigern will be the rule unless the parents wish for exemption.

Fees are inclusive, since our object is to give the fullest possible education to all under our care. Exceptions will arise when coaching for examinations necessitates the purchase of special text-books; for advanced music and art lessons from visiting masters; and for special medical attendance in case of accidents or infectious disease. Motor transport will also be an extra charge.

Excursions will be of great importance, giving experience of hill-craft and of the sea, and using at first-hand all the rich historical and literary traditions of the Lake District and the Border. These may be day expeditions or week-end camps, and will be run as economically as possible.

Physical health will be a first consideration. The development of a spirit of hardihood, which it is desired to foster in boys and girls alike, and the elimination of unreasonable fear, is closely linked with a healthy body. Excursions and an outdoor life will be relied upon to give this rather than any special school of physical training. There is an open-air bathing pool.

Games will be encouraged, also folk-dancing, especially in winter.

Delicate children will receive every care. There is a doctor within easy reach and a trained nurse on the staff.

The diet will be ample and varied, fresh fruit forming a daily portion of it. Vegetarian diet can be provided if desired.

The school year will be divided into three terms. Fees are payable in advance. A half-term's notice is required before removal of any pupil, and it is requested that the fullest possible notice will be given in the interests of the pupil and out of courtesy to the staff.

Parents are invited to visit the school and to take part in its activities at any time, but children may not be absent during school hours. There is a Guest Cottage which can be taken for limited periods.

Inclusive Fees –

Boarders:	Over 12	£37	per term.
	7 – 12	£35	„
	Under 7	£27	„

Weekly Boarders by arrangement.

Day Pupils (tuition only), £5 per term.

Telephone: ONE, CALDBECK

The list of twenty-nine referees included Professor Patrick Geddes, his daughter Norah, now Mrs F.C. Mears (wife of the architect), her old colleague Valentine Bell, Miss Cross of Kings Langley, Professor J. Arthur Thomson of Aberdeen, John Hargrave ('White Fox' of the Kibbo Kift Movement) and her sometime climbing partner, Dr Arthur Wakefield of Keswick.

Mabel started off with a small group of little boys. Among the early pupils were her nephews Lindsay, Chris and Moris, sons of her brother Arnold and his wife Madge, who ran the Oddfellows Arms Pub at Caldbeck, as well as the Post Office, the local garage, and the bus service to Wigton. Lindsay and Moris still live in cottages at Friar Row. Also among the first pupils were two nephews of Gertrude Walmsley, Brian and Graham Wilde, from Buxton. Graham was only four years old when he first came to Friar Row, and his older brother five. Brian was handicapped at birth, and although the condition was not named, it would today be called cerebral palsy. There was little or no educational provision for such children in those days, and his parents were desperate to find a way of helping him develop. The boys were at the school for two years. Graham has many memories of spending time in the local woodland and on the fells, and recalls that he got to know the local environment very well. He thoroughly enjoyed it, but remembers that even though his brother could manage to walk, he was always cold and was unable to make the progress that everyone had hoped for. After two years, Mabel felt that she was unable to help Brian any further, and the two little boys returned to Buxton. Graham's memories of the times remained vivid, and he believes that he gained an excellent start to his education. He commented wryly that although Gertrude taught domestic science, it was a subject in which she had little skill herself. When he grew up, he came back to visit Mabel in the Lake District every summer, and later settled in the area himself.

Lindsay Barker also remembers his early days at the school. He also felt that Friar Row School gave him a great start in life. 'Everyone who went there turned into good citizens,' he remarks. He remembers that they learnt as they went along – Mabel would stop to point out different flowers or wildlife or rocks or ancient remains. They would all sit round a big solid wood table, one that Franz Nevel had made at his Betula woodworks, and which survives to this day. She could read stories brilliantly; he always felt as if the events were really happening. One of the stories he remembers was Hiawatha, after which they all built a wigwam. Camping was a part of school life, especially the annual camps at Seathwaite. He was taken up Scafell Pike at eight years old and Mabel took the opportunity to go climbing while they were there. When she got down, the children had eaten all the sandwiches. 'She could play war!' he remembers. 'She knew the fells like the back of her hand. One day half a dozen of us kids were coming down off Great Gable in thick fog. She was on her own with us. She told us, 'Whatever you do, don't step to the right or left. There's a 300 foot drop and you're right on the edge of it. Walk exactly where I walk.' He remembers that they regularly used to play charades and that the children used to take part in the cooking. 'Eve's pudding every Monday,' he remembers with a smile. 'If it was a nice day, we would just get up and go out.' They were always taught to look after the countryside, and to leave it in perfect condition.

The children were always active and busy, and helped with some aspects of the renovation. Photographs show them taking part in a host of activities including: climbing on boulders, tree-climbing, making a loom, drawing, studying the church architecture, digging potatoes, brambling, staining the cottage floor, making a dam, climbing High Pike, painting the gate, studying quarries and mines, keeping rabbits, digging a pond, constructing a rock garden, making marmalade, building an igloo, making slippers out of raffia and clay modelling. They even had one lesson on the school roof. 'We would dig trenches behind the school and divide into gangs to fight a mini-war with wild rhubarb stalks,' says Lindsay. He remembers Mabel riding off on her belt-driven motor cycle, called Amy. Later she acquired a Rover called Molly, which had a canvas hood. Once, when they were camping, a cow chewed the hood. 'She didn't care!' says Lindsay. 'She wasn't a very good driver. If something was in her way, she would just back into it. Our father said that we weren't to go in the car with her, but we did!' When Lindsay later went to Secondary School at 11 years old, he was top in French, top in Latin, third in Art, but bottom in Maths. 'Mabel didn't have much time for it!' Graham Wilde also comments on the differences he found on returning to an ordinary school in Buxton. He was not used to having to sit in his desk all the time and do book work. 'The other children could not believe that I had done things like tree climbing in my last school.'

Two years on, the school was fully established, and Mabel answered enquiries with the following:

> Friar Row is not an experimental school in the sense in which that term is ordinarily used ... We do not use Montessori, Dalton, or any other specific methods; nor do we profess to attain to so-called 'free discipline'. The affairs of life leave none of us free from the daily discipline of duties; and this the children are led to discover as quickly as possible ... We have acres of ground, still only partly reclaimed from waste, and affording endless scope for inventive, and active youngsters. But beyond this we are in a land of woodlands, fields, commons and numerous streams; and within easy reach of the great fells. Excursions by motor are made at intervals to these, and to whatever of interest and beauty is necessary as illustrative of, or as a starting point for some aspect of the work. The value of this interplay of manual occupations and 'bookwork' is proving itself on the rather surprisingly rapid progress of the group of little boys who have been with me from the beginning; and in the zest

> with which they enter into everything. The old distinction between 'lessons' and 'play' is almost lost.
>
> It follows from what has been said that much time is spent in the open air, and that physical health is a first consideration. We have been, so far, quite free from infectious illness; and the appearance of the children, their appetites and energy are a constant source of pleasure to me (who am myself a keen mountaineer and camper). I can assure the parents of town children who are in need of a country life that they will find here most healthful conditions ...

Graham remarks: 'A school as unconventional as Friar Row must have attracted a good deal of comment locally, not all of it complimentary, but it made a lasting impression on the pupils who went there. So many years on, the powerful personality of its principal is still remembered in terms of her enthusiasm and teaching ability. She was capable of bringing subjects to life and generating interest that far outlasted the detailed memory of discipline.'

Too Large a Land to Rule

As the school expanded, Mabel took on more staff, several from Europe, to give the children first hand experience of other languages and cultures. Committed as she was, this also meant that she sometimes had the freedom to take off and leave the school in the hands of others. She was able to take advantage of good weather and the availability of climbing partners; over the next few years, she was often to be found close to the scene of action. During the course of 1927, she started to explore Carrock Fell, which was her local stamping ground. In her 1932 Fell and Rock article on the subject, she gave a typical detailed description of its geology and structure, explaining about the many minerals found there. She wrote:

> But for many of us, the continuous human interest of this little fell outweighs that of its structure, for man has made his home here from a far distant past. Upon its summit (2,174 feet) is an enclosure of about seven acres. Its origin, purpose and age are unknown as yet. It may be an Iron Age Hill Fort, and if so the only one in this part of Britain. All we are sure of is that the great dykes of loose stone were made by human hands, as was the double tumulus towards the east end of the enclosure. But on the moorlands round the feet of Carrock are very numerous tumuli and artificial heaps of stone – over 200 having been noted and mapped – and this last summer we had the thrill of a small bit of excavation. One tumulus proved to be a burial, containing burnt bones and much charcoal with a scrap of copper among them and some copper slag; while the other, originally a saucer-shaped depression, is a beautiful little stone structure – a hut, we hope. Carrock teems with unrevealed secrets and unsolved problems.

A poem fragment, scribbled in pencil, was found in Mabel's copy of her FRCC journal, describing a later experience of excavating the Howthwaite Cairn in 1934, which proved to be empty except for some small worked flints:

The Howthwaite Cairn

Not e'en the shadow of thy bones is ours –
Thou has arisen: nought beneath the stone –
'Earth unto earth' – then earth to grass and flowers
Breathing upon the fell that was thine own –
No answer from thy cairn: athwart death's portal
Nothing save this (we dimly understand) –
Thou less than dust, there yet remains immortal,
The tiny weapon wrought by thy dead hand.

17/8/34 MMB

In her 1932 article, Mabel continued: 'I climbed Carrock in deep snow, more years ago than I can quite remember. But I first went there to look for a playground with Franz Knefel on May 1st, 1927, and found one, and went again in August with George and Arthur Wood-Johnson; since when we have had many a day on its kindly rocks.'

Mabel went on to describe the climbs she discovered there. The first was 'Eighty Foot Slab', which she climbed with Lochhead and Airey in 1927. The next was 'Three Tier Climb', put up with Nancy Ridyard and Tony Musgrave in 1931. In July 1932, she put up 'Juniper Crack' with the same party. More routes were to come after the writing of her article. In April, 1933, she put up 'North Trough Buttress', with Briggs and Lochhead, and 'Slape Crags Arête', again climbing with Lochhead. In August 1934, she made solo first ascents of 'Rose-tree Route' and 'North Climb', and in the summer of 1935, came 'Maeve's Crack' and 'South Trough Buttress', both with Arthur Wood-Johnson, and 'Slape Crags Direct' with Alan Horne. Mabel loved her local fell, and rounded the article off by saying: 'A day on Carrock ends with a visit to Mrs Lister at Stone Ends Farm. She ranks high indeed among hostesses for climbers. And for those who camp there is a site so lovely that I shall say no more about it here.' There is a story told by Graham Wilde, in the booklet *Caldbeck Characters,* relating that much later in life, Mabel was driving with her brother Arnold along the fell-bottom road that passes under Carrock Fell. At the base of the crag, she spotted a group of young men who were discussing the possibilities of a climb. Mabel asked Arnold to stop the car, and accosted the group, suggesting that she would lead them up a climb. The young men were so astonished that they yielded to her request. Climb completed and back in the car to resume their journey, Mabel said quietly to her brother, 'I think that will be my last.' And so it was indeed her last climb, and in due time Arnold scattered her ashes at its foot.

Mabel was also involved in the exploration of Castle Rock of Triermain with Graham MacPhee. MacPhee was a Professor of Dental Surgery at Liverpool University, known to be a difficult character to get along with; he was brusque, had a sardonic humour and could make cutting remarks. However, Mabel seems to have got along with him well, and the two put up four new routes on the south buttress during the spring and summer of 1928. MacPhee wrote about this in the FRCC journal of 1929. Mabel's touch is evident in this article, which mentions the ancient history of Castle Rock and its geology. Wrote MacPhee: 'It is surprising that in this age of intensive rock-climbing in the Lake District nobody seems to have climbed the Castle Rock. None of the experts who were consulted had ever even heard of the crag ... When I did arrange to visit it with George Basterfield 'some fine day' to climb in rubbers, the weather during the summer of 1928 was unkind and no fewer than ten times successively did our plans come to nought. 'The Secret Crag' became a standing joke.'

MacPhee, however, was determined to 'explore its scansorial possibilities' and had more luck when Mabel volunteered to join him. At first they concentrated on the main central face.

> We started gaily in boots up a small crack, but progress was slow and was finally arrested about 40 feet higher owing to the cold, wet condition of the rock. A second attempt was made farther to the north, traversing up to a ledge and then surmounting a bulge. A large mass of rock was well tested but failed to support my weight, and shattered itself and our *morale* by crashing on the screes below.
>
> This was rather different from our optimistic visions of making a couple of routes up a brand-new crag, and we felt more surprise than anything else at such complete and ignominious defeat almost before the battle had begun. Obviously the Castle Rock required more preparation before the next assault,

such as exploration with a rope held from above. Somewhat crestfallen, we decided to do something on the South Castle Rock, which had at first seemed scarcely worth looking at, but we found even this crag by no means easy ... A direct route up the centre of the face was explored and climbed partly on a rope, but it has not yet been led all the way, as circumstances, chiefly meteorological, have so far always frustrated my attempts.

The three climbs that Mabel and MacPhee did together were Yew-Tree Climb, Slab Climb (led by Mabel) and Scoop and Crack. MacPhee commented: '... Our humble efforts on the Castle Rock attracted quite a crowd of spectators, and on one occasion fully a dozen cars were drawn up at the roadside.' This was the first phase of opening up the crag, which was taken up later by Jim Birkett, Charlie Wilson and Len Muscroft, with Overhanging Bastion and Zigzag, in 1939. Mabel clearly kept abreast of later developments on the crag, as she is mentioned in the ensuing arguments in the local press, somewhat sensationalized, about who were the first to climb the crag and their motivation for doing so.

Mabel continued to hold camps every year, at Seathwaite and further afield. She became an active member of the Ladies' Scottish Climbing Club, and in 1929, wrote an article for their Journal entitled *A Camping Holiday in Iona and Staffa.* Once again her writing gives the full flavour of her experiences:

In August of last year Hilda Burton took a bungalow in Iona for 1928, and asked me to bring a camping-party to join her there. It needed little persuasion to make us yield to the magic in that name. I had always, I think, intended to go to Iona.

But some folks were rather surprised and incredulous. 'What *are* you going to do in Iona?' 'Is there good climbing there?' I murmured 'Archeology,' and some members of our party made – beforehand – slightly facetious suggestions about running round the island twice before breakfast.

Iona was all that I had ever expected it to be, and then far more. I am not going to write here of its great and unique history, its far-reaching spiritual power, its picturesque ruins and Celtic art, past and present, or of the happy and kindly life in it now. These things have been described by many and able pens, and fill volumes. All I have to say is a very little about the more than imagined beauty and interest of Iona itself – of the little island as it is, and would be, had it no human story, or none beyond that of other isles.

Asia and all imperial plains
Are too little for a fool;
But for one man whose eyes can see
The little island of Athelney
Is too large a land to rule.

How can I ever hope to know my own Lakeland or the great mountain regions of Scotland, since life would not be long enough wherein fully to know Iona? It is a little cosmos, varied and alluring, with all manner of fair and intriguing things in every corner of it.

We camped on the comparatively sheltered and flat east coast at the foot of Achabhanach croft. Before us, across the sound, were the lovely red rocks of Mull, with the thatched cottages of Kintra easily seen through glasses on a clear day. Behind us lay the strip of croft with potatoes and hay, and the hospitable farm of the MacArthurs at the head of it; and then Dun-I, so near that we could run up on to it to see the splendid sunsets (and not be more than an hour or so late for supper). From our camp itself, almost at sea-level as it was, we could just see the tips of the Cuillin.

There was never a day in our three weeks, I think, that my feet were not on the rocks somehow. For example, the tiny cliffs of sharp Torridonian slates offered a variety of routes to the morning bath. One could increase this variety and make them into 'severes,' by such devices as a canvas bucket of fresh water in one hand and a sponge-bag in the other, a towel forgotten on the far side of a gully, just too wide to reach across on bare feet. The adjusting of one's bath place with the state of the tide and the position of Charley and the kine also kept the proceedings from any danger of monotony.

There are some good pitches on Dun-I. I planned several routes, which I never did from sheer laziness and lack of time! There are little traverses and chimneys and face climbs even among the rocks beside the White Sands at the north end of the island. All over the interior one could ramble and scramble, never exhausting the infinite variety of ways, never exploring sufficiently all the craggy hills, never learning the routes *round* the bogs. The old sea cliffs edging the machair to north and south I did no more than look at in passing. They await another holiday, and according to Professor Jehu they are of great geological interest.

But it is the west and south coasts, where the Atlantic calls and booms and breaks, that offer the most inexhaustible variety of coves and bays, cliffs, caves, and headlands, of rocks varied in colour and kind, rich with treasures for botanist and geologist, artist and climber; where on many a little jewelled beach (and not only the traditional Bay of the Coracle) one can find the 'lucky' green stones and treasures besides. There is a fantastically rocky little corner overlooked by a knoll called Dun Mhanannan, surely the sanctuary of a far older faith than that brought to Port na Curaich. It has a spouting cave and a dark gully, rich with *Asplenium marinum*, and giving a short climb right on to the top of the Dun. Also in this cove is a small replica of the Napes Needle! It is perhaps half the size of the one on Great Gable, but remarkably like it. We made two routes up it, that to the north being quite easy, the south distinctly difficult. The rock seems sound, but the whole thing is a lovely rock-garden, draped grey with lichens and coloured with clumps of Saxifrages, sea-pinks, Cochlearias, and Sedums – so lovely that the necessary 'gardening' for handholds was done reluctantly and carefully. I should like to see it again in the floral beauty of early summer. Quite near here is the 'Silver Rock' of Iona, a vein of beautiful green 'marble', which we sought for on several days and found at last.

In a sort of side aisle on the west of the Bay of the Ruins we found a 'chimney', really a long, narrow and roofless cave through which one got a remarkably framed view of the bay. There is a nice little climb up to it – two pitches of about twenty feet each. On a second visit we brought a rope, and I took my friend of the bungalow up it in what was intended to be the orthodox manner. Unfortunately, all the midges in Iona had awakened to life and met there that day, so our interest in the climb was divided. There is a similar deep cleft near the Marble Quarry; rather forbidding we thought it, perhaps because we came on it from the top, and found ourselves in the company of a cow whose position seemed perilous.

The Marble Quarry and the coast beside gave good and interesting scrambling, but it is a sad place with its rusting and perished tackle, so much beautiful stone spoiled and left, and its tale of human endeavour abandoned. It struck a note of waste and frustration that seemed especially wrong in Iona.

We made a little pitch from the lower to the upper Pigeon Cave, and had much scrambling on the rocks, spending a sunny day there. On one occasion only did we go right round Iona, taking about five hours to do it on a lovely late afternoon towards the end of our stay.

But the great adventure of the holiday was camping in Staffa. We were told – I do not know if it is true – that the *Fusileer* would not leave us there, but would take us off again. So five happy mortals went off one Tuesday afternoon in Captain Maclean's motor-boat, with tents and food for more than the two days we planned.

O beautiful and wonderful Staffa! Why is it uninhabited? Not only because, as one of its last inhabitants is reported to have said, 'A great hand came down the chimney one night in a storm, and we were afraid and left Staffa,' but because the general ebbing tide of population in the Highlands and Islands has left such small patches to be pastured by a few sheep brought from a larger island. It is about three-quarters by half a mile, and, considering the stern aspect of it usually seen in pictures taken from the sea, is wonderfully gentle and friendly in the interior. We found it so at least, and a winter storm can be terrible anywhere.

We camped in shelter behind the ruins of its one building, near water. Our supply of driftwood for fires was lavish indeed after the careful economy of it, eked out with heather and coal in Iona.

The surface is gently undulating, with one valley forming a waist across the whole isle and giving easy access to bays on the east and west. We really did walk round the whole island frequently, and got down to the sea wherever it was easy. This is not in very many places, for the vertical basalt columns are not climbable – not solo anyway. Captain Maclean had viewed my rope with much suspicion, hardly believing the assurance that I did not use it to get myself into danger but to keep my companions out of it!

We saw Fingal's Cave in sunlit calm, in faint and lovely moonlight and in a grand swell which leapt to the roof, drenching us with spray. Could two days have given us more? Long, precious days they were, every hour of them piling up new and precious memories to keep for all our lives.

From Port a' Fhasgaidh on the west we climbed round at low tide into Cormorants' Cave, and from it went by the narrow and dark passage leading into Mackinnon's. We came out suddenly into a wide and lofty chamber floored with pools and islets, gorgeously coloured and fantastically worn; while the squarish opening framed basalt cliffs and sunlit sea.

The puffins we had hoped to meet had all gone – very recently, I think, judging by the relics we found – but the cormorants were a joy to watch, and so were the occasional seals.

Wind and swell got up on Wednesday night. On Thursday the boats from Gometra never came near Staffa, and the *Fusileer* steamed past. We were not sorry. But Captain Maclean was to rescue us as soon as opportunity offered if we did not return to Iona by that boat, and we thought – or most of us feared – that he would probably try to get us that evening when the tide went down. I do not think he really trusted the tents or the rope or the ample supply of food! Anyway, when we had almost given up expecting him – it would not be true to write 'given up *hope*' – and were having tea, we heard a whistle off the east side. We were told to pack quickly, did so, and were collected from a rocky little bay. There was just enough risk and thrill about it to make us realise the Captain's skill and courage and kindness in coming for us at all that evening.

It was rather disconcerting to return to Iona (with all the sensations of coming home after a long absence), from two days of the easiest and pleasantest camping I have ever experienced, to find that we had created quite a little stir there, and that folks behaved as though we had done something rather wonderful. The only person who had done anything in the least degree dangerous and difficult was the Captain!

But is it mere fantasy to feel that something of us remains in Staffa and Iona, as in all places of the earth that one has loved and touched and slept upon? At least it is true that something of them goes with us, entering into our very being and forming part of us through life; so that whether we ever return to them or not, we shall never say farewell to the waves beating on the Herdsman, the cry of the sea-birds, and the songs of the people of the Isles.

Life in Caldbeck

Not only was Mabel active on the crags and in the outdoor sphere, but she also participated fully in the local community. In 1928, she founded the Caldbeck Drama Group. She was a strong character on stage, her striking appearance and strong voice, with its clear diction, commanding the attention of the audience. In this, she enlisted her little brother, Pat, who was a very keen amateur performer (and whose son, Tim, later became a professional actor). On holiday in Caldbeck in 1930, she roped him into producing and acting in two plays with her at a 'Party' at the school. Despite the fact that they were rehearsed and performed in three days, Pat's diary records that they both went off well. To anyone who lacked confidence, Mabel would say 'Of course you can do it. Anyone can do it!' and occasionally would have people bursting into tears. The Group entered many festivals in the county, very popular in the days before television. The competitive elements involved independent adjudication and were supported by large audiences. Mabel was not afraid to be vocal about her own point of view. At one festival an adjudicator criticised a female lead on the grounds that her make-up was too heavy, thus presenting a rosy-cheeked image that was out of character. In fact, the girl had naturally strong colouring and was not wearing any make-up at all. Mabel was not afraid to stand up immediately and offer an uncompromising correction. Graham Wilde wrote, 'Her comments on the performance of members of casts could be brusque, although everyone knew that they overlaid a sympathetic nature. She was quite capable of sharply criticising even a young part player for fluffing lines at a rehearsal and then, seeing the child upset, of putting her arm round young shoulders to soothe hurt feelings.' Lindsay, her nephew, remembers a time when he went fishing instead of turning up for rehearsal. 'She played hell with me next day,' he said. 'She didn't half play hell.'

Mabel also joined the Women's Institute and was President from 1934-6 and again in 1937. Wrote Graham Wilde in *Caldbeck Characters*: 'She was sensitive to the relationships that connected local people to lifestyles in which they may have had little choice, but that did not stop her from recommending change where she thought it was necessary. Inevitably, as a strong character, she found that the community was often in two minds about her.' Craft Classes were held at Friar Row on Wednesday afternoons, where members of the community could take part in basketry, book-binding, embroidery, batik-dyeing, leather work, raffia work, stencilling and painting wood, and making Christmas calendars. These were run by Mabel and the craft teacher at the school, Elsie Manners, and the cost for 10 sessions was 10/6d. Mabel was also an enthusiastic participant in Scottish folk dancing. She took part in summer schools at Cockermouth Castle, and also took every opportunity to get local people involved. Lindsay remembers: 'She could do a wonderful sword dance. She was a very skilful dancer.'

One of her major achievements was the writing, organisation and presentation of a pageant based on a history of Caldbeck from pre-Roman times up to the 20th century. Wrote Graham Wilde: 'Caldbeck folk, including some who felt that they had little aptitude and still less inclination to take part, nonetheless found themselves recruited to take part in a procession as the pageant wound its way up the hills and along the roads in the village.' Another theatre event in the open, still remembered by some of the cast and the audience, was a performance of 'A Midsummer Night's Dream' in 1935.

Graham Wilde tells an anecdote about the time when Mabel was asked to judge a fancy-dress competition being held in the Parish Hall. 'Although not so popular now, such events were at one time the subject of very careful preparation and keen competition. An important feature was the choice by entrants of the characters they were to represent: success was likely if the competitor had more than a passing resemblance to the original. It was probably on this basis that some friends of a local man urged him to appear as The Poacher. Dressed in the kind of coat favoured by the trade, face part hidden by a beard of sheep's wool and carrying some snares and a couple of gutted rabbits on his arm, the competitor entered the parade circle accompanied by a lemon-coloured whippet. The dog was a favourite companion and could be relied on to walk at heel. Mabel watched the procession carefully, awarded first prize to The Poacher and then picked up the whippet, embraced it warmly and declared it to be 'the most handsome female in the room'. Coming on top of the decision about the first prize, this pronouncement was less than enthusiastically received by a number of good-looking ladies who had put a lot of effort into their own appearances.'

Meanwhile, Mabel continued writing articles for various journals. In 1929, an abridged version of her thesis was published in France, and found a group of followers in teacher training establishments there, especially in Paris. She continued to write annual reports for the Regional Association, and contributed her ideas on education and prehistoric life to a number of journals and books. In 1933, the broadsheet *Discovery*, which she had edited with John Hargrave, was published in a new edition entitled *Exploration*. Nearer to home, she wrote an official guide to Wigton and District, and in 1934, an article for the Cumberland and Westmorland Archeological Society, entitled *Tumuli near Carrock Fell*.

When her godfather and mentor, Sir Patrick Geddes, died on April 17th 1932, Mabel paid tribute to his life and achievements. Perhaps she intended to write a book about him, but in the end her efforts were directed towards classifying his prodigious body of work. By 1931, he had finally been offered and accepted a knighthood in acknowledgement of his pioneering work in a wide range of disciplines. The later years of his life had been spent in India, from 1914 to 1924, where he met Gandhi, and formed an enduring friendship with the poet and educator Rabindranath Tagore. He also met and discussed ideas with Mrs Annie Besant, (whose views were well known in the field of sex education and family planning). This was a time of growing interest in a fusion of the wisdom of east and west, and she formed an organisation to follow the teachings of Krishnamurti, the Order of the Star in the East. They believed that Krishnamurti was a prophet who, as they put it, carried the message of the Coming World Teacher. Both Mabel and Valentine Bell had earlier written articles for their magazine, *The Herald of the Star*, although were not followers of the movement. Geddes spent the final years of his life at the college he had founded at Montpellier, and it was there that the funeral was held. Mabel always retained her admiration for Geddes, and remained loyal to him throughout her life. When he died, she worked hard to ensure that others had access to his body of work, which still attracts worldwide interest. As Lewis Mumford put it,

Geddes paid the penalty for being a pioneer; many of his ideas were simply too early for people of the time to understand their full significance.

In 1934, Mabel's father, Henry Lindsay Barker, died, aged 80. He had lived an active and fulfilling life, never willing to conform to anything that he did not agree with. Well known in Silloth, he looked after his workers, and deliberately rode his motorbike on the Sabbath to annoy the local minister. The family story goes that he used to ride over to the Oddfellows Arms in Caldbeck every other Sunday. He was quite unstoppable on his motorbike, wearing a big fur hat with earflaps. Once he had a crash with another vehicle, which had a sidecar full of paint, and arrived at Caldbeck covered in it. Each time he arrived at the Oddfellows, his son Arnold would slow down the timing, but Henry always got it fixed again on his return to Silloth. Mabel exasperated her father sometimes, but both were very similar in temperament – holding strong opinions and with a tendency to be short-tempered. Henry was buried in Silloth. Many years later, during the war, a bomb fell on the graveyard and blew him out of his grave. 'Henry would have thought this was hilarious,' says his grandson, Lindsay.

New Frontiers in Education

From our viewpoint a hundred years on, it is easy to forget the bravery of the educational pioneers of last century, sometimes working in difficult conditions, taking risks, questioning the accepted practice of the day. Experiential learning, outdoor education, work experience, education for citizenship, school councils, and so on, are all such well established parts of school life that we take them for granted, but they had to be fought for. Mabel was well acquainted with the work of those who did so, and of course, deserves to number among them.

The 1920s and 30s saw a ferment of new ideas and experiments in education, many of which originated in Europe and further afield. Some of these movements were influenced by the educational philosophy of Jean Jacques Rousseau, who first popularised ideas on child-centred education, acknowledging the need for individualised learning, the idea that children go through developmental stages, and the importance of the environment on a child's education. His belief that the individual was corrupted by society's institutions struck a chord with Mabel, especially after the horrors of war.

In the States, John Dewey, who had once been a student of Stanley Hall, was an eminent educational reformer. At the Laboratory School that he ran with his wife, Alice, at the University of Chicago, he emphasised the importance of learning by doing. Mabel was certainly aware of Dewey's early work, and agreed with many of his ideas on interaction with the environment, his belief in children taking a democratic part in decision-making, and his thoughts on vocational learning. She was also familiar with Helen Parkhurst's 'Dalton Plan', published in 1922. This idea had three objectives: to tailor each student's programme to his or her needs, interests and abilities, to promote independence and dependability, and to enhance the student's social skills and sense of responsibility towards others. Students were presented with opportunities to make educational choices about their learning from an early age and, in the process, how to identify their interests and take responsibility for pursuing them.

Another contemporary educator, who profoundly influenced Mabel and many others, was Jean-Ovide Decroly, a Belgian biologist who founded a

Laboratory School in Brussels. Originally, he had been asked to became the head physician of a small 'clinic' for the care of abnormal children, and agreed to do so only on the condition that he could take these children into his family's home. His Institute of Special Education opened in 1901 and later moved to a small country property on the outskirts of Brussels, the 'Vossegat' or 'Fox-hole'. In 1907 he also opened a school for 'normal children' which became a renowned school called the 'Ermitage'. In 1927, this transferred to a rural, wooded neighbourhood on the outskirts of Brussels. The same methods were employed at both schools, questioning all aspects of the current educational system.

Like Mabel, Decroly denounced the position of the classical 'humanities', and stressed the notion of synergy between individuals and their surroundings, and the importance of activity for growth. He felt that the children needed to develop ease in all forms of expression, in their bodies and senses as well as manual skills, having plenty of contact with things other than books. He warned against the danger of compulsory education that paid little heed to technical and vocational training, or to social and artistic education. He talked of the traditional teacher as being the 'unconscious executioner of the child's intelligence', saying that the current education system destroyed the future of many of those entrusted to it and accusing schools of imposing silence and immobility on people who must learn to act and express themselves. Decroly believed that the first objective of the school was to ensure that every individual had opportunities for success in the life that awaited them.

Little by little, he saw the classroom as a last resort, while the natural environment represented the real material capable of awakening and stimulating the forces hidden within the child. He wanted to do away with the 'fenced-in monastic universe' and throw the doors of the school wide open. He freed his schools from subject matter, timetables, deadlines and textbooks, believing that it was necessary for children to actively participate in their own education, so that they could play an important part in determining their own curricula. Decroly spent all his life dedicated to education, and became a leading figure in the field. His methodology was widely accepted, and was a driving force in many educational innovations in Belgium and elsewhere. He also played a part in teacher training, and published many books and articles, urging the need for teachers, doctors, psychologists, and social workers to work together.

Another example of educational experimentation was A.S. Neill, who for some years ran the Journal of Progressive Education, *The New Era*, together with the theosophist Beatrice Ensor. After spending some time in Austria and Germany, Neill founded Summerhill School in 1924. At this boarding school, lessons were optional, the children being allowed do whatever they wanted, as long as they did not interfere with the freedom of others. Children and adults had equal decision making power. Neill felt that traditional schooling repressed children and that it was important to respect and follow the interests of the individual. His way of thinking became better known and more popular in the 1960s, but Mabel was certainly aware of his work, although did not agree with him on every point. She believed that in the real world, human beings were never free to do what they liked because of the basic needs for food, clothing and shelter, and that children needed to become aware of these realities as soon as possible. She would never have allowed children to opt out of opportunities for learning. What she did like was Neill's notion that 'The absence of fear is the finest thing that can happen to a child.'

Another influential thinker, who applied many of his ideas to education, was Bertrand Russell. With his wife, Dora, he started a model school at Beacon Hill in the 1920s, in an attempt to eradicate possessiveness and warlike psychology. However, his experiment only lasted a few years and broke down as his marriage to Dora also fell apart. Again, Russell gained popularity in the 1960s, particularly for his approaches to nuclear disarmament and to sexual liberation.

The Austrian philosopher, Rudolf Steiner, also had a widespread influence on teaching. In 1919, Steiner gave a series of lectures on education to the workers at the Waldorf-Astoria cigarette factory in Stuttgart, who then asked him to set up a school for their children, which became known as the 'Free Waldorf School'. His approach was very child-centred, its basis being a recognition of the physical, emotional, intellectual and spiritual needs of the developing human being. The aim was to educate the children not just in the '3Rs' but also in the '3Hs' – 'Hand, Heart and Head' – an idea that Mabel took up, although she did not mention him in her thesis. Steiner's philosophy, which he named Anthroposophy, provided the guiding principle for this work. Between the two World Wars, staff at Kings Langley Priory developed an interest in the principles of Rudolf Steiner, and nowadays it operates as a Steiner school.

At this time, Jean Piaget in Switzerland was developing his theories about how children develop and learn, which were as yet unpublished. Piaget's scheme described how children go through different stages of development, starting with the sensori-motor stage, through to the point when their conceptual development is mature enough for higher order thinking skills, such as hypothesising; to move through these stages they needed plenty of practical experience in their environment. His theories therefore had major implications for educational practice. Although Mabel did not cite Piaget's ideas, she clearly gave much thought to concept development and how it should be applied to teaching. She related the following story in her thesis:

'Recently, a child of three, regarding some clothing which he had no wish to put on, because the wool was rough and irritating, asked if it could be given to his little brother of eighteen months instead.

"But if someone has to suffer," I said, "Should it be the big boy, or the little one?"

"But," he responded, "*Baby does not have to be afraid of things making him feel bad.*"

This was an example of abstract thought, and of such good psychology that it surprised me.'

Mabel read widely on the subject of educational thought, and carefully selected aspects she wished to integrate into her own practice. She stayed faithful to the same tenet throughout her teaching career: 'All education can be seen as the expression of personal experience, in a broader and broader radius throughout life.'

Youth Movements of the 1920s and '30s.

Closely connected to social and educational change between the wars was the development of youth movements, some of which have survived to this day in various forms. In Britain, the Scouting Movement continued to grow, at first supported by a young man called John Hargrave. Hargrave was born into a Quaker family in 1894 and grew up in the Lake District, where he had a minimal amount of formal schooling and by the age of twelve, was already providing professional illustrations for books, including those of John Buchan. In 1908, at the age of fourteen, he joined the Boy Scouts, and began to study the writings of Ernest Thompson Seton, the American naturalist, who first drew attention to Red Indian culture and philosophy and its relevance to modern society. The young Hargrave soon formed his own Boy Scout troop, which may have been the inspiration for a troop featured in Buchan's novel *The Hunting Tower.* After moving south, Hargrave progressed through the hierarchy of the Scout Movement, and wrote a regular column on Woodcraft for the Scout magazine *The Trail.* At seventeen, he was chief cartoonist for the London Evening News, and at nineteen, his first book, *Lonecraft* (1912), was published to some acclaim; the sons of George V even visited him at his campsite to find out more about outdoor craft. As a Quaker, Hargrave enlisted in the Royal Army Medical Corps when the First World War broke out, serving as Sergeant of the stretcher-bearers in the Dardanelles, but was invalided out in 1916 due to malaria.

After the war, Hargrave was appointed as Boy Scout Commissioner for Woodcraft and Camping by Baden-Powell. However, as a pacifist who dreamed of a new world order, he began to find the Scout Movement too militaristic. In 1920, he wrote a book called *The Great War Brings it Home,* and founded his own organisation, called Kibbo Kift – Kentish for 'a proof of great strength'. Expelled from the Scouts, and with a following of other anti-war scoutmasters, he set about building an alternative and very different movement. The new Kibbo Kift involved old and young, male and female. It aimed to promote outdoor education, physical training, the learning of handicrafts, the reintroduction of ritual into modern life, world peace, and the regeneration of urban dwellers through open air life. Also important was the preservation of all wild species of animals. Hargrave hoped to do nothing less than create a new world civilisation. He was an admirer of Patrick Geddes, and at some point met Mabel. The two did some collaborative work together, writing leaflets about education. Clearly, their ideas closely overlapped, and one wonders to what extent the two colleagues influenced each other.

Mabel listed the essential aims of the Kibbo Kift movement in her thesis:

1. To camp and live in the open air as much as possible, and to strive for perfection in the human body.

2. To be ready to give practical assistance to everyone; to learn, therefore, the skills of practical work as much as possible.

3. To work for peace in the world, and the fraternity of humanity.

Members of Kibbo Kift were called Kinsmen, (and, one also presumes, Kinswomen). A great deal of time and commitment was expected of its members, who were organised into Clans and Tribes, and were given Red-Indian style woodcraft names. Members had to make their own costumes, which included cloaks, hoods and jerkins. Camping was elevated to an almost spiritual level, full of rituals marked by language reminiscent of the Norse Sagas and Saxon archaisms. Kinsmen had to make their own lightweight, one-person tents and to decorate them with symbolic designs. They also had to design, carve and paint their own totem poles.

Hargrave was charismatic, with a somewhat poetical bent, but he was also autocratic, and had many critics. D.H. Lawrence criticised him as being impractical, ambitious and full of hate, even though he respected what he was fighting for. In 1924, there was a split from within the ranks by members who had strong socialist views, leading to the formation of the Woodcraft Folk, which eventually outlived its parent movement.

Hargrave's following at various times included such high profile names as Professor Julian Huxley, Havelock Ellis, Maurice Maeterlink, the Bengali poet Tagore, H.G. Wells, and Emmeline Pethick-Lawrence, the suffragette leader and revival Morris Dance leader. In the '20s, Hargrave's woodcraft books were popular in translation among the large German youth movement, with contingents of young people visiting each other at youth gatherings. Later Hargrave also wrote novels, all critical of the society in which he lived. These achieved considerable success, and Patrick Geddes reviewed them favourably.

One rather bizarre incident occurred when Hargrave was summoned to Denmark to the castle of Baron van Pallandt, a member of the K.K. Advisory Committee. The other guest was the young Indian mystic, Krishnamurti. As the Baron had no heir, he had decided to leave his fortune to one of these young men, both of whom he regarded as potential world saviours. The Baron finally decided on Krishnamurti as his heir. From the mid-1920s onwards, Hargrave's ideas focussed on economic solutions, and he became convinced that 'Social Credit', where everyone would receive an unearned income as their birthright, was the solution. Here there were links with the Sociological Society, in which Patrick Geddes and Victor Branford were the leading lights; Branford's wife Sybella, and an accountant colleague, John Ross, both lectured extensively on Social Credit. In 1933, the movement mutated again to become the Green Shirts, or Social Credit Party of England and Hargrave increasingly turned his attention to the urban working-class unemployed. Although members marched in the streets and wore uniforms, it remained an anti-fascist, anti-communist and anti-imperialist organisation.

Hargrave wrote his most highly acclaimed novel, *Summer Time Ends*, in 1935, which was positively reviewed by Ezra Pound and John Steinbeck, but sold few copies. With the onset of war, and the banning of uniforms, Hargrave found a new vocation in the field of psychic healing and continued with a variety of other projects, including writing and cartoons. In 1976, he won a court battle proving that the moving map display in the new Concorde plane had been his idea, but failed to win any monetary reward for it. Finally, when a rock musical was created about the Kibbo Kift movement, Hargrave, then in his 80s, managed to attend performances and inspire those he met. He died in 1982; one wonders what Mabel made of the trajectory of his life while she was alive!

Another early movement was The Order of Woodcraft Chivalry, founded in 1916 by Ernest and Aubrey Westlake, a father and son team of Quakers. They had also been inspired by the work of Ernest Thompson Seton, and offered a recapitulatory curriculum 'providing appropriate conditions and suitable environments for the impulses and characteristics of the child as they appear and develop in regular sequence, corresponding, as is believed, more or less closely to the "culture epochs" of the human race.' This movement later established Forest Schools. For some reason Mabel did not support the movement, and despite what would seem an overlap in philosophy and aims, it was not mentioned in her thesis. A letter from Aubrey Westlake to Patrick Geddes, written in December 1927, commented: 'I do wish Dr Mabel Barker looked upon us i.e. the O.W.C. with more favour as we should have been delighted to have cooperated in the practical subject of her thesis.' Perhaps the ideas of the I.O.C. were too strong for Mabel; some of their philosophies on social behaviour and groupings were rather unconventional, and their ideas of 'learning by doing' even extended towards sexual activity for young people.

The person who had the most enduring impact on the growth of outdoor education, however, was Kurt Hahn. Hahn was born in Berlin in 1886 and founded the Salem Schools in 1920, in a section of the castle belonging to Prince Max von Baden, Germany's last imperial chancellor, who had to negotiate terms with the victors at the end of World War I. His first pupil was the Prince's son, but Hahn did not want the school to be elitist and introduced a graduated fee system. His approach emphasized self-discipline, character building and working together for a common cause, such as giving service to the surrounding communities. He, in turn, had been influenced by meeting a group of Abbotsholme pupils in 1903, while on a walking holiday in the Alps, and became very interested in the ideas of Cecil Reddie, its headmaster. At Salem climbing, hillwalking, canoeing and sailing were all on the curriculum.

Climber and educationist Geoffrey Winthrop Young first met Hahn in 1919, and later sent his son, Jocelin, to the school. Geoffrey and his wife, Len, who was a founding member of the Pinnacle Club, both spent a few months teaching there in the summer of 1932. Hahn was a vociferous opponent of the Nazis, never afraid to speak out against authority, and was arrested in 1933 after denouncing the murder of a young communist. High level negotiations took place, and with help from his British friends, he was finally released. Being Jewish, Hahn was very lucky to escape when he did. Geoffrey Winthrop Young did all he could to help him settle in Britain, and Gordonstoun was founded in April 1934, with Prince Philip being one of the first pupils there, having transferred from Salem. The school naturally attracted a lot of interest. Hahn introduced the Moray Badge, which would later became the Duke of Edinburgh's Award Scheme, with John Hunt (leader of the Everest expedition) as its first director. During wartime, the school moved to Aberdovey, and here the Outward Bound Movement was first formed. Challenging courses of 26 days were given to boys from industry, where the boys were 'impelled to experience' in sea training and coastguardship. The skills learnt by the young men were seen as very useful in time of war, gaining wide acceptance and a prestige that has survived to this day.

Another visionary whose work was flagged up in Mabel's 1926 thesis was Kingsley Fairbridge, who was born in South Africa in 1885. In 1903, at the age of 17, he visited his grandmother in England and was deeply moved by seeing children living in poverty in the slums of the big cities. While on a scholarship to Oxford in 1909, he established the 'Child Emigration Society,' later to become known as the Fairbridge Society, in underpopulated Rhodesia. He said 'I saw great Colleges of Agriculture (not workhouses) springing up in every man-hungry corner of the Empire. I saw children shedding the bondage of bitter circumstances and stretching their legs and minds amid the thousand interests of the farm.' He aimed to provide the children with a sense of self-worth, and the training and skills necessary for their future. In 1912, he received an offer of land in Western Australia, and he and his wife Ruby established the Fairbridge Farm School at Pinjarra, 50 miles south of Perth, where they received the first party of orphan children from Britain, aged between 7 and 13. Finding funds was made even more difficult due to the war, but afterwards he was sponsored by the Prince of Wales and his brother princes, and the Farm School began to flourish and expand. Kingsley Fairbridge died in 1924, at the age of 39. Three years after his death, there were over 200 children at the school, and this number continued to grow. Mabel admired his work, and wrote of it in her thesis. Such experiments are seen differently now, of course, and by the 1950s the scheme began to founder, ending in 1973. However, Fairbridge's mission is still going strong to this day. The Fairbridge Drake Fellowship continues to help disadvantaged young people from inner city areas using a range of programmes, designed to provide them with social experiences and vocational training.

During the 1920s and 30s, youth movements were also growing throughout Europe. In Britain, the Youth Hostels Association was established in 1930, and meant that ordinary people could get out to the countryside and afford to stay there. This was modelled on an idea popular in Germany. There, the *Wandervogel* movement continued to flourish, despite the loss of a generation in World War One. However, many members were critical of the Versailles Peace Treaty and the Weimar Court, and the movement split into factions. The number of youth groups exploded, becoming the focus of political parties, both left and right wing. Unfortunately, it was the popularity of such youth groups, with their love of the outdoors and nature, which paved the way for Hitler Youth. This group was formed in 1926, adopting the *Wandervogel* pattern of youth leading youth. After 1933, the Nazi party abolished or absorbed all other youth groups and their facilities were seized. Some individual groups remained in contact with their members, and eventually became nuclei for youthful opposition to the Third Reich. Many children, however, were bullied into joining Hitler Youth, and by 1939, attendance was compulsory. Mabel had close links with Germany, often having German students staying with her at Friar Row. She would have discussed these events with them, and must have felt a deep sense of unease at the sinister trends developing in their country.

On the Fells in the Dark

Mabel continued to climb as enthusiastically as ever throughout the 1930s. Her love for the Highlands and Islands never waned, and when possible she tried to organise camps there. In 1931, she was back in Skye, having as good a time as ever with her friends Nancy Ridyard and the Musgrave brothers. She traversed the ridge again, and was visited by her old friends, the Mears family. In 1931 she went to Eriskay, with two friends Nancy Greenhaulgh and Helen Burton. There she tried to learn Gaelic and made friends with many of the islanders, who wrote to her afterwards. She went to Skye again in 1934, and in 1936 went back to Glen Brittle and on to Ullapool, taking the opportunity to climb many of the mountains of the north, including Ben More Assynt, An Teallach, and Suilven. She also met up with her old colleague, George Morris. In 1939, she visited Arran, where she studied the archaeology and climbed some of the hills.

There were also climbing adventures closer to home, and regular summer camps at Langdale and Borrowdale, as well as occasional visits to Wales to sample the climbing there. In 1933, she joined the Pinnacle Club, and attended the Easter meet at Wasdale. On September 9th to 11th that year, a number of Pinnacle Club members joined her for a meet at Friar Row, including Blanche Eden-Smith, Alison Adam, Molly Fitzgibbon, Marjorie Wood and Lilian Bray, where they remembered having a hilarious time. Mabel later became an honorary member of the club. As well as her exploration of Carrock Fell, and her participation in archeological excavations there, she was also in the first ascent party on Hell Gate Pillar on Gable in June 1934, with Balcombe and Cooper, and did the first ascent of Alpha Variation on Gable with Arthur Wood-Johnson in 1935. In 1937, she took part in exploration on Gill Crag with Nancy Ridyard, Charlie Wilson and Ward. In February of that year, she put up Left Ridge with Wilson. The whole team put up Main Slab Route (to the Perch) and Flake Buttress on June 20th 1937. She also put up Corner and Wall with Ward on the same day. In July, she and Nancy Ridyard were with Jim Birkett when he put up The Tarsus on Dove Crag.

It was Nancy Carpenter (née Ridyard) who was to write Mabel's obituary in the Pinnacle Club Journal many years later. Nancy talked of having learned much of her climbing from Mabel. She wrote: 'For some years we camped and climbed together in Wales, the Lake District and Skye, having unforgettable days on the new rock-face climbs and in the classic cracks and chimneys. Even when in old boots with nails missing Mabel was faultless and had delicate and perfect balance. It was delightful to rest on a sunlit summit whilst she talked of the structure and history of the different rocks we were climbing or of matters of archeological interest in the locality. Her many friends included the Mallory family and, as all climbers know, Mallory and Irvine were lost on Everest, a later party finding Mallory's ice-axe not far from the summit. This ice-axe came into Mabel's possession and she later gave it to me. Needless to say it is my most highly-prized treasure.' This axe is now housed in the National Mountaineering Museum at Rheged.

Jack Carswell remembers his first meeting with Mabel Barker in 1934, when he was 19 years old and she was coming up to her 48th birthday. Now past 90, he lives at Grune Point, Skinburness, not far from where Mabel grew up. He looks back over a life that has spanned over seventy years of climbing, including the Alps, Himalaya, Kenya, Peru, Morocco and Jordan, having made his last trip to the Alps just before his eightieth birthday. Growing up in Workington, on the Cumbria coast, he says, 'I never wanted to do anything but climb.' He first walked to Loweswater when he was ten years old. 'You had to do it to get accepted into the gang,' he points out. At twelve, he got his first tent and as soon as he got a bicycle, would go to Wasdale over Styhead, and take the bike with him. 'Sometimes we had only one bike between us,' he remembers. 'We would take the train to Keswick, and then took it in turns to ride the bike and leave it by the roadside for the next person. You could leave anything in those days, and no-one would touch it. I didn't get a car until after the war.' After long days on the fells, his Grandpa would wait up for him, smoking a pipe, checking that he got back safely.

Jack was first introduced to climbing by Ieuan Mendus, a solicitor who took digs with his aunt. 'In those days, you could be maligned for stepping out of class if you went climbing. Climbers were a race apart. They were seen to endanger the lives of policemen and keep farmers away from their work,' he says. The situation was not helped by a reporter called Inkpen, of *The West Cumberland Times*, who was opposed to climbing and influenced public opinion in a very negative way. He wrote articles with headlines such as 'Mountain Madness'. 'But once you were in the group, everyone just mixed in. It didn't matter whether you were a professional person or not. Everyone was equal. There was no sexism in those days. They were just climbers.' Jack was an engineering apprentice, earning a few shillings a week, with one week's unpaid holiday. There was certainly not enough money to cover drinking as well. 'Rubbers cost sixpence each in Woolies then,' he remembers.

On the day he met Mabel, he was camping at Wasdale with Sid Wilson, a fruiterer from Maryport. One fine summer's evening they were exploring the Pinnacle face of Scafell, when they heard voices singing not far away. 'That was one of my biggest pleasures in those days – climbing there in the evening with the sun on it,' he says. He traversed along to Moss Ghyll, where he found a group of German students and Mabel Barker sitting on a large ledge, singing German songs. 'She looked like a gypsy, very dark-skinned. She wanted me to go and climb on Esk Buttress straight away, even though it was late in the day! In the end, we persuaded her to settle for Moss Ghyll Grooves.' He remembers that Mabel was always in the forefront of what was going on, and knew lots of people. She was completely at home with the younger generation, always good company, and never patronising or condescending. A few months after they met, Jack remembers attending the FRCC New Year meet at Buttermere. They went to The Fish Inn to find accommodation, and were asked if they wanted double or single rooms. Mabel, it seemed, was impervious to the connotations of such a request, and did not bat an eyelid. Her home at Friar Row became the headquarters for a group of climbers who would later form the Carlisle Mountaineering Club, including Charlie Wilson and Nan Hamilton. If the weather was bad, they would spend the time doing play readings instead. He remembers that in the 1930s, Mabel had a motorised scooter, and her dog, Roc, would run behind it. Roc, a black labrador, would stay with her rucksack all day. However, on one occasion, Roc was not where he was supposed to be, and it turned out that he had eaten the whole of the Hargreaves family's provisions at the new

FRCC Hut at Brackenclose. After this, a rule was made that no dogs were allowed in the huts! In fact, Mabel had to bale Roc out on more than one occasion, for eating forbidden meat supplies.

Jack also remembers the 1936 Easter weekend at Wasdale, held to celebrate the fiftieth anniversary of the ascent of Napes Needle. Seventy-six year old Haskett Smith was to repeat his historic climb, with the help of Chorley and Speaker, and 300 people gathered to witness the occasion. Jack had arranged to meet Mabel at the Napes, but on the way joined three lads who were climbing on Tophet Bastion. The leader had a fall and broke his femur, and Jack became involved in the rescue operation, missing Haskett Smith's ascent. Sadly, the lad later died. Mabel, however, did witness the ascent and took many photos. She no doubt took part in the light-hearted banter when the old gentleman reached the top. 'Tell us a story,' shouted one of the spectators. 'There is no other story,' Haskett Smith shouted down, obviously none the worse for his efforts. 'This is the top storey!'

Jack asserts that with Mabel, everything turned into an epic. She was completely safe, and no-one ever got hurt, but nonetheless she had a penchant for climbing in all weathers, and thought nothing of being benighted. Mabel was the first to admit this in her article in the Pinnacle Club Journal of 1935, entitled *On the Fells in the Dark*.

> One evening last summer, a friend who was waiting for me at a farm at the head of one of our Lakeland dales remarked to the farmer's wife that I had refused to give any definite time at which she might expect me, to which the experienced old lady replied slowly, '*She* never comes down very early.'
>
> Well, that time I did, rather to their surprise, this occasion being evidently the exception proving the rule.
>
> I have a reputation among climbers for getting benighted: not on the rocks, of course, which would be the dangerous result of bad judgement, but on the way down from them.
>
> In winter this is almost inevitable, and a perfectly common habit of climbers. The light is so short and precious, and we are as safe, at any hour, on a mountain track as on a road – indeed, in these days, much more so!

But to me it happens in summer too, as many can testify who have unwarily trusted themselves to my guidance, or innocently taken me into their company.

Well, let me say at once that I *like* the fells in the dark. There is then an added magic and mystery about them, and a feeling which it is hard to explain. Perhaps it is a sense of power in oneself, and of communion with the hills. One belongs to them, like any other animal: one knows discomfort and hunger and weariness, but never *fear* of the hills in the dark even when alone, and in a storm, or in torrents of rain.

I have no stories of terrifying or dangerous experiences to tell, for nothing of that kind has ever happened to me in all the years, and they are many now, in which I have walked the fells by day or night.

And while nowadays I generally carry a flash-light, I do not use it except in an emergency. It is apt to confuse one's sense of direction, and one cannot see so well afterwards if it fails. Once I crossed from Grains Ghyll to Langdale in a thunder-storm. It was magnificent, but I had a companion who used a flash-light, and we missed the track in the wet patches on Esk Hause. After some vague scrambling the lightning showed us Angle Tarn a little beneath us, and all was well. Placidly we sat eating chocolate at the top of Rossett Ghyll at midnight before descending to Middle Fell.

Years ago, before the Scafell Pike track was cairned and marked as it is now, or there were any flash-lights, I set out from Seathwaite with another girl, to go to its summit for the first time, and descended in mist and darkness; and how this first experience of the fells in the dark gave me a feeling of entering into my kingdom: of being given the freedom of the hills by day or night, I have told elsewhere.

I recall a night return of a party from Pillar. The party included a young schoolmaster, a football enthusiast, who was at the outset rather scornful of the slowness of our pace. But once at Pillar, while some climbed, *he* went to sleep! And on the return in the evening I sent the rest of the party (which included children) ahead, and formed a rearguard to bring him in slowly (I think, to be fair, that a damaged knee had something to do with this). It was dark long before we were half-way home. Slowly we went round the head of Ennerdale along Moses Trod, down into Gillercombe, and down Sour Milk

Ghyll. When, at the foot of it, we suddenly walked into camp, he confessed to the utmost astonishment, for he had not had the slightest idea where he was, and what was more, had not believed that *I* had either, and thought my confident progress the merest bluff!

Quite recently, five of us started up a big climb on Scafell late on an August afternoon. We were far too late, but all on holiday, full of the joy and return-when-you-please freedom of campers. We finished our climb just in time. Ten o'clock found us back on Mickledore, laughing and joking , congratulating our leader and everyone else – (particularly the last man, who was short-sighted, had carried a camera, and had come last across a delicate traverse in the dusk). Not only was it getting dark but mist had come down, and while we were changing from rubbers to boots and devouring the scraps left in our rucksacks, it began to rain. The boys were camping in Wasdale in two parties, one of them with his mother: my party was in Borrowdale. I wanted to go alone over the Pike, but they wouldn't hear of it. 'Very well then: the Corridor Route, and all together to the Sty Head Pass.'

But once on the Mickledore screes it was impossible to find the start of the Corridor Route. 'Never mind, then – all down to Wasdale.'

None of us will forget that journey. Stumbling along over boulders, down steep grass slopes, crossing streams and wondering which they were, losing and finding each other, calling, disputing as to where we were, elated with our triumph, increasingly tired and wet, we made our way down slowly; to come at last out of the mist and see far below us a tiny light moving in the valley. Said A.H.*(Alan Horne)*:

'That's mother going to see if I am at the other camp. Wait a minute.'

He sent a ringing shout into the void: 'Mo-ther'!

We listened tensely, and from far away came a faint answer: 'A-lan'!

A chorus burst out: 'She heard,' 'She answered,' 'Did you hear?' 'She'll know we're all right.'

'Yes – wait a minute. I want to speak to her.'

Then, very slowly and deliberately: 'Go back to camp. We are all O.K.'

And so, with our one concern, the thought of that waiting mother, set at rest, we continued on our weary but happy way: coming up against a wall, finding a stile we all know, and so striking a path at last. We reached camp in Wasdale about 1 a.m.; and after I had been fed and partially dried, A.H. motored me round to Seathwaite – fifty miles to make a point five miles away over the pass! The light came as we sped up Borrowdale.

We might have walked over, but I was very weary. I suppose it may be taken as a compliment that my own party had all gone to bed without the slightest anxiety!

I have never unintentionally spent a night out on the Lakeland Fells, and once only in Scotland. That was when I first felt the Black Cuillins of Skye. I cannot say *saw* them, because they were hidden in mist. Ardently desiring to see Coruisk, we, a party of two, had gone round to it by the coast, and were trapped crossing the Main Ridge by a track which is marked on the half-inch map, but in fact does not exist. We worked our way up as far as possible in the fading light, and then decided that the only thing to do in this strange and relatively dangerous ground was to wait through the short hours of darkness. We spent the night, and actually slept a little, on a narrow rock ledge, wet to the skin, and suffering most from the fact that we had eaten our lunch many hours ago. A determined search through the wet debris in the rucksack when daylight came was rewarded by about two squashed raisins.

Fortified by these, we continued over the ridge. I have passed the place where we crossed it many times since, and always feel that we had the proverbial luck of lunatics in that adventure: for of the Black Cuillins it cannot be said as of Lakeland that progress in dark and mist is safe if you go slowly and with caution.

We left our inhospitable ledge about 5 a.m. and after an exciting descent over the glaciated slabs of Coire na Creiche arrived at the farm, where we had *not* occupied our booked beds, about 10 a.m.

Coire Banachdich, in the dark, seems to have some special attraction for me. Several times I have come down it, not by the scheduled route under the slopes of Sgurr Dearg, but right down its central boiler-plates, which is good fun and provides a lot of moderate climbing. I have done this with parties that were game enough, but so slow that light failed before we were out of the Coire. I remember two girls who, as a matter of course and with touching trustfulness, simply came on the rope whenever it seemed convenient. In thickening dusk I slung them both down a chimney somewhere near the bottom: I couldn't find it again in daylight.

And once I came down with a young Swiss girl, she enjoying the whole adventure immensely, and quite unperturbed all through; but towards the end slowing up through sheer weariness. When we were well down on the grass she suddenly said:-

'It's a lovely night. Can't I just sleep here till morning?'

I said no, because it would become very cold in the early hours: and anyway, we were packing up for home in the morning and wouldn't have time then to retrieve lost property left lying about on the hills. But we were only about two miles from camp, so I suggested that she took a rest while I went back to camp for a flash-light.

'But how will you find me if I go to sleep?' was the only objection.

'Well, I'll shout and show the light and you'll have to wake up,' said I, and set off without more ado.

It was quite dark before I reached camp, where Nancy Ridyard was preparing a delicious supper.'

'I've left Rita parked in Coire Banachdich and I'm going back for her.'

'Have supper first; she'll be all right,' said Nancy: and such indeed was my intention.

We took our time over it and were joined by Van, who had been into Portree about repairs to the car (which is another story). We took all the best batteries remaining in the camp at the end of the holiday: put some supper for Rita in a can: left Van to his well-earned meal, and Nancy came with me.

Finding the way back over those two miles, now in total darkness, was a more difficult business than I had anticipated. We saved the lights for later use. Whatever the nature of the going I had a constant illusion of rising ground just ahead, and I remember Nancy's boots were not comfortable. And when we were actually on the first terrace of the great Coire the finding of our objective seemed indeed a forlorn hope, though I had tried, before leaving, to note her position in relation to the sky line on either shoulder.

> We called – our voices seemed lost in the void: we flashed our lights – they were pin-points in a great darkness.
>
> But we got an answer at last, for really we had almost hit the mark.
>
> Rita had been soundly and placidly slumbering till our calling aroused her. She had seen deer on the sky-line: watched the marvel of the stars: slept, and altogether enjoyed her rest. We gave her a little time for supper, and then, using the flash-lights (for now we could not miss our direction) made good time back to camp.
>
> 'The night is but the shadow of the earth,
> Which spins in glory – '

Jack had been with the party on the occasion when they came down to Wasdale in the dark. He remembers that Austin Barton was still on the Flake when it started to rain and night descended. Jack then had to do the last of the climb in one long run-out to get them off. Later, Mabel was to write Alan Horne's obituary when he died in 1960 at the age of 50. She mentioned this event once again.

> It must have been in the early 1930s that, when I was camping with a party of children and students, we came in contact with Alan and his mother, also camping; and so began a happy rock-partnership and a friendship lasting for the rest of his life. His mother was also a wonderful person, not a climber, but a great camp 'second' to Alan, backing him up in everything and never betraying the least anxiety ... In August 1935 he was camping with his mother in Wasdale, and I with the usual collection of children and students in Borrowdale. He came over to us on 8th August with two friends from another camp, suggesting an ascent of the Central Buttress. I gladly agreed, and we set off. But we amused ourselves on the way by doing some 'first ascents' on a crag to the left of Corridor Route (a crag to which I cannot give a name, nor say if our own light-hearted scramblings were indeed 'firsts')
>
> The result was that we arrived rather late at our main objective. Nevertheless we did it, Alan leading with his usual grace, patience, and care for the safety of all his colleagues; but by the time we were off the rocks it was 10p.m., dusk was falling and it was beginning to rain! I proposed to go the shortest way back to Seathwaite, but the boys would not hear of it. We decided to go all together

as far as the Corridor Route, or any path at all, so all went down to Wasdale, increasingly wet and tired, but full of triumph and joy not withstanding.

It was this 'stopping off on the way', always wanting to squeeze in that extra bit of climbing, that Jack Carswell became so well acquainted with. One such minor epic occurred when Jack was climbing with Mabel and Tom Stobart (who later climbed on Everest and Nanga Pargat) on Deer Bield Crack in the rain. Jack remembers that they couldn't get up the crack and had to use Mabel's rope to get down. Unfortunately, the rope also got stuck. It was the same one she had used with Claude Frankland. They had to buy her a new rope in haste, as she was due to leave for Skye a few days later.

However, Mabel was always very conscious of safety and felt a responsibility to all the novices on the crag. She could often be found organising parties other than her own, soloing up and down, and making sure that they were doing things properly. Jack remembers that, in those days, if you were on a hard climb and saw another climber, you always knew who they were. 'You just did not know what was possible and what was not,' he says. 'So there was a high sense of risk, of absolute adventure.' His friend, Austin Barton, made a film in the mid 1930s, taken around Gable and in other places. There is a very brief glimpse of Mabel, climbing in the snow. 'You didn't have the same protection from the elements in those days,' he remembers. 'We had no hats or gloves, even in the snow. And we never used crampons then.' Mabel did have a belay device, something which was unheard of in those days. It was a pulley with a short length of rope attached, engraved on one side with *Arthur Beale, London as sole agents*, and on the other with *Schermuly's neo-belay*. A patent for this (Pat.15998/15) had been filed in 1915, but the problem was that no-one could understand how to use it. Perhaps it had been given to Mabel by her German friends. At some point she passed the device on to Jack Carswell, and it was then given to the FRCC for the 75th Anniversary Exhibition in 1981.

Climbing Down

It was in 1936 that Jack and Mabel had one of their greatest adventures together; this was recounted in the FRCC Journal of 1937. It was entitled *From Both Ends of the Rope'* and was in two parts. The first part by Mabel was called *Climbing Down.*

'We don't climb down often enough.' This remark may be true in more than one sense, and certainly it applies to our treatment of most of the more severe routes in Lakeland. We go up them, and come down by some easier way, neglecting in consequence the technique of descending. This seems a pity, and means that one maxim of a great climber – never to make a move which cannot be reversed – is often neglected.

As a result of a discussion round this point the idea was born of descending the Central Buttress of Scafell. Jack Carswell suggested it – at first tentatively, for it sounded rather crazy; then hopefully as the details were thought out. The main difficulty, the Great Flake itself, could at a pinch be roped down. (I believe this has been done before?) Apart from that, the most severe pitches of the climb are generally admitted to be the traverses: and why should they not go just as well from right to left as from left to right? Nobody had ever tried them that way; they might even be easier.

Therefore I was not too much surprised when on an evening in June, Jack Carswell and Ieuan M. B. Mendus arrived at Friar Row proposing that we try it next Sunday.

We duly met at Seathwaite, but we did not descend C.B. We went up one pitch of Gillercombe Buttress, got soaked to the skin, went home, and spent the rest of the day drying ourselves and our clothes.

But the following Sunday, June 21st, was perfect. We wandered slowly up the Corridor Route: left our spare gear in Hollow Stones, and went up Broad Stand, feeling rather like conspirators. This feeling was heightened by meeting with friends on the top to whom we talked evasively. Having got rid of them, we hunted nervously for the top pitch of Central Buttress, and perhaps our excitement was responsible for the difficulty we had in locating it. But once found, we spent no time in contemplation, but got over the edge as quickly as possible.

Jack Carswell, the originator and leader of the enterprise, naturally came last: but one advantage of climbing down is the increased responsibility at the other end of the rope. The first down has certainly more of the job in hand than the third up: and being in that position I had all the fun of working out the route backwards. To begin with, I went down the first (14th) pitch rather too far left: met wet and rotten rock, and a foothold came off. 'Nice sort of start,' I thought: but could of course warn the others against repeating my error.

When Ieuan joined me at the belay in the Bayonet-shaped Crack there came what proved to be, for me at least, the most difficult part of the whole climb. The route (Pitch 13) lies down part of the Moss Ghyll Grooves to a small but good stance with no belay. This has to be left for the first traverse and no belay is available till the V-Ledge. It looked, and was, extremely thin and exposed, but went delightfully, the rope being eventually carried over a small bracket visible on the sky-line from the M.G.G. stance. But the footholds by which this is reached when ascending to it from the V-Ledge are well underneath, and cannot be seen from above. I looked at the thing almost too long, for I began to be afraid that it would take more nerve than I possessed to hang on the bracket by my arms alone, in faith that an invisible foothold would materialise. Moreover, I was then so far from the belay in the Bayonet Shaped Crack that Jack and Ieuan could not hear me. I could not even, for some time, get them to give me enough rope for the next move (which would have to be made soon if I was not to fall from sheer fright!) At last I managed to 'get over' a suggestion that Jack should come to the belay, and then hold Ieuan on the M.G.G. stance, whence my rope would be horizontal and well supported by the bracket (which is no use as a belay, but is slightly hooked, and a rope so held *might* stay in it if a climber came off here). This move was carried out, and I then slipped over onto the V-Ledge, finding as usual that 'the difficulties are purely mental.' Ieuan then followed easily, taking my word for it that there were footholds: and I suppose Jack made nothing of it, for I heard no comments from him.

The vertical crack from the V-ledge to the second traverse (11th pitch) looks horrid from above, but its bark is worse than its bite. The traverse also really does go more easily, I think, from right to left: perhaps because one is making for such an obvious and comforting belay. The third traverse (10th pitch) also went beautifully and was a pure joy. We were making good time, and everything in the garden was lovely. But when we all assembled round the Cannon we became aware of an obstacle to our triumphal progress. There was a party coming up!

We arranged ourselves in a prostrate row on Jeffcoat's Ledge, and spent the next hour and a half as pleasantly and patiently as might be. We could not see much of A.T.H. and his party, but could hear quite well, so the wait was not monotonous, and pleasantries were being exchanged long before Ruth appeared and traversed over our recumbent bodies to the belay beyond them. With subsequent members of the party of four (led by S.Cross), we traded chocolate for cigarettes, for both Ieuan and I left ours in Hollow Stones, expecting to rejoin them sooner or later – but had not thought it would be so *much* later; and our self-denying ordnance was dissipated in smoke.

When the last foot of the ascending ropes had passed over us we prepared for business.

So far Ieuan, as middle man on the traverses and carrying a spare rope, had had the least interesting time perhaps, but this was a co-operative affair, and now his turn came. Our order was changed: Ieuan went first along the Flake: Jack next, and I waited at the far end. Ieuan disappeared, belayed by Jack, and after much wangling with ropes announced with what breath was left to him that he had reached the chockstone, and had climbed all the way down. It took some time, and much discussion between the men for him to get the ropes round the chock and himself arranged to their complete satisfaction – (these details I leave to my partner to explain more lucidly than I can) – but when all was ready I passed Jack on the outside of the Flake, and with all the cold-bath thrill that one can get in such a moment, climbed down after Ieuan. We all three climbed this quite clean, without coming on the ropes at all: but when on Ieuan's shoulder, my right foot (I being quite unable to see where it was going) went on and on for a long time into space with no bottom to it. Eventually it found a foothold in what proved to be the poor lad's stomach! So it had to be got out again, with some agony to both, and carried round behind instead. At last, to his great relief, that feat was accomplished, and I went right down to the Oval. That descent is extremely thin, but naturally not so exhausting as an ascent, and one found oneself at the bulge (Pitch 4) with a sort of incredulous relief. The end of the spare rope was thrown down to me, its other end going through the loop on the chockstone and up to Jack. He then climbed down clean (leaving no loop behind on the Flake), over Mendus and down to the bulge, belayed by me. At the bulge he waited while Ieuan untied the loops, save one detached loop over the chock in which he stood and which finally carried the running belay by which Ieuan descended, passed Jack, and joined me on the Oval. Jack then flicked off this remaining loop, and came down to us, leaving no trace of rope behind.

The rest of the descent we were now in the mood to treat as a joke: but in fact it needed care. Our original order was resumed, and I found time at the bottom of pitch 3 to retrieve some garments lost by the other party. (While on the Oval we could see bits of them on the upper traverses – a foot, or the flick of a rope now and then – and realised how far these traverses overhang the Flake itself.)

Above the last pitch we all met once more. Jack said it went straight down. I said it didn't, and I wouldn't; and after a glance over he agreed cordially. Actually Pitch 1 comes up a good way to the right of the stance we arrived on. It was amusing that our only hesitations over route were with the top and bottom pitches!

Well, it was a great climb!

Jack Carswell wrote his part of the story, in the second part of the article, entitled *B.C.*

'While walking up that agreeable valley which lies behind Melbreak, where my companion was wont to fritter away valuable climbing hours in attempting to obtain photographs of some very refractory buzzards, our conversation turned, as it always does to climbing.

A joking allusion to C.B. as a descent deposited the germ of an idea which rapidly attained maturity as the problem was examined. After all, the major difficulties were concentrated in the Flake and the traverses, and why should a traverse be any more difficult from one end than the other? The Flake however, was not to be disposed of so easily, for the purist in me said that it must be climbed, while conscience with a strong backing of common sense, said I should have recourse to the obvious method and rope down, and the two waged a continuous war up to the very time when we were congregated on the tip of the Flake.

Soon the project developed into a conspiracy with all the secretiveness essential to a good conspiracy. The idea had met with an enthusiastic though not unjudicial support from Ieuan M B Mendus who was to be our second, and together we broke the news to Mabel M Barker. Her reply was never in doubt, and we gathered that all her various inchoate engagements were to remain inchoate until the deed was done. Thereafter, it was a standing engagement for every Sunday.

The first attempt was a literal 'wash-out.' We met at Seathwaite and had Ieaun and I been left to ourselves we would have had the wit not to leave the valley, but Mabel who never lets 'I dare not wait upon I would' silently shamed us into climbing the first pitch of Gillercombe Buttress. Whereupon we beat a judicious retreat facilitated by torrents of water after a classical wetting. The famed hospitality of Friar Row boasts many things but male attire is not among them, and later that day, draped in two blankets apiece, Ieuan insisted that either he had forgotten how to don a toga or the Romans were only precariously decent. True, we attained a certain dignity but it was a dignity that could be maintained only in repose.

The next week-end was glorious and after a delightful Saturday at Caldbeck and on Carrock Fell, Mabel Barker, Mendus and myself toiled up from Seathwaite under a broiling sun with a strong torrid east wind which occasioned some slight misgivings at first till we realised that owing to the tilt of the strata we should be fairly sheltered from any wind from the Mickledore end, as proved to be the case.

The problem of whether or not to bathe in Styhead Tarn, occupied as all discussions on hot days do, just sufficient time for us to get cooled down, a rather lengthy process. The corridor was just as long and dry as ever and it was in a very limp condition indeed that we eventually arrived in Hollow Stones.

We ate a very dry lunch, and after skillfully avoiding a direct question as to our intentions we found the top of the climb, a matter of no small difficulty, and one after the other dropped over the edge.

The downward view from the first few feet of the top pitch (which was unexpectedly awkward) must be unique in Lakeland, and with a wind that made conversation difficult I reflected to myself that we were asking too much, though we could at least have a good day's climbing. The third and second had no difficulty with Pitch 13, but on the next pitch which leads down to the V-Ledge and in its upper portions is common to Moss Ghyll Grooves, our difficulties commenced. Comfortably sheltered at the bottom of the top pitch I listened absently to the full-throated but fruitless efforts of Ieuan and Mabel, who were spaced out below me at intervals of 40 feet, to establish contact in the teeth of the strong wind; both were audible to me and I finally gathered that she wanted him to descend until he was level with her, the better to receive her instructions with regard to the rope. It transpired that Mabel was standing at the V-Ledge end of the traverse (Pitch 12), so while she held to the rock – there being no belay – I joined my second and changing belays with him, let him take up the desired position. He was then able to give her a running belay over the hook on the traverse, after which she descended to the V-Ledge.

This awkward operation reinforced the opinion I had formed at the commencement, and I received warnings as to the difficulty. Thus I was cheered to find the traverse one of the most delectable things I have done, and my second said that he was more than relieved when I appeared with a broad smile on my face. But I found the warnings as to the descent on to the V-Ledge fully justified. The advice to lower myself, suspended on my hands only, to an invisible foothold was scarcely comforting, but I found it sound.

Foregathered on the V-Ledge my friends told me that Sidney Cross, A.T. Hargreaves and others were ascending the climb. Various suggestions were made as to how to dispose of them, none of which would have met with their approval.

Mabel tripped merrily down the right-angled corner and across the traverse to the pinnacle with only the suggestion of a pause on the traverse itself. However, she advised me to have a doubled rope for the corner but the knowledge imparted by two ascents discounted this.

After slinging a 60 foot coil over, Ieuan followed in great style. The holds found are not quite as good as one would like – they rarely are – but we were soon on Jeffcoat's ledge, where we heard voices.

After much precarious craning of necks we discovered that the other party had already reached the Oval, so, not wishing for an audience while manoeuvring at the chockstone, we settled ourselves down for a lengthy wait, and made ourselves more thirsty than ever with chocolate and huge chunks of home-made marzipan (a well-known Friar Row delicacy).

Now commenced a diplomatic exchange which would not have disgraced a Foreign Secretary, the outcome of which, to the dismay of my companions, was the discovery that there were no cigarettes in the party. Thereupon the arrival of the others was more eagerly awaited than ever.

Many were the climbs done and the places visited during the ensuing hour, but immediately a smiling face graced the tip of the Flake an agonized duet rang out saying in effect 'A cigarette, a cigarette, my belay for a cigarette,' which in view of the fact that there were four in the other party might not have been a bad bargain.

The difficulty, or apparent impossibility of accommodating seven people on Jeffcoat's Ledge will be obvious to anyone who has been there, but we did it. The problem of the passage was solved without ceremony in the only possible way, i.e., by their walking over our prostrate bodies and the barbarians actually seemed to enjoy the process. After we had got our respective ropes well tangled they passed on and left us to it.

We changed our order, Ieuan going first, myself second and Mabel last, and leaving her on Jeffcoat's we two edged along the crest of the Flake. The arrangement between us was that Ieuan should climb down to the chockstone and report on whether it was climbable. He lowered himself over the ledge, his hand disappeared; a moment's silence and then a voice gently suggested that I might hold the rope a little tighter if it wouldn't inconvenience me. This, however, was not in accordance with my part of the plan and the rope remained slack, until a voice triumphantly and with not a little surprise announced that its owner had climbed it clean.

It was here that the 60 foot rope, hitherto Nobody's Darling, came into its own. First, while held by me, Ieuan hooked a short loop of line over the convenient spike below the chockstone and stood under in it under the very mistaken impression that it would relieve me of some of its weight. Next he started to tie on to the chockstone, but stoutly denied the existence of the thread. Dialectics ('testing of truth by discussion, logical disputation') even from a lawyer meant nothing to me. I had used the thread twice, and eventually it was found. It is said that mild-mannered, inoffensive people are known to swear on occasion; my second evidently thought this an occasion.

Ieuan, having untied the rope on which he descended, Mabel went down on two ropes, thus disposing of a temporary surplus length. When she was safely on the Oval one length of rope was thrown down to her and the other hauled up by Ieuan, who threaded it through a loop and returned it to Mabel so that she might belay me from below.

I had been perched on the Flake for so long that I was stiff and sore, so I took a short rest before commencing the descent. This I found less trying than the ascent, because by getting the right shoulder in the Crack one can use sundry small holds on the inside, sufficient to control a descent but not of much help when overcoming the excessive friction of an ascent. Once past the chockstone my rope naturally became a doubled one, and I doubt whether it would be wise to attempt to descend this wall without such a safeguard. I stopped at the bottom chockstone and once more the second pulled up an end of my rope after Mabel had untied, undid my running thread and rethreaded the rope, this time through the loop in which he was standing, and cast off the loops from the chockstone and descended on the now doubled rope. I was then able to flick off the loop on the spike and join the others on the Oval, leaving no trace of our passage.

We coiled the 60 foot rope and unceremoniously threw it down to the screes, following later in a much more leisurely fashion. After the mixture of styles above we did not find any trouble with the remaining pitches. The climb, however, maintained its interest until the end, since the bottom pitch is always a pretty problem, and as Ieuan and I stepped off the last foothold we were greeted by Mabel in appropriately feminine manner.

On looking back we agreed that in the previous 5½ hours we had savoured the essence of climbing to the full, and that C.B. had no rival. As to difficulty we formed the opinion that for those who know the climb there is not much to choose between an ascent or a descent providing the party has some experience in descents. The Flake itself is both easier and safer.

Ieuan and I were proud to have had the company of Mabel Barker. We had read her account of her ascent with Frankland in 1925 many times before we had the pleasure of meeting her. She was the first woman up the climb and it was only appropriate that she should also be the first down it.

As we sat in Mrs Edmondson's at midnight that night quaffing tea, Mabel said to us, 'Only one thing remains for you boys.'

'Yes?' we replied.

'To repeat the climb when you are in your 51st year.'

Truly a chastening thought.'

Colin Wells, in his book *Who's Who in British Climbing*, described this as the day when Mabel took part in an 'inadvertently symbolic climb which effectively passed on the baton of women's leadership to the next generation'. Alice Nelson (Jammie), who later married Sid Cross, was in the other party; it was she who made the first female lead of Central Buttress three years later. As Wells puts it: 'Instead of swapping a baton, however, Barker handed over some toffee to Nelson and cadged some fags in return. Those were the days ... '

Soon after the descent of CB, Jack Carswell moved to Bolton to work in an engineering company. The last climb he remembers doing with Mabel was Savage Gully in the pouring rain. At the time she had a lodger and somehow persuaded him to come along too, dressed in his office clothes. 'Mabel being Mabel, must have a climb, rain, wind or no.' That climbed turned out to be an epic, too. Mabel and Jack kept in contact over the following years, but the war disrupted activities. He always knew Mabel as one of a group of climbers. 'Frankland was the only one that she was associated with more than individually,' he says. 'But she never spoke about him. We didn't talk intimately about things like that in those days.'

Throughout the '30s, Mabel was active with the FRCC, attending Annual dinners whenever she could, keeping her copies of signed menus. She also helped with the updating of the FRCC guidebooks. In 1937, she received a letter from her old friend, Ernest Wood-Johnson, enclosed inside a copy of the new Great Gable, Borrowdale and Buttermere Guide. 'You and Kelly are the first to receive these advance copies – treasure it, my dear, as we'll never write another guide!' he said.

Friar Row School was now well established, and it seems that Mabel could occasionally take off when the opportunity arose. At some point in the 1930s, her old friend and colleague, Gertrude Walmsley, left to take up a teaching post in a deprived area of Stockport. Conditions there were very different from those at Caldbeck; Gertrude was appalled to find out that some pupils in her class did not know what grass was – they had never seen any. After the war, Gertrude moved to Essex where her sister was headmistress of the local school. When her sister retired she accepted the headship. Gertrude was replaced by R.H. Hedley, who had formerly been an Assistant Headmaster at a school in Vienna. Friar Row had by now become increasingly international and its brochures were printed in English, French and German.

Friar Row housed a variety of events. A Fellowship of the Kingdom Conference was held there in 1936, and Maryport Nursery School made regular visits, providing an opportunity to teach outdoor education to the very youngest children. Older pupils were not neglected either. Mabel's adult education classes, under the auspices of the W.E.A., included taking her students up mountains, such as Helvellyn and Cat Bells. She took part in further excavations, and in 1939 held a gathering of the Association of Women of the World at Friar Row.

Mabel must have seen the war clouds gathering, especially through contact with her friends and colleagues in Germany, France and other parts of Europe. She did, however, manage one final adventure before the onset of war brought all normal activities to a halt. This was the Border Walk of May 31st to June 6th 1938, which is recounted in the FRCC Journal of 1939, entitled *The Border Line.*

The Border Line (In Mabel's own words)

There had been some talk in the local paper of a pilgrimage along the Border Line. This did not come off, but the suggestion of it led to some debate on the question 'Could it be traversed in a week?' The W.E.A. Local History Class in Carlisle was interested in the Border, and out of our discussions arose the idea that some of us should try to walk it, not necessarily in a week. Whitsuntide was the only time available, and as it turned out, exactly a week and no more was ours in which to carry out the plan. For various reasons most of those who first hoped to do it were unable to come, and the party was eventually reduced to Miss M. Short, myself, and Roc the dog, and as things turned out this was just as well.

We began at the east end, arguing that if any must be omitted it would be easier to complete it at a later date at the home end.

So we went off on a Monday morning, by train to Newcastle and bus to Berwick; and after a delightful evening in that lovely town, began the real business on Tuesday, May 31st.

The first surprise to one bound on this adventure (and that in spite of much study beforehand) is the large amount of England lying north of the Tweed. Buses on the Great North Road proving few in number we walked the three miles to Marshall Meadows: and the day was hot, and our packs were heavy. Once there, however, the fun began. With some local help we found a hole in a field, and popped down it like rabbits, into a red sandstone tunnel which brought us out onto the rocky shore by the North Sea. The tide was out, and for half a mile we scrambled along, looking for the wall which here marks the Border Line.

Time passed, but no wall appeared. We came to a great mass of fallen cliff, and saw two men on top of it.

'Where is the Border Line?' I called. They pointed back.

'Then I'm in Scotland?'

'Ay, ye're in Scotland.'

On the grassy terrace just above the shore was the wall, very 'sore decayed.' We solemnly sat on it, took photographs, and made for the top of the cliff, where the men awaited us. They greeted us in friendly fashion and came as far as the railway, where the Border is marked clearly enough. Only twice does the Line actually cross the metals.

At Lamberton Toll an old man was working in his garden.

'Are you in England or Scotland?' we asked.

'Ah'm in Scotland. The March is *there*,' he said decisively, pointing to his garden fence.

So we followed the March, over fields and along stone walls, leaving the sea behind. We were a bit uncertain (not for the last time) as to which wall was *the* wall; but lunched about the highest point, looking over the battlefield of Halidon Hill; and at Mordington Church came down onto the road, where Messrs Binns informed us exactly which country we were in.

From here we followed the Bound Road, the only piece of the Line which is actually *on* a road, so that for about a mile one could walk in England and the other in Scotland. This road degenerates to a sunk lane, running down to the Whitadder. Here there must once have been a ford, but neither ford, ferry nor bridge could we see now, though traces of the lane continued on the other side: so round we had to go to the bridge on the main Berwick road. It began to rain, and kept it up steadily all day. At Paxton Old Toll we came back to the Bound Road, which runs down to the Tweed and stops. Well, the Line was safe now in the middle of the river, and not likely to get mislaid for many a mile; so we set off to follow the Tweed, charmed by its rare beauty, and interested in the number of fishermen. We pushed through woods on the steep concave banks, and walked over grass in the great meadow-filled meanders; but even here the going was not too good, owing to the rain which made the mud slippery and deep. We crossed into England by the Union Suspension Bridge, first of its kind in Europe; and took to the river again below Horncliffe.

The pouring rain could not damp our joy in Norham Castle, and we lingered too long over the magnificent ruin, so that we decided to stay the night at Ladykirk instead of pushing on to Coldstream. This was our first mistake, and we hereby advise all successors to stay in Norham. Ladykirk proved to be the most inhospitable little hamlet ever: clustered round an enormous church, built by James IV because he was not drowned in the Tweed. We vainly sought shelter in every house in the place, including a large farm and a very large empty manse, but nobody would offer so much as a settle to sleep on! Wet, weary and hungry, we set out for Coldstream: had another shot at a house on the way, and jumped at its owner's offer to take us in his car to Coldstream. Thus we missed the walk past the mouth of the Till, but hot baths and supper at the Crown Temperance Hotel were welcome indeed.

Next morning we turned upstream to Coldstream bridge (which shares matrimonial honours with Lamberton and Gretna), and followed the Tweed again through woods, private grounds, on the road, and over grassy meadows. At Baa Green the Line is actually the north hedge of the road, for here a scrap of Scotland is south of the Tweed. We rested on the mound which was once Wark Castle, the greatest fortress on the Border, and reputed scene of the Garter episode. Near it is a deserted graveyard with one stone standing in pathetic loneliness. And so on to Carham Church, shortly after which we reached the Redden Burn, and bade farewell to the Tweed.

The Redden is so insignificant that we were doubtful of its identity: but some men in the first field it crossed assured us that we were indeed on the March.

After going under the railway the Line makes a very curious salient, and a bit of England is consequently north of Scotland. Here we did our duty by it as faithfully as we could, but its behaviour was puzzling, and we were glad to verify our locality at a hamlet called Nottyless, where the inhabitants gave us help with interest. It was not possible, however, to follow it meticulously just here, for the fields were under springing crops, so we followed a track across them, as near as made no difference. Just over a fence a gypsy woman sat by a winter tent of wattle and blankets.

'Now are you in England or Scotland?' was answered by, 'Well, this is English ground, lady.' But it wasn't. We were just west of our Line there.

At Holefield Farm, where they were busy sheep-shearing, we sought hot water for tea, for there was no inn or village for far enough.

A little farther the Line touches the road, and then crosses 'No Man's Land.' A car drew up, and its driver courteously asked where we were going. Our answer intrigued him. He knew Logan Mack (whose 'Border Line' was our book of words, though its weight precluded its presence); insisted on taking us up the half-mile of road before us, and gave us much helpful information and good advice.

Thanks largely to this, the Line was not difficult to follow over the moors to Bowmont Hill. These were chiefly remarkable for the great number of hares we saw on them.

Over Bowmont the Line passes between two camps, and I went up for a look at the English one. Parallel earthworks cross the hill, and at its end is a circular work with some stone visible. It would be a fine place for excavation.

Below us now lay Bowmont Water; and we could study the morrow's route (we hoped), for from Yetholm Mains the Line runs up into the Cheviots. For the night we had to go on to the town of Yetholm, where we found refuge from the rain, then beginning, with Mr. Sutherland and his daughter.

But the following morning, June 2nd, was perfectly foul. Rain fell in sheets, and the wind howled. Miss Short decided to go by road to Cocklaw Foot. I felt that if I did not then and there follow the Border Line onto the Cheviots I might never again have the chance to do so, and that to omit this section would, in a way, spoil the whole adventure for me. So I set off with Roc on what was, perhaps, the maddest walk I have ever undertaken.

I was wet through before reaching the end of the village street. I passed Church Yetholm, and in Yetholm Mains, to keep the map dry, asked for direction from a woman who must have been one of its famous gypsies: and then from a shepherd, who told me to follow the Halterburn – 'That's the Bound,' said he, adding that when a line of trees ended a wall could be followed right up.

I had a look at map and compass in comparative shelter before leaving the burn.

The course seemed clear, and I took to the sheltered side of the wall, just able to see the col on Coldsmouth Hill, after which was thick mist and utter solitude.

The wall played up until I judged that we were on Whitelaw Hill. Then it ought to go down, of course, but seemed to be overdoing it. Still, I dare not leave it: and it might be as well to get out of the mist and have a look at things. They turned out to be a farm in a lonely valley by a raging burn. The farm was not in the bond, but I made for it. I got over the burn by a sheep hurdle. Roc with one look at me, went in, and to my relief came out on my side, some way farther down.

The farmer stared in amazement, and to my rather faltering request for the Border Line bade me come in.

'Where are you making for?'

'I wanted to follow the Border Line onto the Cheviot.'

'But you're not going onto the Cheviot to-day?'

I simply dared not say that I was! I would go as far as I could – and where was I, anyway?

It was Burnhead: the stream was the Halterburn: the Line was the divide between it and the Curr Burn. They were most anxious for me to take the easiest way to Cocklaw Foot.

By this time the kettle was boiling. I thankfully drank hot tea with my lunch, and had a good look at the map. I had gone too far west off Whitelaw, and was about half a mile from the Line.

Once out of sight of the farm, I made for the divide. I was not any too confident, for in the mist all landmarks were lost again: but on what felt like the divide was a wall once more, and it seemed to go in the right direction. Wind and rain kept it up well, and the wall ended ...

Then a few rocks, enormous in the mist, began to emerge and a huge cairn loomed up. This, I found later, was the Schil, second highest on the whole range.

The next section was open flat moor with no indication of any divide or Line whatever. The compass was of little use with nothing to take readings from. But after a while, like a faint streak in a negative, a dark line developed. Into my mind came the recollection of something Logan Mack said about posts on the moor. It was a post all right, and after what seemed a long way another appeared – and another. Carry on!

At last came a wire fence: and this began to go up steeply. It *must* be going onto The Cheviot – or rather (for the Line does not actually go onto the summit of Cheviot, which is in England) onto Auchencairn. It went up, and up – interminably up, into thicker mist and howling wind. I dare not leave it, and it seemed endless. Roc toiled up beside me – no wall or stone now, to shelter either of us. And suddenly it ended. Whether this was the highest point of the Line or no, I could go no farther. But in a sudden lightening of the mist I got a glimpse of a great white streak to the left. It must have been the 'Hen Hole.'

So working round to the right and down we came to a stream. Going down that valley, Cheviot Burn as I hoped, was the coldest and most unpleasant part of the whole day. The wild waters were all over the place, and it was difficult to get round the concave bends. At a low level I met a shepherd.

'Where am I making for?'

'Cocklaw Foot.'

'Thank goodness!'

Round the next bend was the farm. Miss Short would be there, and all arranged. Not a bit of it! The door was opened by a very stout and surprised woman, who had never heard of either of us – and she doubted if she had room. Well, might I come in? Of course: and while she got me some tea we discussed the situation. She was sure that my friend would have been unable to get up the flooded road. She contemplated me while I ate bread and cheese ravenously: and suddenly said:

'If you're not that particular about seeing her again tonight, I could mebbe air a bed for ye.' Rather! And in no time she had a roaring fire in the room off the kitchen, and I had the jolliest evening and the most comfortable night ever.

The rain stopped. Next morning brought sunshine, a good breakfast, dry clothes, and Miss Short about 10 a.m., with her own story of the day before. Unable to get up the road, which showed only as a line of telegraph poles, she had stayed at Mowhaugh. A shepherd bound for Cocklaw Foot had tried to take a message, but he couldn't get there either. They assured her that I could not possibly make it – no experienced shepherd would go onto the Cheviot on such a day. (Well, perhaps not. It sounds fine, but after all, shepherds are not in the habit of steering in mist by map and compass.)

We went back up the much-reduced Cheviot Burn, and took up the Line at the end of the fence where I had left it. About 100 yards beyond it were the big cairns on Auchencairn. The Cheviot lay before us – a great flat peat moor. We decided not to try for its summit (which indeed is a moot point), but did our best by the Line, which here has no demarcation. The peat bogs were extraordinary. They always seemed to intoxicate Roc, but he was the only one who appreciated them.

We doubled back and found the Hanging Stone where East and Middle March meet; and below us could see a bedraggled fence following the divide. We were indeed on the tops of the Cheviots, and now every mile was one nearer home.

So with little incident we passed Crookesdike Head, King's Seat, Cocklaw and Windgyle with its huge cairns. From this a green ridge led north-west with the headwaters of Coquet Dale on our left. The day was clear, the views perfect, and all we had to do was keep on the divide: though some of it was pretty hard going through peat and heather and – worst of all – ground covered with high tussocks of grasses, which, we were told later, the shepherds call 'bulls' snouts'.

The Line makes a curious rectangular bend onto Rushy Fell. It is fenced here, and easy to see even from a distance: and is memorable because we saw a horseman with a dog: one of the two human beings we saw on the Line from Yetholm to Kershope Foot: the other being a shepherd near the head of Kershope.

Descending a little to the west of Blackhall Hill, we struck Dire Street, running from Hunnam-on-the-Wall to Newstead and pointing to Inveresk. It took us straight into the 'Ad Fines' Camp. In our all too short inspection it seemed that camps of several periods and curious outlying earthworks cover a large area. It is strangely situated in the bottom of a high valley, and on the headwaters of the Coquet Burn. This Dere Street is the road blocked at Hunnum in Kipling's vivid story, saying 'Finis' to Parnesius. The camp must have been falling to ruins then and the road overgrown, away behind the Wall in the late days of the Roman period: but the main crossing of the Cheviots was *here* and not at Carter Bar, when the Province of Valentia was a going concern, and this place must have been a centre of activity for the Roman legions.

It was good to find clear running water in the infant Coquet, where for the first time since Yetholm Mains the Line, for a very short way, follows a stream. After some boggy going over Harden Edge and Hoggerel Hill we left the Line for the night, and went down Spithope Burn to Byrness. It was a long valley, but less wearisome than the main road at its foot, and the long search for rooms. We were advised to try Catcleugh Farm, but knew as soon as we saw it that it was too large to have any room for us! Finally we found a kindly hostess in one of the cottages near Catcleugh Reservoir. A larger party would have had yet more difficulty in finding resting places; and for a really big pilgrimage the problem would be serious.

We went up again by the Hawk Burn next morning, making Hungry Law and Catcleugh Hill. The way was easy to see between the headwaters of the Ramshope Burn and Kale Water: but on Lap Hill we were just saved by a timely look at the compass from following a fence too far north. From Ark's Edge – a long and rather featureless shoulder – we came down to the main road over Carter Bar, and lunched on the site of the Reidswire Raid, now occupied by road-menders' tackle, while cars passed and we were once more informed by Binns as to the whereabouts of England and Scotland.

Round the shoulder of Catcleugh Hill and Carter Fell we followed a nice old road, not marked on the map nor referred to by any writer that I can find. We left it to climb to the big cairn on Carter Fell. From here there is nothing whatever to mark the Border, and probably we began to go wrong quite soon in the great peat bogs. They were beyond anything of their kind that we had hitherto encountered, and in concentrating on the problem of progressing at all we lost our direction. Also we travelled more slowly than we reckoned. (I had by now evolved a sort of inverted system of determining our position: we made about two and a half miles per hour, therefore after two hours' going we should be in such-and-such a place. It worked generally, but not here!)

We saw what we took for a cairn in the trackless moss, and made for it joyfully, but it wasn't a cairn, and led us farther astray. At last a valley beneath us – with a river and farms – but there *should* have been a railway! We went down to investigate. The first farm reached was Kielder Head. We were about three miles from the Line, and at the foot of the Scalp Burn, while we should have crossed its headwaters at Haggie Knowe.

However, the day was yet young, and the distance to Deadwater much the same whether we returned to the Line or abandoned it, so with instructions from the folk at Kielder Head and another map consultation we made up the Scalp Burn, and, rather hot and tired, regained our Line at Haggie Knowe. (At least we did expiation for the mileage in a car on the Tweed!)

And so we came to the Kielder Stone: old meeting place of March Wardens, and a magnificent bit of rock.

Thence up once again onto Peel Fell, whence a view of the Solway can be had, but it was not clear enough that evening. From the edge of Rushy Knowe we looked down on the Deadwater Burn and Farm, our objective. A nice slope seemed to promise speedy and easy going – but once off the steep, the whole valley proved to be part of a huge afforestation scheme, and a network of little drainage channels put the brake on very effectively. However, we reached the desired haven and the promise of supper and bed, just before its folk turned in for the night.

On the following morning, Sunday 5th, we could for the first time start right on the Line with no retracing of our steps. It comes down from Ruch Knowe by a wall which had been on our right the night before: and here for the second time crosses a railway at Deadwater station. There was once a spa here, still marked on the maps as a 'Bathing House.' It is now a small unattractive sulphur spring among the ruins.

We climbed Thorlieshope Pike, came down a little burn past Blackhope, and, cutting a funny little peninsula of Scottish ground, came gladly to the lovely Bells Burn. This is a charming part of the Line, and it was good to follow a real running burn after all the peat bogs.

But we had not finished with these, for on leaving the burn we met them again on Buckside Knowe: 'bulls' snouts' also, and very wet going. A wall takes the Line over Larriston Fells, but after a sort of half-hearted look at them it leaves their summits to Scotland. So we left it, and went onto the tops whence the views are glorious. Below lay Liddesdale, and clear in the distance were the Solway and the Lakeland Hills.

We rejoined the Line at Bloody Bush, marked by the big obelisk which was a toll bar on the road from Dinlabyrein to the North Tyne. A fence could be followed for a time, but it died away, being literally drowned in a bog which waxed as the fence waned. I forgot Logan Mack's advice to avoid this section and seek higher ground, and we walked doggedly through the thing. A single upright stick in a waste of bog was the last ghost of a fence.

In time it began to grow firmer, and to gather into the headwaters of Kershope. The Line was once more safe on a river, good to be followed for miles without brain work or reference to the compass. We came to a cairn, the county boundary of Cumberland, and were in home waters.

'Dinna ye cross ... , my man, or there'll be a toom chair at the Redheuch.' The quotation kept running in my mind as we took whichever side of the growing burn seemed best. 'The *wrang* side o' Kershope'! May it be that some day all national boundaries will matter as little as this once turbulent frontier does now.

We kept by the water, and the following of it was a pretty rough job. From Kershopehead (now deserted) both sides were afforested. Roc found a dead deer and wallowed in it, surprising us by his smell, and by the fact that of the afforestation commission allowing deer to remain in their infant forests.

After a cheery chat with the inhabitants of Scots Kershope we pressed on, now on the English side, and suddenly came to a road, or what has the intention of being one in the future. It is being constructed up the valley by the unemployed in camp at Kershope Foot, for use when the timber is grown. After a bridge, annotated by Binns, we followed a charming cycle track to where, under a railway bridge, the Kershope joins the Liddel, and transfers to it the responsibility for the Border Line.

After a fine night at Under Burnmouth Farm we set off on our last day's tramp. To enquiries as to the best side on which to follow the river, our hosts replied rather uncertainly, and said it would be difficult. Feeling that the end was well in view, I said rashly that it would probably be like walking on a bowling green after what we had been over.

Soon began the same game that we had played with the Tweed: difficult passages of steep wooded banks, and easy going on flat ground in the concave bends. We had chosen the English side, but crossed at Watleyhirst. For a time all went well, and a little path led us into lovely woods. But the path died, and the woods became a jungle, and while we fought through it on the steepest slope we had yet met, the hoot of a train on the other side sounded derisively, while Miss Short said something about a bowling green!

We climbed out of it, and abandoned the Liddel for the moment.

But a few fields brought us to Penton Bridge: whence easy paths through those lovely woods brought us to Rowanburnfoot. Here was the problem of the Whitadder again, for the Esk had to be crossed, and hope of a footbridge failing, we had to go back to Canonbie, where we fell for the first café. So fortified, we attacked a road walk to the end of Scots Dyke.

This curious earthwork, now wooded, divides the Debatable Land between Liddel and Sark, having been constructed in 1552 by a joint commission from both countries, with the French Ambassador as umpire. It runs in a straight line for three and a half miles, and we expected pretty plain sailing; and so it was for the first mile. Then a detour had to be made to cross the Glenzier Burn on a sheep hurdle; and after we regained the Dyke it was more overgrown. Tangled thickets, bogs and growing weariness slowed us down. After the Glenzier Beck we came to open fields on the Scots side, and a ploughman told us that the March followed the edge of the wood; so by a path along it we came at last to a road at Craw's Knowe where the Scots Dyke joins the Sark, and the Line is in its keeping to the Solway.

At Sark Hall, Miss Short decided to make for Longtown and a bus to Carlisle. I wanted to finish out now, so took to the grass by the Sark. It proved an unexpectedly pleasant and interesting little river, with small but steep cliffs of boulder clay.

But after the Black Sark joins it at Newton came Solway Moss – another peat bog!

On the river bank it made real peat scenery. There was a peat cliff about twelve feet high; a gully in it with a waterfall: a huge peat 'boulder' at its foot, and a sort of peat cave in which I sheltered for a while from the rain which was now coming down steadily. Under the Longtown road, under the railway and the Gretna road went the Sark carrying the Line: then over flat green pastures, and through a marsh dyke with great red sandstone pillars: a last meander in the salt marshes – and then its waters mingled with the Solway.

On the Monday evening, just a week since we left the point 'where the sea takes charge' at the eastern end of the Border Line, we walked on Solway sands.

We had covered about 136 miles in the seven days from sea to sea.

The Onset of War

Mabel's plea that national boundaries should matter as little as the Border Line was indeed heartfelt. In September of that year, Chamberlain signed an agreement with Hitler, promising 'Peace in our time'. Soon afterwards Europe braced itself for war. Mabel must have been particularly sickened, given her vision of education changing the world and averting war. In February of 1939, Elsie Manners visited, an old friend who had worked at Friar Row several years before, and who now ran a Preparatory School in Leeds, St. Martin's Kindergarten. The two must have discussed contingency plans in the event of worsening conditions in Europe, and the following Whitsun, she brought a group of her pupils to visit the school. By September 1939, Friar Row School was forced to close as staff and children had to hurry home before borders closed; at this point St. Martin's Kindergarten was evacuated to Friar Row. Perhaps it was no coincidence that many of the children at the school were Jewish – Mabel was surely aware of climate in Germany, and wanted to provide a safe haven for all vulnerable children, no matter what their race or nationality. No doubt, had world events turned out differently, Mabel would have done all she could to protect and hide such children. In the event, many of the children stayed for varying lengths of time from September 1939 onwards. Meanwhile, her three beloved nephews, went away to fight in the war. Her half-brother, Pat, had written a novel called *Inglewood* which was printed in 1939, but never distributed due to the war. It was a historical romance set in medieval Cumberland and based on one of the Border Ballads.

These were uncertain times, when no-one could predict how long the war would take to reach its close. During the Phoney War, which lasted from September 1939 to the following May, it seemed that bombardments of the large cities were inevitable and invasion highly likely. The School now became Friar Row Kindergarten and Junior Preparatory School, with brochures advertising garden and orchard, with good water supply, modern sanitation, central heating and electric light. 'Caldbeck is a safe area among the mountains, and is easily accessible, being connected with Carlisle and Wigton. Physical health will be the first consideration and much thought given to diet, fresh fruit forming a daily portion of it.' Inclusive fees were £30 per term for 8-10 year olds, £27 for 6-8 year olds, and £25 for children under 6. References could be obtained from a Miss Richardson, of Allerton High School, Leeds, Harold Cherry of King Lane, Alwoodley, Leeds, and Mrs Berg of Harrogate Road, Leeds.

War-time Evacuation

2003, Leeds, England

Now, I myself had been a pupil of Allerton High School, Leeds, and my mother had attended the school during the war. Furthermore, the two other referees lived less than a mile from my own home. Questions about whether my mother remembered a Miss Richardson among the staff did not bear fruit. I decided to turn detective. A friend's mother had also attended the school, and while at the house for a family get-together, I posed a few innocent questions:

'Did you know a mistress called Miss Richardson when you were at Allerton High? I'm doing some research, you see, on children who were evacuated to the Lake District during the war.'

'I was evacuated to the Lake District,' chipped in Uncle Harvey immediately, now in his 70s. 'Let's see, it was a place called Caldbeck. We went with our teacher, a Miss Manners. I would have been about eight or nine then.'

'You didn't happen to stay at a place called Friar Row, did you?' I said.

'Yes, that was it.'

Coincidence seemed to play a strange part where Mabel was concerned. It was time to get out my pen and make some notes.

Harvey Frieze was at Friar Row from September until Christmas 1939, and then returned to Leeds.

'Miss Manners was a small plump woman. She was very kind. I remember going on a ramble, and someone trod on a wasp's nest. The wasps ended up in Miss Manner's hair. She was in bed for three weeks. I've been terrified of wasps ever since.'

'Do you remember someone called Mabel Barker?'

'Not very well. She didn't teach us, but she was around. She was a horsy woman, very well respected, a bit like a village squire. She was kind, but you knew not to mess with her. There were ropes hanging around the place, and climbing boots.' He shook his head, musing. 'I hadn't thought about it for such a long time.'

Uncle Harvey knew of others who had been evacuated. For Maureen Camrass (née Berg), my questions brought up long-buried memories. She was eleven years old when she went to Friar Row, accompanied by her little brother and her nanny, Miss Webster. She stayed there for a year. She remembers a harsh winter and a big freeze-up, when she went skating on the village pond at night, wearing a pixie hat. She remembers that Miss Webster and Miss Barker got along tremendously, but that Miss Barker seemed terribly old. Miss Manners tried to teach them; she had a cat that wheezed all the time, and it joined them for lessons. They made sweets and little boxes to put them in.

Brian Zimmerman remembers being asked in school one day who wanted to be evacuated. He put his hand up and went to Friar Row for nine months. He remembers Mabel as a tall lady with two plaits curled round the side of her head. He has good memories of his time there. His parents could only see him once every six months, because of petrol rationing. Mabel was in charge of the house, but Miss Manners ran the activities. They went on long walks through the woodlands. There were few formal lessons. They made collages with Miss Manners. Sometimes they looked at Mabel Barker's climbing photographs, but it seemed like a different world.

The evacuated school children eventually all went back to Leeds; at some point Mabel worked again at Garlands Emergency Hospital in Carlisle, as she had done 25 years earlier. Friar Row became a hostel for refugees. One of these refugees, Helgard Schröder, came to Caldbeck at the age of twelve with the Czech Refugee Trust. She had first arrived in Britain from Prague in 1938, staying with an English family in Sussex until it was possible to be reunited with her parents, who were forced to live in conditions unsuitable for children. Many Germans were interned in camps, but her family was sent to Caldbeck. She recalled: 'The village was suitably situated for 'aliens', being far away from important centres. There was a curfew and permission was required to leave a 5-mile radius (e.g. to go shopping by bus to Carlisle, about 13 miles away.) The refugees at Friar Row came from different countries (Czechoslovakia, Hungary, Poland and Germany) having fled from Nazi domination. Most of the single men lived on the premises, the other refugees all had rented rooms in the village ... There were lots of contacts and very good relations with the local population. The refugees gave concerts in the Parish Hall, we were active in the Women's Institute, I became a Girl Guide etc. Elsie Manners is the only name which tells me something. She was the hostel warden for a certain time – I heard her being described as rather helpless with so many forestry workers who cut pit props for the war effort. Later, in 1942-4, she was our Art Teacher at the Thomlinson Girls' Grammar School in Wigton ... Our family moved to Glasgow in 1944, where my father worked in a factory for the war effort and I completed my education in 1946 with the Scottish Highers. We returned to Dresden, my parents' home town, in September 1946.

'All these years I have remembered with gratitude the kindness and hospitality extended to me as a refugee from Nazi Germany by the people of Caldbeck. Since Europe has become united I have often returned to Caldbeck to see my old friends and we feel as if we said good-bye only yesterday – there is no time barrier and our friendship is just the same as it used to be when we were school-girls.

'I have been an English teacher in Berlin for over 50 years and one of the things I try to imbue to my students is a love of and for everything English in order to help improve understanding among people.'

It is difficult to say why Mabel started a new job in Peterborough, but when the Spring Term opened on January 20th 1942, she took up the post of Geography Mistress at The King's School there. She most probably had contacts who persuaded her to join the staff; certainly, at least one of the staff, H. Somervell Robinson (Robbie) had mountaineering connections. The King's School was a school for boys, but did have a sister school, Peterborough High School. Is it coincidence that this school claims to have established the first ever mountaineering club for girls, the Westwood House Mountaineering Club, soon after Mabel's time there? At the King's School, Mabel continued to teach her pupils enthusiastically, no doubt somehow managing to integrate the different subject areas of the curriculum, rather than simply teaching towards examinations. The school ran a Scout Troop, and Mabel possibly had some involvement. The school magazine, 'The Petriburgian' records that in 1945, '... In conjunction with the Natural History Section the society (Science Society) enjoyed a most interesting lecture by Miss Barker on 'Fell Climbing.' This was illustrated by slides which were really most impressive.' However, the Petriburgian of 1946 records that 'To our great regret Miss Barker was taken seriously ill with arthritis and was unable to return to teaching here. We are glad to say that after prolonged treatment in hospital in Carlisle she is now much better and even talks of resuming her interest in rock climbing. She is spending her convalescence in writing a biography of her godfather ...' Upon retirement, Mabel received a cartoon drawing showing her scaling the blackboard, complete with ropes, nailed boots, and ice axe, with the caption 'Watch me, boys. This is the great wall.' It is signed by her colleagues. Mabel was extremely proud of this, and its viewing by visitors was obligatory. In 1952 The Petriburgian carries a note that Dr Barker ('Auntie Mabel' to her admirers) had paid the school a visit, and it is likely that some of her colleagues and ex-pupils continued to visit her in the Lake District. She was to spend the remainder of her life in Caldbeck.

La Maison de Sèvres

Across the channel, one experimental school crystallized Mabel's ideology in a way that she could never have foreseen. This was a school born out of necessity, with a unique clientele, which saved the lives of many children and helped them reintegrate into society afterwards. The Maison de Sèvres was to become a model of education and resistance well beyond the war.

Yvonne and Roger Hagnauer were teachers who had trained in Paris, strongly influenced by the ideas of Dewey, Decroly and others. They also cited Mabel Barker's work as a major influence; in many ways, her methods and ideology were better understood in France than in England, where they had become part of what was known as *L'Education Nouvelle.* Roger and Yvonne were both passionate about educational renewal and were also very active within the trade union movement, being on the extreme left politically. Yvonne was an English teacher who had studied at Cambridge. Before the war, both were involved in experimental work, including self-government in schools and teaching French to foreign workers. Both took an active part in movements for peace.

At the onset of war, both Roger and Yvonne were disqualified from teaching as a result of their activism. Nonetheless, Roger was mobilised, received a medal for his work with the wounded, and was taken prisoner in June 1940. In this way he avoided having to declare that he was Jewish, as was then required by law. When released in November 1940, and having been suspended from teaching, he obtained a post with *Entr'Aide d'Hiver,* the Parisian section of *Secours National,* an organisation established to help the civilian victims of the war. By the end of 1940, it was under the direction of Marshal Pétain and the Vichy Regime, and was used as part of their propaganda. Many of Roger's old trade unionist friends worked for this organisation, and helped him go undetected until March 1943. Said Roger, 'When one comes face to face with a regime such as Vichy, which could collaborate with the Nazis, I regard disguising the truth as a totally honourable tactic ... there were those who believed me, but most just pretended to believe me.'

From then on, this disguise was used as a key tactic against the Vichy Regime. In July 1941, Yvonne Hagnauer took charge of a *Colonie de Vacances* at

Charny. When, at the end of the holiday, many parents failed to reclaim their children, *Secours National* funded the Maison de Sèvres, based a few kilometres west of Paris. Some months before, this building had been inaugurated as a Training Centre for Active Teaching Methods. Yvonne became director, her job being to look after and educate these abandoned children, some of whom were orphans or from families that could no longer look after them, while others were runaways, or petty criminals. All were traumatised.

However, the next wave of children came for a different reason; these were the ones who had to flee from a regime that had decided they had no right to exist. 'The first clientele of the children's homes was composed of the human wrecks of a soulless proletariat which had not settled down since the exodus,' wrote Yvonne. 'But in 1942-3 the others arrived ... those who came up the lane hugging the walls, those who were taken in during a favourable 'black out' and who kept for months their walled-in faces of hunted children, unfamiliar with their assumed names, living, at first, with the terrifying urge of running away to be set free.' In order to reduce the risk of anyone revealing their true identity, Yvonne instituted the use of totem names for all who lived there, including the adults who were also forced to hide. Yvonne and Roger became *Goéland* (Seagull) and *Pingouin,* and would in fact keep these names for the rest of their lives. Likewise, the pathways that brought the children to Sèvres had to remain a mystery.

The house had originally been the home of nuns. Yvonne Hagnauer wrote: 'We immediately saw how we could put to good use the cells of the nuns, the big chapel paved in grey which would become our ward, and we duly appreciated the whitewashed walls, the bare rooms, as we had known summer camps set in manor houses; emblazoned gates, covered ceilings, and the shocking contrast between the campbed and the useless and anachronistic magnificence of the place. Didn't we have the changing magnificence of the hills which stretch their long softened hilltops onto the horizon, the deep woods and the leaden touch of Corot's ponds under the willows? ... The premises were no doubt a little cramped, the garden was not very large, but the belt of woods nearby surrounded the house with the mystery favourable to the rambles of teenagers.'

The children in this school were cemented together by common needs and grief. Sèvres gave Yvonne the opportunity to conduct many experiments for the benefit of these children. The teaching was founded on observation, freedom, and the development of their own areas of interest, in order to generate active participation. It was a synthesis of many ideas, individualising methods of learning, giving creative power to each teacher, using active methods already in use in the rural schools. Life in this school was not at all normal, yet the work was done with tremendous hope and courage, with the idea of normalising the children and re-adapting them to life, giving them solid skills to preserve their dignity and one day rediscover their place in society. Yvonne felt it was important to liberate the creative potential of the children and give them responsibility, using self-government methods. The children looked after the house, participated in cooking and took care of the animals. They learnt respect for life and love of nature despite the horrors of the outside world. They were involved in many kinds of creative work, including printing, drawing, modelling, film-making, weaving, puppetry, singing and dancing. From the start, a poster was displayed at Sèvres, proclaiming 'Liberty or Death!' and was not removed even when officials visited the school – an enduring symbol of the will to challenge the Vichy Regime. Ironically, the school was the subject of an article in *La Gerbe*, a collaborationist newspaper, praising its methods, and one General who came to inspect decided that it should be used more extensively as an instrument for propaganda. Fortunately, the war came to an end before this was possible.

In 1941, the underground networks had brought Jewish children individually, but after that the arrivals took on a more systematic character. 'These made up the permanent hard core of our Home and brought an element of indisputable wealth: first because we had now become their family and, with the flexibility of mind and ability to assimilate that characterized them, they felt the need to settle down; then because they came from all over Europe, nay, from the ghettos and concentration camps as well, and thus brought through their variety all the human elements a child community could wish for: enthusiasm, a taste for culture, slight differences and oppositions of characters so rich that our work as educators was made more alive and more attractive. The third wave which came up against our walls brought a mosaic of cases – children suffering from emotional confusion (the aftermath of war), children maladjusted after the storm, orphans – all social cases to be studied individually and whose stability can only be secured by individualized care in every field.'

The Maison de Sèvres was at the heart of a clandestine network. One visitor to the house was Marcel Marceau, later to gain world renown as a mime artist. He was born Marcel Mangel in Strasbourg in 1923, and worked with his brother Alain as a courier for the underground, marching children over the French Alps to Switzerland, pretending to be a Scout Master. In 1944, he attempted to take one group of children over the Swiss border, but was forced back, so brought them to Sèvres instead. He stayed until September 1944, himself fleeing the regime. He would act and mime for the children, and was described as 'a ray of sunshine in the stream of our misery.' Marcel's own father died in Auschwitz. Small wonder that he became such a master of disguise, and that he taught others how to say so much by keeping quiet. As he said, 'Do not the most moving moments of our lives find us without words?'

Roger Hagnauer himself was denounced in March 1943, but thanks to the help of friends, he managed to flee and hide in the free zone until Liberation. There was a growing chain of complicity among some of the bureaucrats of the regime, who appeared to support Vichy, but in reality were diametrically opposed to it. In this way, the Maison de Sèvres functioned throughout the Vichy Regime and the German Occupation with its 80, and later 100 children 'in an atmosphere of eager research and creation, enhanced by the mystery of our life, so isolated behind grey walls and a curtain of thick trees.' Life was not easy and without cares. Supplies were difficult to get. At one point they had to go along bombed roads and pull up tons of carrots at night, to keep themselves through the winter. There were problems of admission into hospital for children with fake identities, and there were nerve-racking visits of representatives sent by the Commissioner for Jewish Affairs. Luckily no one ever found them out, and the experiment flourished during and after the war.

Immediately after the Liberation of Paris, Yvonne gathered everyone together and climbed onto a chair. 'Now it is over,' she told them. 'We are free. Everyone has a right to their own name.' And so it was that the children and adults all recovered their true identities. But the ordeal was not over. Roger told how many of the children became silent. They followed with their eyes the American planes, carrying survivors, which they could see from the terrace. But they waited in vain for their parents to return. The terrible nightmare unfolded. Only one mother returned from the camps, and she was in a terrible state. The children waited for a long time, and at last had to resign themselves to the truth – that all they had left were pictures of their loved ones.

For many of the children, the Maison de Sèvres remained their only family. In the face of destruction throughout Europe, the children kept their humanity, enthusiasm, culture and rich character, made so by the education they had received. Many did not leave the house until they married. As Yvonne Hagnauer wrote: 'An old door, never closed, that one pushes to enter, and here is the stopping place, until the departure for a life that one will be able to start, this time, with a new and confident soul.'

After the Liberation, the Maison de Sèvres was able to continue its work with the help of *Entr-aide Francaise.* The children venerated Pingouin and Goéland as if they were true parents, throughout their lives. Here was a family, it was said, where there were never crises, recriminations or aggression, but instead a profound *joie de vivre*, made up of over 100 boys and girls from no-one knew where, from the most diverse environments, their only common background being a store of terrible memories. If this was the outcome of *L'Education Nouvelle,* it was exactly as Mabel had envisaged. I have no doubt that, had the war taken a different course, she would have acted with the same degree of courage.

The Final Years

After the war, Mabel settled down to a quiet life in Caldbeck. Friar Row became separate cottages, and Mabel lived in one of these, Bar Cottage. Its two rooms were lined with books, and these she treasured, keeping them long after other possessions were gone. There, she chose to live simply, surrounded by her animals. The place was untidy, yet she could always put her hand on what she wanted. As Mina, her nephew's wife, says, 'The welcome was better than the abode.'

Mabel had no interest in the usual domestic possessions, and there were few concessions to comfort. Nor did she have any money. She cooked on a primus stove, slept on a folding campbed, and her furniture was simple. She still went out walking whenever she could, and made enthusiastic attempts to get the village folk out on the fells. She continued to smoke heavily, as she had done all her life, and spent her time writing articles and letters to her many friends. She also assisted with the classification of the prodigious archives of Patrick Geddes. She prepared manuscripts for books entitled 'History of Caldbeck' and 'Mills of Caldbeck', but these drafts were lost when lent to a local schoolmaster and accidentally destroyed in a fire. Mabel was devastated, and the work never replaced.

Mabel's sparse way of life was reminiscent of her old friend, Millican Dalton, with whom she continued to correspond, and whose obituary she wrote in 1947 for the FRCC Journal:

> In all the later years, up to the outbreak of the last war, we met from time to time. He gave up the campsite at High Lodore in favour of Castle Crag. There he was to be found, summer after summer, and we could tell when he was 'at home' by the blue smoke curling among the trees, easily seen from the Borrowdale road. But it was none too easy to find, and some of us will remember adventurous treks from it, when the charm of his campfire and coffee, and his (increasingly argumentative!) conversation delayed departure till the dusk caught us. When we climbed together it was rather a shock to find that I was expected as a matter of course to take the lead. But he never regarded himself

as past climbing, even in his 80th year. Nor did he ever change much in appearance. I have some rather jolly photographs taken about 1935.

Many in these days will have less comfortable housing accommodation than he had in his 'Aladdin's Cave', where traces of his occupation will surely be found. He was no believer in 'roughing it', but an adept at achieving comfort wherever possible, and a great believer in down quilts as a necessary part of camping equipment.

His cave will be waiting for him this summer on Castle Crag; his fireplace ready, his seat built up beside it, gadgets in plenty for suspending tins, fresh water collecting in his pool, and a bed of dried leaves in one corner. There is an upper cave, reserved for guests. It will wait in vain – perhaps. But his picturesque figure and loveable personality have surely become part of the heritage of Lakeland so long as the hills endure and men love them.

It was the fact that both shared so many values that inevitably led each of them to a simple life where material possessions were of little importance.

In the same issue of the journal, Mabel published a final poem:

ENNERDALE

O weary long is Ennerdale,
And bleak and bare its barren fells,
And far the way down Ennerdale
To sound of kindly Christian bells.

O dark is night in Ennerdale,
With clinging mist and sodden ground:
While Gable crags stand sentinel
To guard the hidden ways around.

A dreary dale is Ennerdale.
Through stony wastes the white becks creep;
Like ragged ruins demon wrought
The Pillar Rock looms gaunt and steep.

At eventide in Ennerdale
    A mystery and a magic drave
Adown the dale, athwart the hills,
    And we were whelmed beneath its wave.

At eventide in Ennerdale
    With golden water foamed the ghylls,
And golden air from Tir-nan-Og
    Was pouring down upon the hills.

O clear to us in Ennerdale
    Beneath a sea of crimson fire,
Magnificently wrought, arose
    The City of the Heart's Desire.

MMB

Throughout her retirement, Mabel delighted in visits from old friends and their growing children. Graham Wilde, who had been a student at Friar Row when it first opened, visited her each summer.

'She couldn't care less for formalities,' he says. 'She had a very strong personality. Sometimes it was difficult to have a discussion with her. She had her own opinions and beliefs, and never changed them. World War II was an enormous blow to her, and she was convinced that the right thinking, especially in education, could stop these conflicts. She certainly had a touch of genius, but she just couldn't understand why everyone else didn't think the same way. She was a socialist of the pure kind, and made no compromises. She believed that if there was something wrong, it was your moral duty to do something about it.' Mabel believed strongly in social progress for women. 'She could and did meet men on equal terms,' says Graham. 'She sensed that if she had married, she would have had to behave as women were expected, and she wanted to live on her own terms. She believed strongly in votes for women, but she was not the banner waving kind. She made her mark by personal example. Perhaps that's why she smoked. All the women in that group smoked. It had primarily been a man's thing, so they were making a point. At that time, wearing breeches was also making a statement. Perhaps, in previous times, she would have been branded a witch. Her forthright opinions, which sometimes went against the norm, could arouse a lot of suspicion.'

Her nephew, Tim Barker, the son of her half-brother Pat, also remembers meeting her during those years. His father was extremely fond of her, although he chuckled about her attitudes and approach to life. He remembers that she was very direct in manner, wore tweeds and had her hair in coils. Nonetheless, she always had a sense of fun, and wanted to engage with young people. He sensed that she wasn't ordinary, and that she thought deeply about things. He has memories of two outings they went on together. One was a drive around the Caldbeck Fells, pointing out the tumuli. The other was a visit to Hadrian's Wall and Birdoswold Fort, where he remembers her casually picking up a shard and giving it to him saying 'Oh yes, that's a bit of Roman pottery.' For birthdays, she gave him books such as Jacques Cousteau's *The Silent World* and Laurens Van Der Post's *Venture to the Interior*.

Mabel was fond of animals all her life. She always kept black Labradors and black retrievers, although as her nephew frequently says, these pets 'did as they liked'. But Graham Wilde suggests that 'her dividing line between domestic and wild creatures was often blurred.' Nestlings were brought to her and cared for until they were ready to be returned to the wild, but one, a jackdaw named Johnnie, stayed and became a pet. Johnnie was a bit of a comedian. He would take cigarettes from her and put them under his wing, or fly off with them. Another time, she looked after a pet badger named Judy, while its owner was on holiday. Judy was an orphan who was taken into care, lost her fear of humans, and lived a domestic life with the village doctor. Attempts to return her to the sett were unsuccessful, as she would return to the doctor's home before he did. At Mabel's house, Judy hid under a chair in a corner. Eventually, deciding that she needed food and exercise, Mabel put her hand under the chair to try to get her out. Mabel's hand had to be stitched and bandaged. In the end, she was given to London zoo, where, unusually for a badger in captivity, she gave birth to cubs. Mabel maintained an interest in wild creatures to the very end, even when terminally ill. Despite not being able to walk steadily, she insisted on showing visitors a pair of spotted flycatchers nesting at the bottom of her garden.

During her years of her retirement, Mabel's brother, Arnold, would knock on her door every day, and they would go for long walks in the woods. She also went walking with other villagers, pointing out plants and wildlife as she went. When a chain was put on the gate, threatening to deny access to the fells, she filed it off. Instead, she put a padlock on it and gave the key to the Rector. Mabel hated boundary fences. She had a theory that people could live without fences, like a commune. Naturally, families did not agree with her because they wanted to be able to fence their children in for safety reasons. One of her deathbed wishes was that rights of access to the fells would remain.

Just before Christmas 1958, Mabel entered into correspondence with Lyna Kellett, the FRCC archivist. Lyna had received a request from the author Ethel Mannin for reminiscences of C.D. Frankland, to assist with a book she was writing. Ethel Mannin had written a mountaineering novel called *Men are Unwise* before the war, and had also written *Late Have I Loved Thee*, published in 1946. Mabel did her best to help, although when she looked back at her journals of those times, she 'felt as if it was the story of someone else'. She wrote in early 1959 that her new labrador pup, named Bran, had been 'a bit of a deterrent of leaving home! He is now eating my boot and must be dissuaded!' Nonetheless, she went to some trouble, and wrote a long, fourteen page account of the times she spent with Frankland, enclosing the poem 'On Great Gable –1927'. It appears that Ethel received more information than she intended. She wrote back to Lyna, rather disingenuously, saying that 'it would be tactful to show interest in the poem', but with little feeling for the historic and personal importance of the notes, or the deep friendship shared by Mabel and Frankland. Luckily, they were kept in the FRCC archive. However, Mabel's journals and other pieces of writing were not kept, as the family had nowhere to store them, and did not envisage a resurgence of interest in them.

Many years of heavy smoking eventually took their toll. When she became ill with lung cancer, she lived life quietly. A neighbour voluntarily kept an eye on her, making sure she had what she needed. She loved knitting, and would always have a garment on the go. Children loved to visit her, including her great-nieces and nephews who lived nearby, and she would tell them stories and show them things of interest, such as the prisms hanging at her window that played with the light. 'She was smiling right until the end,' says Mina. 'She was knitting something for the children, and was worried that she would not be able to finish it. I took it off her, and this seemed to take a weight off her mind.' Even at the end, when in hospital, she still had a healthy disregard for the rules. When Lindsay and Mina came to visit, their three children waited at the other side of the glass window. 'What are they standing out there for?' she said, ignoring the signs that said children were not allowed. 'Tell them to come in!' And so they did, and were able to say their last goodbyes. Mabel died peacefully in hospital on 31st August 1961.

A Rite of Passage

Caldbeck, 1979 or thereabouts

The address on Mabel's letter to Mary Frankland struck a chord immediately, for I had visited Caldbeck long before I knew of her existence, during my degree course as a student of Psychology and Education. A university friend, Jonathan, had completed his Philosophy degree some months earlier, and knew not what to do with the rest of his life. 'I feel lost,' he wrote, 'and impatient to be stepping out on some road with resolve, in faith that it leads me through the enrichment of encounter and achievement to my spiritual home.' We decided to take a long walk from north to south of the Lake District, to contemplate the future and our life's work. Since Jonathan's father was the Rector of Caldbeck, we would start from there.

My memories are hazy. I remember Jonathan meeting me at Carlisle, and the amusement of seeing him with a neat haircut, after three years of long, flowing locks – his nickname had always been 'Scruff'. We spent an afternoon walking round the village, he showing me where he used to play as a boy. We crossed the river on the old stone bridge, and walked along Friar Row to the pond, where you could bathe in summer and skate in winter. The village enchanted me, for it seemed the ideal place to run free as a child. My strongest memory, however, was climbing up into the tower of St Kentigern's Church, Jonathan's secret hideaway. There we hunkered down like stowaways, smoking, trying to resolve the conflicts between our upbringing and somewhat profligate student lives. We both came from traditionally religious homes, though with different faiths, and sometimes it felt as if we led double lives. But now he had a strong sense that it was time to contribute to society in some way, and did not know how or where. I think it was then that I mentioned Botton Village, a Rudolph Steiner Community in the North Yorkshire Moors, which I had visited with the University Conservation Society. Might he be interested? By now it was getting dark, and was time to return to the Rectory for tea with Jonathan's family. From our dusky vantage point, we surveyed the countryside once more, Jonathan pointing out Carrock Fell and the mountain ranges to the south, with the river Caldew winding its way towards us.

Early next morning, after saying goodbye to Caldbeck and a last look at the iron gates and long driveway of the Rectory, we made our way up to the fells on a perfect, late summer day. I don't remember what we talked of as we walked over the Dodds to Helvellyn, over Nethermost and Dollywagon Pikes. Perhaps there was little need to talk, as we surveyed the ever-changing views. At nightfall we put the tent up at Grisedale Hause and cooked a meal, suddenly shy at our close proximity, having always been part of a larger friendship group. We were young and attracted to each other. 'I sing and smile inside when I see you,' he later wrote. 'This you must take on trust until the day my demeanour and behaviour betray the fact.' We also held a deep respect for each other; neither wanted to tamper with this friendship. Ours was a different mission. So we sat quietly in the evening warmth, witnessing the fading light, knowing that otherworldly feeling one gets on the fells in the dark.

The next day we walked over Helvellyn and Fairfield, across the broad backs of the mountains and back down to civilisation. We said goodbye fondly at a bus stop near Windermere, and went off in our different directions. My own pathway in life would soon retrace our mountain steps, this time leading school children along them.

Perhaps we wrote or met occasionally over the next few years. Sometimes there was news through mutual friends. Jonathan went to Botton Village and stayed. He was the first of our group to marry and start a family. Mabel's letter acted as the perfect catalyst to track him down. Sure enough, a long letter soon arrived, and so we met again at Botton after more than twenty years. He was just the same, still thoughtful, funny, and a little mysterious. He had indeed found his spiritual home there, living with his family, running the Eurythmy School, and caring for handicapped adults who live as part of the farming community. Jonathan provided the initial key to the folk of Caldbeck, and with that I was able to start unlocking memories.

In a final, fitting twist, it was Jonathan's father who conducted Mabel's funeral service in 1961. Nowadays, his children are boarders at the Steiner school at Kings Langley, the site where Mabel taught for so many years.

O Nature Take Me

I am sorry to say this, readers, but the subject of this biography did not have a complex, tortured personality. She did not lead a scandalous life, nor was she famous. Though a supremely skilful climber and gifted teacher, her place in history is small. So, why have I written a book about her? The day I read her letter to Mary Frankland, something of her spirit climbed off the page. I sensed deep inner strength behind those words of consideration and reassurance, hope and courage. Intrigued, I found myself tugged backwards across the span of years. I knew that she had more to say and was impelled to find out what it was.

Mabel being Mabel, must have her say. Some of her writing was exquisite. Indeed, she became increasingly voluble, her sense of humour and 'incurable hope' soon endearing her to me. There was much to admire about her: independence and the determination to live on her own terms, according to her own beliefs; her wonderful spirit of generosity, which had nothing to do with material goods or money, although these she would share without a thought; her physical and moral courage. I admired too the way she shared her deep love of nature and respect for the earth with those around her, introducing scores of people of all ages to climbing and the outdoor world. Like Millican Dalton, she too, had worked out her theory of life, and stuck to it, merging her working and climbing life so that together, they became a source of joy and fulfilment. No stranger to loss, and ever resourceful, she squeezed the maximum enjoyment out of every situation. Perhaps she was too idealistic, but she never lost her faith in human nature and her zest for renewal.

Recently I noticed an advertisement by English Heritage in a teaching journal. 'Citizenship is right up your street,' it read. 'Your local environment links the present, past and future and is the ideal starting point for a rewarding citizenship project. Looking at real-life issues that affect the community – such as new uses for old buildings and what is worth preserving – can involve your class in weighing evidence and making informed decisions on what they want their local neighbourhood to be like. To get you started, our unique new teacher's guide is packed with case studies, schemes of work and a 'toolkit' to help busy teachers plan and carry out successful projects on your doorstep.' 1924 or 2004? Although never mainstream, Mabel's influence on educational thought has surely percolated down to us today, through her articles, her lectures, the conferences she organised, and not least through the teachers and children she worked with.

But what would Mabel make of recent educational changes? What would she say about the mounds of paperwork to be tackled before a child sets foot outside the school gates? What would be her view of the prescribed curriculum, or the way that schools are pitted against each other in competition, as if SATs levels or the number of A to Gs at GCSE were true measures of the value of education? What would she say about the way that technology has replaced connection with nature for so many children? Is education feeding the hand and head, but losing its heart? And if so, what will be the effect on future generations?

Alexander Farquharson, one of the leading lights of Le Play House, said this in 1930: 'If I ever were asked to establish a test for disciples in the survey movement, I should make each one repeat to me the sentence: 'O Nature take me.' I should know by intonation, glance, gesture as these words were said whether the disciple was for life only a 'torch bearer' or was to be one of the few mystics.'

Well, Mabel was more than a torch bearer. Her whole life was a hymn to the fells and the wild places she loved. She lived to the full because she did not fear death. If she had a message to give today, it would be this: 'It is the experience of the earth that gives us the comprehension of life ... We return for the moment, to the one real and simple fact, that there exists *nothing* but The Earth; we have no other means of production, and all aspects of our existence are the results of actions and reciprocal actions between humans and the earth.'

In her 1926 thesis, she cited an Irish myth where the hero, Lugh (the sun), prepared to struggle with the dark forces. Some warriors betrayed the peace agreed between themselves, and assassinated Lugh's father. The cry of Lugh, Mabel said, should be uttered by us all: 'Oh Earth, forgive this broken bond!'

I hope we can listen before it is too late, before human damage to the earth escalates further. Mabel believed that education must play a vital part in conserving the earth for those who come after us. I see her now, walking across the fells in the dark, striking a match, and beckoning us to follow. The mountains were always her spiritual home, and still are.

List of First Ascents

Year	Date	Climb	Party
1923	Aug 12	Bracket and Slab, Gimmer	Lyon, Barker & 4 others, inc. Herbert
1924	Aug 4	Frankland's Gully, Skye	Frankland, Barker & Hughes
1924	Aug	Girdle Traverse on Scafell, wrong way round	Frankland, Barker
1924	Aug	First female ascent of Central Buttress, Scafell (4th ascent)	Frankland, Barker
1925	Aug 19	Tricouni Rib, Napes	Frankland, Barker
1926	Aug	First female traverse of Skye Cuillin Ridge	Frankland, Barker & Hughes
1927		80 Foot Slab, Carrock Fell	Barker, Lochhead & Airey
1928	Mar 31	Yew-Tree Climb, Castle Rock	Barker, Macphee
1928	July 3	Slab Climb, Castle Rock	Barker, Macphee
1928	July 3	Scoop & Crack, Castle Rock	Barker, Macphee
1931		3 Tier Climb, Carrock Fell	Barker, Musgrave & Ridyard
1932	July 9	Juniper Crack, Carrock Fell	Musgrave, Ridyard, Barker
1933	April	North Trough Buttress, Carrock Fell	Barker, Briggs, Lochhead
1933	April	Slape Crags Arête, Carrock Fell	Lochhead, Barker
1934	June	Hell Gate Pillar, Gable	Balcombe, Cooper, Barker
1934	Aug 5	Rose Tree Route, Carrock Fell	Barker
1934	Aug 5	North Climb, Carrock Fell	Barker
1935	April 21	Alpha Variation, Gable	A Wood-Johnson, Barker
1935	July 22	Maeve's Crack, Carrock Fell	Barker, A Wood-Johnson
1935	July 25th	South Trough Buttress, Carrock Fell	Barker, A Wood-Johnson
1935	Aug 21	Slape Crags Direct, Carrock Fell	Horne, Barker
1937	June 20	Main Slab Route (to the Perch), Gill Crag	Ward, Wilson, Barker, Ridyard

1937	June 20	Flake Buttress, Gill Crag	Barker, Ward, Ridyard, Wilson
1937	June 20	Corner and Wall, Gill Crag	Ward, Barker
1937	July 25	The Tarsus, Dove Crag	RJ Birkett, Barker, Ridyard
1937		First Descent of Central Buttress, Scafell	Barker, Carswell, Mendus
1937	Feb 6	Left Ridge, Gill Crag	Wilson, Barker

Bibliography

Journals

Fell and Rock Climbing Club of the English Lake District; also FRCC Climbing Guides

Yorkshire Ramblers' Club

Ladies' Scottish Climbing Club

The Herald of the Star

Cumbria Magazine

Books

Angell, S. *The Pinnacle Club: A History of Women Climbing* (Glasgow: Pinnacle Club, 1988)

Barker, M.M. *The Use of the Geographical Environment in Education* (Unpublished Phd Thesis 1926, translated by J. A. Levi)

Birkett, B. & Peascod, B. *Women Climbing* (A & C Black, 1989)

Brittain, V. *Testament of Youth* (Virago, 1978)

Cox, F. Mabel the Mountaineer, (*Cumbria Life*, 89, August 2003)

Dubreucq, F. Jean-Ovide Decroly, *Prospects*; the Quarterly Review of Comparative Education (Paris, UNESCO: International Bureau of Education, vol 23, no 1/2, 1993)

Entwistle, M. *Millican Dalton, A Search for Romance and Freedom* (Mountainmere Research, 2004)

Evans, D.F.T Le Play House and the Regional Survey Movement in British Sociology 1920-1955 (unpublished M. Phil Thesis, City of Birmingham Polytechnic/ CNAA, www.dfte.co.uk/ios, 1986)

Gambles, R. Cave-Dwelling Rebel with Many Causes *Cumbria and Lake District Magazine* (December 2000)

Gifford, T. Millican Dalton, Professor of Adventure (*High* June 1994)

Graves, R. *Goodbye to All That* (Penguin Books, 1960)

Hankinson, A. *A Century on the Crags* (Dent, 1988)

Hankinson, A. *Geoffrey Winthrop Young* (Hodder & Stoughton, 1995)

Jones, T. & Milburn, G. *Cumbrian Rock* (Pic Publications, 1988)

Mairet, P. *Pioneer of Sociology, The Life and Letters of Patrick Geddes* (Lund Humphries, 1957)

Marrot-Fellague Ariouet, C. Les Enfants Cachés Pendant La Seconde Guerre Mondiale aux Sources d'une Histoire Clandestine (www.lamaisondesevres.org/cel/cel6.html 2005)

Mazel, D. (Ed.) *Mountaineering Women* (Texas A & M University Press, 1994)

Pilley, D. *Climbing Days* (The Hogarth Press, 1989)

Simpson, C. The Professor of Adventure *Cumbria* (October 1995)

Smith, C.J. John Hargrave – "White Fox" (Kibbo Kift Foundation, 1995 www.kibbo kift.org)

Smith, K. Epitaph to a Cragsman – A Profile of Claude Deane Frankland (*Climber and Rambler* February 1978)

Smith, M.K. Robert Baden-Powell as an Educational Innovator (The Encyclopedia of Informal Education www.infed.org/thinkers/et-bp.htm 1997;2002)

Treacher, K. *Siegfried Herford, An Edwardian Rock-Climber* (The Ernest Press, 2000)

Wells, C. *Who's Who in British Climbing* (The Climbing Company Ltd, forth coming)

Wilde, G. Dr Mabel Barker in *Caldbeck Characters* (Caldbeck and District Local History Society, 1995)

Wilson, G. *The Central Buttress of Scafell* (Millrace Books, 2004)

Index

And I wish I could tell you how deeply he had won the hearts of all my rather mixed little camping crowd — men & women & lads & lassies. They have written of him & spoken to me in a way that is a touching proof of his greatness, as a man, not only as a climber. One boy (with us in Skye in 1925) writes "Cumberland is dearer to me than ever — & Great Gable will always be a monument to one of the finest men I have ever known". Another said "He was the kind of man you meet once & never see again" — & a boy with me this year & 2 years ago, exploded over some stupid tourist criticism of climbing with "How dare they! They are not fit to mention his name"! May Steele seems